Southern Living®

2002 Garden ANNUAL

Golden groundsel butters the woods' edge in a Greenville, Delaware garden. (See page 89.)

Southern Living®

2002 Garden ANNUAL

Oxmoor House®

Southern Living 2002 Garden ANNUAL

©2002 by Oxmoor House, Inc.
Book Division of Southern Progress Corporation
P.O. Box 2463, Birmingham, Alabama 35201

ISSN: 1048-2318
Hardcover ISBN: 0-8487-2503-4
Softcover ISBN: 0-8487-2504-2
Printed in the United States of America
First Printing 2002

SOUTHERN LIVING
Garden Editor: Gene B. Bussell
Senior Writer: Stephen P. Bender
Associate Garden Editors: Ellen Riley, Charles Thigpen
Associate Garden Design Editor: Glenn R. DiNella
Assistant Garden Design Editor: Troy H. Black
Assistant Garden Editor: Liz Druitt
Senior Photographers: Van Chaplin, Allen Rokach
Photographers: Jean M. Allsopp, Ralph Anderson, Tina Cornett,
William Dickey, Laurey W. Glenn, Meg McKinney Simle
Production Manager: Katie Terrell
Editorial Coordinator: Bradford Kachelhofer
Editorial Assistant: Lynne Long
Production Coordinator: Kathryn Korotky

OXMOOR HOUSE, INC.
Editor-in-Chief: Nancy Fitzpatrick Wyatt
Executive Editor: Susan Carlisle Payne
Art Director: Cynthia R. Cooper

SOUTHERN LIVING 2002 GARDEN ANNUAL
Editor: Susan Hernandez Ray
Copy Editor: L. Amanda Owens
Contributing Designer: Rita Yerby
Editorial Assistant: Diane Rose
Contributing Intern: Megan Graves
Contributing Indexer: Katharine R. Wiencke
Director, Production and Distribution: Phillip Lee
Books Production Manager: Larry Hunter
Production Assistant: Faye Porter Bonner

To order additional publications, call 1-205-445-6560.

Cover: Daffodils, pages 58–59
Back Cover: page 75

Contents

*Petunias
(page 68)*

Snapdragons and geraniums (page 53)

Rudbeckia (page 225)

Chinese pistache (page 182)

elcome to the *Southern Living 2002 Garden Annual*. In this one book, you will see all the gardens we were fortunate to explore during the past year. You will learn to know our new friends—both plants *and* people. We hope you will find some new friends of your own among these pages.

From "Starting Seeds" (page 33) to "Fall's Finest Flowers," (page 181) use this book to help create your garden, month by month. The letters to the editor and garden checklists will give you reassuring guidance and sound advice as you plan your garden. Also included is a plant hardiness zone map and source lists for products and plants featured over the past year.

Any gardener who digs in the dirt knows how fast the year can pass and how gardening is a measure of that year, as well as our lives. Enjoy.

GARDEN EDITOR

*A whimsical purple house serves as the
backdrop for a festive garden with a
Southwestern flair
(See pages 96–101.)*

Lenten roses (See pages 12–14.)

January

Checklist for January

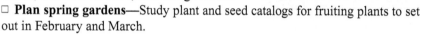

TIPS

☐ **Bulbs**—Spring-flowering bulbs, such as narcissus, hyacinths, snowflakes, and tulips, should be emerging shortly and will profit from an application of water-soluble 20-20-20 fertilizer. Also, cottonseed meal applied at a rate of 5 pounds per 100 square feet of bed area provides an organic and slow-release form of fertilizer that is excellent for vegetables, bulbs, roses, and other ornamental plants.

☐ **Citrus**—In the Lower and Coastal South, it's time to harvest early-fruiting citrus, such as grapefruits, tangerines, and 'Hamlin' and navel oranges.

☐ **Dividing**—Many deciduous shrubs, such as forsythia, spiraea, kerria, and winter honeysuckle, can be divided now. Each twig that has a root is a new plant to share. You can dig the suckers from the sides of the shrub, or lift the whole plant from the ground and divide it into several parts.

☐ **Lawn mower**—Now's a great time to tune up your mower. Sharpen and balance the blades, clean the air filter, and change the oil.

☐ **Plan spring gardens**—Study plant and seed catalogs for fruiting plants to set out in February and March.

☐ **Vegetables**—Purchase seeds of cool-weather vegetables for early-spring gardens. Good choices include lettuce, kale, collards, beans, English peas, and cauliflower. Select a planting site that gets at least five to six hours of sunlight a day.

☐ **Water garden**—Scoop debris from the bottom of your water garden. Trim off any leaves damaged by cold. Remove dead flower heads and seedpods. Divide water plants that have started growing.

Leatherleaf mahonia—Noted for its stiff, prickly foliage, this evergreen shrub opens fragrant, yellow flowers this month. Wait to prune until early spring, when the blooms are finished and blue-black fruit has developed.

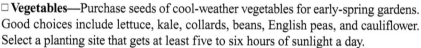

PLANT

☐ **Flowers**—Even on cold January days in the Lower and Middle South, you can still plant sweet William and English daisies. Don't worry too much about freezing temperatures. Work the soil, plant, and water thoroughly as you would with any other annual. Mulch heavily if a hard freeze in the teens or below is predicted for your area.▶

◀**Herbs**—Many herbs prefer the cooler weather. Basil, dill, chives, fennel, savory, Mexican tarragon, and watercress are good choices. Plant in containers with well-drained soil, or mix them into the garden.

☐ **Nut and fruit bearers**—Pecans, peaches, pears, grapes, and blackberries may all be set out at this time in the Lower, Coastal, and Tropical South. Choose a sunny, well-drained location, and consult your county Extension agent for the recommended selections for your area.

☐ **Paperwhites**—As the holiday round of paperwhites stops blooming, most stores still have a supply of bulbs. You'll probably find them on sale. Select firm bulbs that have not sprouted. Place in a watertight container, and spread gravel around the bulbs to anchor them. Add water up to the bulb bases, and place in a sunny location indoors. In a few weeks, the blooms will perfume the room.

☐ **Shrubs and trees**—This a good time to plant new shrubs and trees. Evaluate your landscape, remove unattractive plants, and replace them with others that you prefer. If you need a new landscape plan, go to southernliving.com (AOL Keyword: Southern Living) for our custom landscape plan service.

Azaleas and camellias—In the Tropical South, visit garden centers while these beauties are blooming to choose the right color. Azaleas, such as the large 'Southern Charm,' do best in shady places. *Camellia japonica* does well in shadier locations, *Camellia sasanqua* in sun.

PRUNE

☐ **Trees**—Remove deadwood and crossing branches from shade trees. Also remove lower limbs to make lawn mowing easier. Prune dormant fruit trees, cutting off any branches growing towards the center. Wait to prune your spring-flowering woody trees and shrubs, such as camellias and azaleas, until after they flower. "Topping" is a bad practice that destroys a tree's natural form. A better approach is to remove weak, twiggy growth from inside the plant. Thin out branches that are crossing, and reduce overall size by selectively removing some of the longer stems. ▶

FERTILIZE

◀ **Pansies**—Pinch off withered and cold-damaged blooms. This will encourage the plant to keep new blooms coming. When night temperatures continue to remain above 40 degrees in your area, feed pansies with a liquid fertilizer, such as 20-20-20, every other week to both encourage growth and promote blooming.

CONTROL

☐ **Lacebugs**—These ⅛-inch insects are known to attack azaleas, sycamores, and avocado trees in the Tropical South this month and next, causing the leaves to look dusty, turn yellow, and fall from the plant. Spray with a product labeled for those plants, such as acephate (Orthene), or dimethoate (Cygon).

☐ **Turf**—A dry winter day is a good time to mow a dormant, warm-season lawn. Not only does this groom the lawn, but it also removes fallen leaves and pine needles that have lingered over the late fall and winter. Once you've mowed the lawn, inspect your yard for winter weeds. Control them by spraying when the weather warms in spring.

January notes:

_____

_____

_____

_____

_____

_____

_____

_____

_____

_____

_____

_____

_____

_____

_____

_____

_____

_____

_____

_____

_____

❧

TIP OF THE MONTH

Each winter I start my tomato plants indoors inside frozen orange juice cans. When it's time to transplant them to the garden, I just remove the bottom from the can and stick the can in the ground. I find plants started this way grow bigger and produce longer than store-bought plants.

OPAL DUNCAN
CALVIN, KENTUCKY

*As seen at left, an astonishing variety of blooms
is available among the Ashwood hybrid Lenten roses.*

the lenten rose

Stunning new colors for a perennial favorite deserve a place in your garden.

Blooming in winter, Lenten roses push nodding buds through chilled soil to join the season's earliest bulbs. Unlike other flowers that fade within days, Lenten rose *(Helleborus orientalis)* stays colorful for several months. Not a rose at all, but an evergreen perennial, it blooms in subtle shades of white, pink, and rose that fade to green as spring progresses. Thanks to recent breeding efforts, their flowers are getting even showier. Lenten rose hybrids have graced the shaded beds of Southern gardens for generations. Gardeners treasure their winter foliage, early flowers, and seeds that drop and grow into seedlings for transplanting or sharing.

BY LINDA C. ASKEY / PHOTOGRAPHY VAN CHAPLIN

Because plants multiply by seed, conscientious growers sell only after seedlings flower and show their colors.

"You don't have to water or fertilize, and deer won't eat them," says Sam Jones of Piccadilly Farm in Bishop, Georgia. Sam, alongside his wife, Carleen, runs a nursery that specializes in Lenten roses. These plants' sturdy character and long blooming season have meant ever-increasing popularity. They make a hardy evergreen ground cover in shaded areas. Naturally drought tolerant, they endure the summer and then put on a flush of new growth in fall and again after flowers appear in late winter and early spring.

With greater demand comes opportunity for nurseries to make improved selections. Judith and Dick Tyler of Pine Knot Farms in Clarksville, Virginia, started with the Piccadilly Farm Mix and continue making crosses and strains using Lenten roses they bring home from annual visits to England. Through work with this breeding stock, they have been able to offer the Ashwood hybrids, plants with more vivid and varied colors and flower forms. Exciting innovations include doubled and anemone-flowered blossoms, outward-facing flowers, picotee flowers (a lighter or darker edge), brighter pinks and whites, and new colors such as green, yellow, apricot, and dark velvety purple.

Success with Lenten roses requires some advance planning. Here are a few guidelines to aid your endeavor.

Choose the right spot. Lenten roses need light shade and well-drained soil. Plants prosper from the Upper to Lower South and into Central Texas. North Florida and coastal gardeners need to provide full shade, fertile soil, and perfect drainage. Sam says that calls from customers who have lost plants usually reveal that they have used automatic sprinklers that kept the roots too wet.

Don't plant too deep. The crown of the plant should be sitting on the surface of the soil. If set too low, the plant will decline. Likewise, years of heavy mulching or a buildup of fallen leaves will have the same effect.

Give them a good start. Prepare the soil deeply. Work plenty of organic material, such as compost, mushroom compost, soil conditioner, sphagnum peat moss, or rotted manure, at least a foot deep into the planting bed.

Shade-loving Lenten roses bring the waning days of winter into full bloom.

Also mix in a timed-release fertilizer at the rate recommended on the label. If your soil is acid, add a half-cup of dolomitic lime per plant as well. In winter every year after, sprinkle a handful of lime around the plant.

Choose the right colors. Although the dark purple or slate (sometimes called black) Lenten roses are intriguing, they don't show up well in the garden. White flowers carry the best at a distance. Pink and rose colors add interest during a season when flowers are so rare.

Groom plants in small gardens. If your plants are close to a walk or terrace, remove any ragged foliage that has been damaged by winter. The flowers will show up better, and new growth will quickly emerge.

Editor's Note: You can see hellebores blooming and buy the colors you want at Piccadilly Farm. Call (706) 769-6516 for details. For information on Pine Knot Farm, call (804) 252-1990 or visit their Web site at www.gloryroad.net/~hellebores. ◇

LENTEN ROSES
At a Glance

Light: shade of tall trees
Soil: organic, well drained
Moisture: tolerates drought, but not wet
Spacing: 30 to 36 inches between plants
Propagation: transplant seedlings in fall
Nice to know: deer and vole resistant
Expect to pay: $4 to $35 depending upon size and selection

Cover Crops
Go Underground

If you sowed a cover crop in your vegetable garden last fall, it's time to take off that heavy winter blanket. Cut plants such as clover, ryegrass, and vetch, and then turn them back into the soil. Remember it takes about four weeks for these so-called "green manures" to break down. Till now, and your garden will be ready for spring planting.

If you didn't plant a cover crop last fall, you can still sow cowpeas, buckwheat, oats, or alfalfa in the early spring. They require a little extra work, but cover crops help hold the soil while the garden is idle and keep it from washing away. They also help pump life back into tired soils.

When it's time to cut, use a lawnmower or a string trimmer to remove the top growth of your cover crop before you till. If you don't, your tiller will likely become tangled in green stems and leaves, making the job difficult, if not impossible. Some gardeners prefer to cut their cover crop and let it lie on the ground and wilt a few days before turning it under.

Turn your garden thoroughly, mixing all the green vegetation evenly into the soil. You can use a turning fork if your garden is small. Don't till when the soil is wet and tacky or if it's extremely dry. The ground should just be slightly moist. It will take the masses of green manure a few weeks to break down, but the process eventually increases the amount of organic matter in the soil. Cowpeas, vetch, soybeans, and some of the clovers are legumes that have the ability to take nitrogen from the air and store it in their roots. The nitrogen will then be available to future crops. ◇

Grown to enrich the soil, this cover crop of clover needs to be cut and turned under before it begins to set seed.

Gardening Is Great in January

This is a good month to till, plant, plan, and dream.

Spring isn't the only season for solace in the garden. Cold weather may sometimes bring a blanket of the blues, but shake off those winter excuses, and stay in an active frame of mind. Whether you're inside or out, gardening can lift your spirits and soothe your senses—even in January.

COME OUTSIDE

Jason Powell, owner of Petals from the Past in Jemison, Alabama, opts for winter gardening outdoors. "January is an ideal time to be outside," he says. "It's the best time for planting all types of fruit trees." Jason orders apple, pear, peach, and plum trees in bare-root form, which is usually cheaper than container-grown plants. The trees come in plastic packages filled with sphagnum moss. To plant, unwrap

the roots, and soak them overnight in water. Cut off any broken roots. Dig a hole 2 to 3 feet wide, spread out the roots, and cover with soil. But be careful not to plant too deeply. The graft union, marked by the crook in the trunk near the base, should remain 1 to 2 inches above the surface of the soil.

Working with your soil is another useful January chore. "Whether you are turning it over or tilling, it's an excellent time to prepare the soil," states Jason. Test your soil with a kit from your county Extension service. Turn fall leaves into your beds so they will be composted by planting time. Tilling brings insects to the surface, where they will be victims of winter temperatures or food for hungry birds.

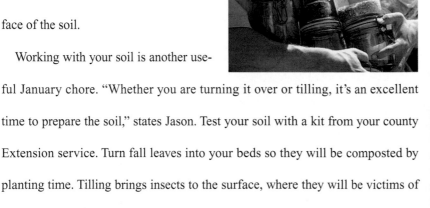

PHOTOGRAPHS: TINA CORNETT, CHARLES WALTON IV/STYLING: CINDY MANNING BARR

ABOVE: *Get some exercise outdoors by working on your soil.*
LEFT: *Start tomatoes from seed to plant in the garden later.*

STAY INSIDE

If you prefer to stay warm indoors, try starting a windowsill vegetable garden. Plant tomato, eggplant, and peppers from seeds; then place them in the garden after the danger of frost has passed. Don't forget to pull the plants back a little from the window; tender leaves will die if they touch icy panes.

Creating winter potpourri from saved Christmas tree needles is another indoor gardening idea. Allow needles to dry completely by spreading them on newspapers in a well-ventilated area. Collect hemlock cones, juniper berries, and other fragrant items from outside as well. You can even stuff a small pillow with the short needles of a Fraser fir.

Judy Lowe, a garden writer and resident Tennessean, battles her winter blues indoors. "I bury myself in a towering stack of garden books, old and new—preferably ones with color photographs. I forget the cold and focus on the warm spring weather that I hope is around the corner. I pick up interesting ideas, learn about new plants, and build the perfect garden in my dreams."

Judy also brings the outside in by replenishing her houseplants. "As soon as the lights and ornaments are removed and the Christmas tree is put out in the yard for the birds, I begin to crave greenery. Although I'm not much of a houseplant fancier the rest of the year, in winter I need every room in my house to have a garden presence."

She relies on Dallas ferns to bring life to bathrooms, medium-size specimens such as prayer plant or Chinese evergreen for the family room, and a trio of ficus for the living room.

Orchids in fuchsia and pale pink add subtle color. "Don't let anyone convince you that orchids are fussy or difficult to grow in ordinary home conditions," says Judy. "Both moth and tropical lady's slipper orchids are ideal indoors and couldn't be easier, if you refrain from watering with a heavy hand."

In winter, you may need to water indoor plants more often. The heated air can dry out container plants more quickly than at other times of the year.

With her plants in place, Judy is ready for whatever winter brings. "I am transported to a warmer world where plants are always green and flowering; then I am content to be patient until spring."
Lynne Long

Winter White

The season's surprise is a wealth of pristine blooms.

White is winter's color, crisp as a frosty morning, and fresh as a blanket of newly fallen snow. It also provides a welcome interlude between autumn's intensity and spring's full-spectrum outburst.

The number of white blooms available this time of year is astonishing. Some thrive as houseplants, while others can live indoors or out. Mix and match your options for arrangements that celebrate this seasonally perfect color, and enjoy a wide array of easy-care flowers.

Camellias are unfolding pristine petals and look magnificent when brought indoors. Immerse stems in warm water immediately after cutting. Trim again just before arranging. Christmas roses' clear white blooms are now pushing above their umbrella-like foliage. Choose mature flowers for a longer vase-life.

Forced bulbs, so abundant this month, adapt to arrangements inside as well as out. Purchase crocus, paperwhites, hyacinths, and snowdrops in bud or early stages of bloom. Crocus last only several days indoors, so choose tightly budded plants. Paperwhites may be grown outdoors in potting soil or pebbles, where cool temperatures and good light will keep them stocky and upright.

Primroses love sunshine and cool weather, and will last for weeks outdoors. Inside the house, maintain moist soil, and keep plants away from a heat source. There are several types, with varying heights and flower shapes.

Other white-blooming houseplants are cape primrose *(Streptocarpus)* and cyclamen. Cape primrose must remain indoors unless temperatures are above

ABOVE: *Clockwise from the top in rice paper vases: star of Bethlehem, cyclamen leaves and flowers, and Christmas rose and ranunculus.*

55 degrees, and it prefers a window with early-morning sunlight. Monthly feeding with a blossom-boosting fertilizer will keep it flowering freely through the season. Cyclamen prefers a cool indoor climate, but will easily adapt to life outside under cover from frost.

Take a cue from the flowers, and keep your containers in the same color palette. Paint terra-cotta pots and saucers white; green leaves appear brighter, and blossoms sparkle against them.

Make miniature vases for cut flowers by covering small jars with delicate rice paper. A piece of double-stick tape will hold the paper in place, and a silk cord tied around each jar turns simple into elegance. Small vases require few flowers, so an arrangement can be inexpensive as

well as easy. Use one type of flower in each jar, and then group the containers on a pretty tray. For a more informal assembly, use rounds of white birch bark to cover pots of candytuft, Christmas rose, and crocus.

Bulbs in pebbles and water have a dressed-down look, appropriate both indoors and out. If you use soil-grown bulbs and want the casual appearance of pebbles instead, shake the soil free, and rinse any remaining residue from the roots. Then tuck each bulb into an antique jelly jar or ice-cream dish with pebbles, and add water.

Winter is the season to enjoy a pause from the hurried past, and to catch a breath before spring. White flowers are a lovely promise of this simple season. ◇

LEFT: *Paperwhites and cyclamen love cool days, and a cut camellia blossom is a joy to see.*
BELOW, LEFT: *White bark makes the perfect container for Christmas rose, candytuft, and crocus.* BELOW: *Primroses and cape primroses are diminutive enough to tuck into small places.*

by ELLEN RILEY
PHOTOGRAPHY JEAN ALLSOPP

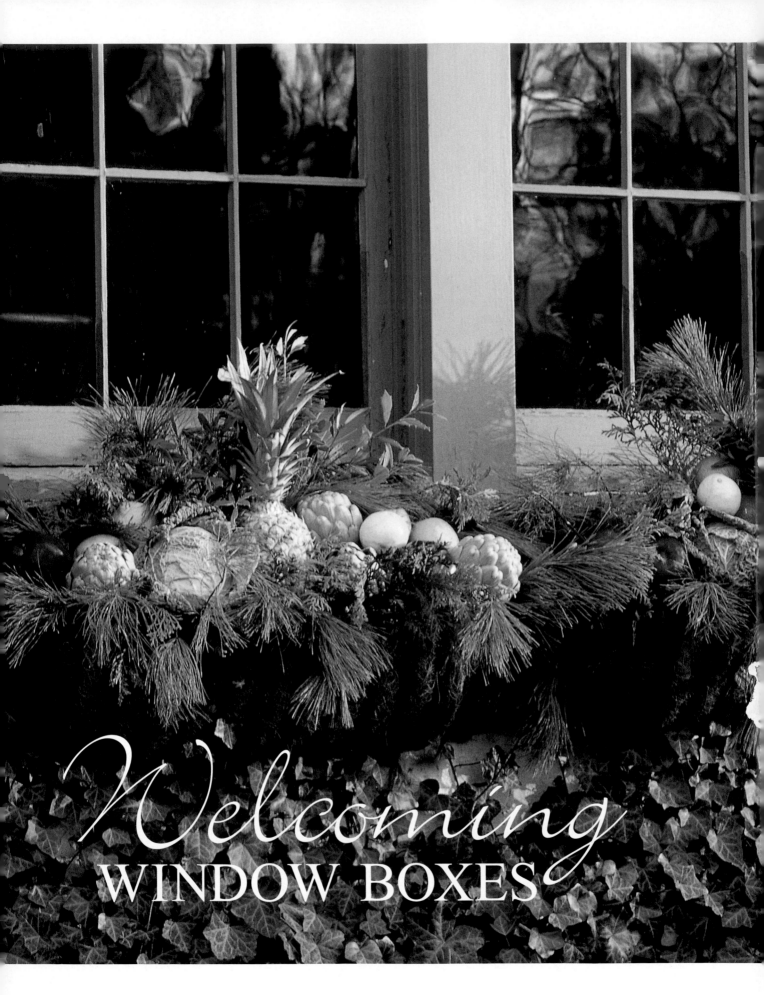

Welcoming
WINDOW BOXES

*Containers don't
last forever, so grab
the chance to mix it up;
take your pick of materials,
and have some fun.*

In January, icy winds flex frigid fingers around the garden, where flowerbeds slumber, dreaming of spring. Window boxes, void of summer's hot colors, hug the house, seeming to search for warmth.

"Winter is a real opportunity to do something fun, when things are really drab," says Barbie Tafel Thomas, a landscape designer with Webb-Thomas in Louisville. "You can also use things that would never work any other time of year." Whether you incorporate fresh fruit, small bushes and flowers, cut greenery, or dried material, your planters will take on a full, abundant look reminiscent of summer's substance.

"When you're having a party, pull out all the stops, and do up your window boxes with fresh produce," Barbie suggests. The containers pictured at left show how festive this can look. Barbie first filled the boxes with cut pine boughs to provide a soft-textured base. She added cypress and holly for diversity and then arranged the fruit. As always in good design, one element should be the focal point. Barbie chose a pineapple to center attention in each box and then built the arrangement around it. Clustered on each side of the main attraction, Chinese cabbage and artichokes add volume as well as additional green textures.

Winter fruit provides glorious color. Sunshine shades dominate citrus, and apples bring a drop of ruby red. For maximum impact, Barbie used citrus as the dominant color family and clustered each type of fruit. "The thing about lemons and oranges is that they're not

BY ELLEN RILEY
PHOTOGRAPHY JEAN ALLSOPP

terribly expensive in winter. They will stay fresh for several weeks, and they still retain color as they dry," she says. She placed apples sparingly throughout the collection for additional pizzazz. Drawbacks to using apples are their susceptibility to freeze damage and their tendency to show up on a squirrel's radar. As a result, they may need to be replaced more often than citrus.

Many garden shops and nurseries stock 1-gallon pots of hardy evergreens such as juniper, cotoneaster, Japanese boxwood, nandina, and ivy. Choose plants with good color, and avoid those with brown tips. Purchase ivy only if it has been outdoors. Greenhouse plants are not ready to face winter winds and will succumb to the first few cold nights.

RIGHT: *Cotoneaster and magnolia complement the dark shutters; dried hydrangeas pick up the stone color.* FAR RIGHT: *Cut greenery in hard-to-reach boxes is a carefree solution.* BELOW: *Conifers make a miniature forest while nandina berries add sparkle.*

ABOVE: *A container of shrubs takes on new personality with the addition of a small bunny and an interesting pot filled with birdseed.*

Barbie designed the stone box (shown at top of page) with a combination of cotoneaster and brilliant pansies for the plant base. "The box required more impact than just the shrubs and flowers. By using cut magnolia, I added a large leaf, which was needed, and gave the box a focal point," she says. Dried hydrangeas contribute additional texture and color, bringing unexpected lightness to the arrangement. "Using hydrangeas, and even cut magnolia, is a temporary thing.

It will last for about three weeks and then most likely need to be replaced. But that's a simple thing to do."

Another application is to use small conifers. A formal look is achieved by repeating one plant type across the back of the box and pansies of one color in front. A more casual look results from mixing the evergreens and using a combination of pansy colors. Ivy is a good choice to cascade over the front. Add texture with clusters of nandina berries or pinecones.

Maintenance can be an acrobat's hobby when a window box is placed in an upper-story location. In such a situation, Barbie employs a combination of cut greenery to fill this vacant space. While it requires occasional replacing through the winter, the

issue of watering is nonexistent. Greenery such as magnolia and holly hold up for long periods before browning, so the box always looks well tended.

An easy-care, whimsical technique is to add a single piece of garden statuary to the window box. Moderation is the secret here. Be sure to focus on one element, and center everything else in the box around it.

"When homeowners place window boxes on the front of their home, they are committed to doing something special and unique with that part of their landscape," Barbie says. Winter is a time when imagination and personality can take over. "Use the boxes to have some fun, and make the winter planting something special." ◇

> With planning and imagination, winter window boxes can be rich and full.

Chinese fringe (See page 31.)

February

Checklist for February

EDITOR'S NOTEBOOK

You're looking at one backward plant—variegated Italian arum (*Arum italicum* 'Pictum'). Unlike other plants that sprout foliage in spring and lose it in winter, this one does just the opposite. During summer, you never know it's there. But come winter, beautiful, deep green, marbled leaves peek out from between the leaf litter. Standing only about 2 inches tall, they form a spreading mat of foliage, adding welcome color to a pretty much colorless season. When hot weather arrives in early summer, the leaves wither, leaving short stalks topped by bright red berries. Italian arum likes shade and moist, woodsy soil, so it's a good plant to add to a naturalized area or woodland garden. And it's easy to share—just dig up a clump, and use your fingers to separate plants. Italian arum proves that it's okay to be backward. That singular thought has kept me going, lo, these 46 years. *Steve Bender*

☐ **Chrysanthemums**—Now is a great time to start thinking about your fall landscape in the Coastal and Tropical South. You'll want to divide, replant, and pinch mums back by about 3 to 4 inches. Also take cuttings of your favorites so they will be ready for a fall bloom. Dip the cut ends in rooting powder, and then stick them in pots that are filled with moist potting soil.

☐ **Cut branches**—When forsythia, quince, star magnolia, and saucer magnolia buds begin to show a touch of color, they are easy to force into bloom indoors. Cut branches, taking care not to destroy the natural shape of the plant. The branches should be in full bloom for several days after you place them in a vase of water indoors.

☐ **Daffodils**—The best time to cut these bulbs for indoor arranging is when they are still at the bud stage but showing a hint of flower color. By cutting then, you can add several days of life to your arrangement.

◀ **Bedding plants**—In the Lower and Coastal South, this is your last chance to plant cool-weather annuals. Dianthus, lobelia, pansies, snapdragons, and violas can still be planted before hot weather arrives.

☐ **Spring annuals**—Plants such as pansies, violas, ornamental kale, cabbage, stock, and snapdragons may still be set out now if they are started from 4-inch or larger pots in gardens in both the Middle and Lower South. Sweet alyssum transplants are available in a variety of colors including traditional white, purple, or blends and are excellent choices for either masses or low borders. Six-inch pots or gallon-size spring-blooming perennials, such as columbines, Shasta or ox-eye daisies, daylilies, purple coneflower, and Louisiana phlox will also perform well if they are planted now.

☐ **Trees**—This is an excellent time of year to plant trees in your garden. Before you plant, think about where you want to have shade in your landscape, and then select a tree that fits your needs. Keep in mind that it's a good idea to have a shade tree near the house to keep out the sun so that you'll save on electricity during the hot summer months. Remember, if you live in areas where the subsoil is hardpan or rock based, you might want to consider a fibrous-rooted tree, such as a maple, instead of a tap-rooted tree, such as a white oak. Ask your nursery to show you which trees' root systems fit your subsoil type before you make your purchase.

Roses—Plant now so they will be well established before hot weather. Lower growing types include 'La Marne' and 'Marie Pavié.' For hedges and background plantings, consider 'Mutabilis,' 'Old Blush,' or 'Mrs. B. R. Cant.' Climbers include 'Fortuniana,' 'Lady Banks's,' and 'Cherokee.'

☐ **Vegetables**—In all but the Upper South, it is time to plant onion sets, lettuce, spinach, and seed potatoes. All of these vegetables are somewhat frost tolerant, so don't worry if the nights are still cold in your area. ▶

PRUNE

☐ **Roses**—Prep your roses for spring bloom. After your last frost date, prune to remove all dead wood and crossing branches. Shorten remaining growth by about a third. Make cuts at an angle about ¼ inch above an outward-growing bud.

☐ **Trees**—Now is a good time to prune trees, except maples and birches. If the limbs are more than an inch in diameter, use the three-step method for removing branches. Make the first cut on the underside of the limb around 6 to 8 inches away from the trunk. Cut about half the thickness of the branch. Go to the top of the limb, and cut off the limb halfway between the underside cut and the trunk. The resulting stub should then be cut within ½ inch of the trunk.

FERTILIZE

☐ **Camellias and azaleas**—Fertilize these shrubs this month. If your azaleas and camellias fail to thrive, check the soil. These two shrubs prefer an acid (pH 5 to 6), well-drained soil containing lots of organic matter. Mulch azaleas well, as they have shallow fibrous roots and tend to dry out easily.

☐ **Palms**—Palms will soon begin active growth in the Tropical South, so feed them late in the month with a specially formulated palm fertilizer. Check the label, and make sure it contains iron, potassium, and manganese.

☐ **Pansies**—Pinch off withered and cold-damaged blooms. This will encourage plants to keep new blooms coming. When night temperatures remain above 40 degrees in your area, feed with a liquid fertilizer, such as 20-20-20, every other week to encourage growth and promote blooming.

Climbing roses—Don't prune these roses now; wait until after the first flush of blooms. However, now is a good time to tie main canes to a support before they leaf out. It is okay to remove stray canes that will not cooperate.

☐ **Poinsettias**—If you added poinsettias to your garden in the Tropical South, cut them back by about one-third. Keep them moist, but be careful not to overwater. Feed with 20-20-20 when new leaves appear.

CONTROL

☐ **Lawns**—Winter weeds are evident in dormant warm-season turf now. Hand pulling and spot applications of post-emergence herbicides are about the only methods of control. When selecting a post-emergence herbicide such as Purge, Weed-Stop, or Weed-B-Gon, make sure you follow label directions and that the product is approved for your particular grass type. Otherwise, you may injure or kill grass.

February notes:

❧

TIP OF THE MONTH

Lots of folks like to save seeds, but how can you tell whether old seeds are still good? Here's one way. Count out about 50 seeds, place them between two layers of wet newspaper, and cover the newspaper with a plate. After five days, count the number that have germinated to determine how thickly you'll have to spread them in your garden. If half are no good, spread twice as many as you normally would.

Mrs. B.E. Abbott
Indianola, Mississippi

IT'S ALL
monkey grass
TO ME

Low-growing, dependable, and green, liriope and
mondo fill in the cracks between seasons.

Do you have *Liriope muscari* or *Ophiopogon japonicus?* Chances are you have one or the other if you live in the South. Before you panic thinking you may have contracted an awful foot fungus or a disease from mosquitoes, relax. These horrible-sounding names are two of the most common ground covers in landscaping.

Both have been used for years to edge driveways, sidewalks, and flowerbeds. Because they spread and are almost impossible to kill, they are often given away as pass-along plants. Many people refer to both plants as monkey grass.

Liriope muscari ranges from 12 to 24 inches in height. When not called monkey grass, it's also known as lily turf or simply liriope. 'Big Blue' is the most popular and available selection. The leaves are ½ to ¾ inches wide. Liriope is usually dark green, but some selections, such as 'Silvery Sunproof' and 'John Burch,' have striped white or yellow leaves. Those selections tend to do better in sunny locations.

'Evergreen Giant' grows tall, usually 2 to 3 feet in height. It makes a nice foundation planting against the house under low windows. It isn't as cold tolerant as other selections and is best suited for the Coastal and Tropical South.

Liriope spicata, sometimes called creeping liriope, has soft narrow foliage. Because its foliage is not stiff, it forms a loose mound. It isn't recommended as an edging plant because it spreads aggressively and will quickly grow into turf areas and flowerbeds. It works well in large beds as a ground cover, where weeds have a hard time competing with it.

Liriope thrives in a moist, fertile, well-drained soil and will take sun or shade. Roots, known as stolons, move underground, allowing the plants to spread. More popular for its foliage, liriope does have attractive summer flowers. 'Majestic' has the showiest, producing spikes of purple that fan out at the top of plants. Liriope blooms are usually violet, but 'Monroe's White' has cream-colored flowers.

Ophiopogon japonicus, commonly referred to as mondo grass or mondo, is very similar to liriope but much smaller, growing 6 to 12 inches tall with ¼-inch-wide leaves. Its fine texture makes it a good ground cover in tight spots.

Mondo grass is not recommended for full sun locations because of leaf burn. A little shade allows it to retain a deep blue-green color. 'Silver Mist' is a variegated form with green-and-white leaf blades. There is also black mondo grass *(O. japonicus* 'Nigrescens') which has very dark foliage. This selection is more of a specimen plant and is slow to establish itself. Dwarf mondo (there are several dwarf selections) is tiny, growing only 3 inches tall. Many times dwarf mondo is used in cracks and crevices of walkways. Its low profile keeps it from interfering with your footing.

Mondo grass and liriope can both suffer from cold damage during bad winters; foliage can turn brown and look rough. You can run a lawnmower set on its highest setting or a string trimmer over them in late February to remove discolored foliage before new growth appears. When trimming, don't cut too close to the crowns of the plants, or you may hurt new

CLOCKWISE, FROM TOP LEFT: *Dwarf mondo, tucked in between these rocks, softens the hard edges. It grows only 2 to 3 inches tall and won't trip up pedestrians. 'Monroe's White' liriope is sun sensitive and prefers shade. Its white spikes help brighten dark locations. Liriope provides a thick edge for this flower border, creating a lush backdrop for annual color. Most selections of liriope have lavender to purple blooms in late summer.*

BY CHARLIE THIGPEN / PHOTOGRAPHY VAN CHAPLIN

DESIGN: HAROLD LEIDNER, DALLAS

ABOVE: *Liriope makes a nice dark green foundation planting under windows and won't interfere with the view.* INSET: *Both liriope and mondo grass form clumps that are easy to divide.* BELOW: *Here you see the size difference between dwarf mondo on the left, mondo grass in the middle, and liriope on the right. Notice the width of liriope's leaf blade.*

foliage. Even when cold damage isn't a problem, it helps to cut these plants back every few years to rejuvenate tattered foliage and promote new growth.

These ground covers are good for more than edging. They make a nice sweep of green in the landscape and can be used as a low-maintenance lawn substitute. They excel under trees where turf grasses struggle. Planted on steep banks, they help hold the soil and prevent erosion. Drought tolerant and rarely bothered by pests, they also look good in pots, planted alone or in a mix.

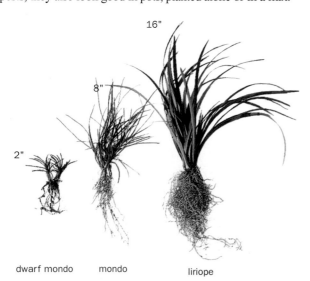

dwarf mondo   mondo   liriope

If you already have one of these ground covers and would like to divide it, don't worry. Liriope and mondo grass can easily be lifted, separated, and planted in other locations. Or you can buy them in flats or small pots. Buying lots of small pots may seem like an expensive way to go, but if you have to buy your plants, you can divide them and get several sprigs from one pot. Use a sharp hatchet or knife to separate tight, root-bound clumps, and then cut off the bottom half of the roots with clippers. This will not harm the divisions, but will promote new root growth.

Space liriope 8 to 10 inches apart and mondo grass 4 to 6 inches apart. Large plantings should be put out in a gridlike pattern. If the soil is loose and you water and fertilize periodically, they should mesh tightly together in a couple of years.

Mulch new plantings with finely shredded bark. Bark keeps weeds out and moisture in. It also allows stolons to move under the mulch so plants can spread.

Try one of these can't-miss ground covers. Don't limit them to just edging sidewalks and driveways. Plant them en masse or where your grass won't grow. You really have nothing to lose—they thrive on neglect. ◇

The flowers and foliage of this pink loropetalum stand out against the white azaleas.

A Lovely, Easy Shrub

Loropetalum (pronounced lor-o-PETA-lum) may be hard to say, but it sure is a pleasure to grow. This large, handsome shrub is a native of China and Japan, but it's pretty happy growing here in the South. Gardeners who want to avoid trying to say loropetalum may simply call it by its common names: Chinese witch hazel and Chinese fringe.

The white-flowering type, *Loropetalum chinense,* has been around for years and is truly a good dependable shrub, but it has never been widely grown. A pink-flowering version, *L. c. rubrum,* a relative newcomer to garden centers, has really popularized the plant. Some of the pink bloomers can be found under names such as 'Blush,' 'Burgundy,' 'Sizzlin' Pink,' 'Razzleberri,' and 'Rubrum.' Their airy ribbonlike blooms are striking, and some selections sport showy purple-green to burgundy foliage.

When you see knee-high plants at the nursery, don't be misled. At maturity some selections will grow up to 12 feet tall and 6 to 8 feet wide. They tend to have a vaselike shape. You can remove lower limbs from older shrubs to make small trees. Read the label or tag on the plants you buy for guidelines and spacing recommendations. They don't waste much time filling out and can grow up to 3 feet in a season.

These shrubs prefer loose, well-drained, acid soil. Full sun to partial shade is needed for plants to maintain a full shape and bloom heavily. Some of the burgundy-leaved selections have high fertilization requirements and need lots of sun to retain their dark foliage.

They seem to perform best in the Middle to Lower and Coastal South. Subzero temperatures can kill or knock plants back to the ground. In cooler climates apply a thick mulch to protect roots, and plant in a protected area.

Loropetalum makes a nice accent plant in a large container or planted in a shrub or flower border. Be careful using them in foundation plantings—many of the pink selections are so new that their mature sizes are unknown.

Their name may be hard to say, but these plants are easy to grow, and they're a great addition to any landscape. *Charlie Thigpen*

LOROPETALUM
At a Glance

Flowers: stringy pink or white blooms in spring
Culture: full sun to partial shade, needs well-drained nonalkaline soil; no major insect or disease problems
Size: 12 feet or more tall, 6 to 8 feet wide (Mature sizes of some new selections are unknown.)
Uses: borders, containers, hedges, specimens

Bare Facts for Planting Bare-root Roses

These plants can unnerve an inexperienced gardener. Here's how to get them growing.

After clipping off any damaged canes or roots, soak your bare-root rose in water for several hours to help it recover from its drying journey.

Spread the roots gently over a mound of soil in the hole so they'll grow at a downward angle. Organic material and water are all that's needed right now.

Keep the graft union a few inches above the soil and mulch level, unless you're trying to establish the rose on its own roots.

PHOTOGRAPHS: VAN CHAPLIN

It can be a little scary the first time you see a bare-root rose unwrapped. Whether purchased with its roots hidden by a colorful bag or received in a shipping box through the mail, once you've stripped off the packaging it seems so, well, *bare*. Your dream of richly colored petals spilling their intoxicating fragrance through a sunny, blooming garden is represented by nothing more than a prickly bunch of sticks.

Don't let the raw appearance dismay you though. Container-grown plants are easier to deal with in some ways, but buying roses or having them shipped while they're dormant and require no heavy supporting soil is very practical. It can also save some bucks (with which to buy more roses). Plus, bare-root roses are conveniently available for purchase during the cool fall, winter, and early-spring months that are our prime Southern planting season. Roses are tough; these sticks actually will turn into the rosebush of your imagination, with only a little effort on your part.

The first thing to do, once you've gotten over your instant of shock, is to pull on your gloves and inspect your purchase thoroughly. Canes should be plump and green, not desiccated and shriveled. Roots should be flexible, with minimal breakage. If everything looks to be in pretty good shape, this is the time to clip off any damaged parts and generally tidy up the plant.

Once you've groomed your rose, drop it (root end down) into a bucket of water to soak. You can, if you feel particularly nurturing, add a few drops of root stimulator, some alfalfa pellets, or a handful of compost, but plain old water is fine. The soaking time can be anywhere from 4 to 24 hours to properly rehydrate the rose without waterlogging its roots. This should give you plenty of time to dig and prepare the planting hole.

The new home you prepare for your bare-root rose should be in a nice, sunny area with well-drained soil. It helps to work plenty of organic material into the planting hole to feed the plant slowly and steadily as it gets established. There's no need to add a stronger fertilizer until the weather warms and the rose begins to show signs of active growth.

You want the roots of your rose to grow at a natural downward angle, so make a little mound of soil under it for support. Keep adding more soil until the rosebush is covered almost up to the graft union. (This is the knobby area at the base, where the rose plant you purchased is grafted, or budded, onto a super-vigorous rootstock to improve the plant's early performance.) Make sure the graft union is above ground unless you want the rose to put down its own roots. Firm the soil, and then water thoroughly to get rid of any air pockets. Add a layer of mulch for insulation. Don't remove the rose's identification tag, but move it if it cuts off growth.

That's it. You are now the proud owner of some carefully planted sticks. And in just a few weeks, when the leaves actually grow and the tempting buds begin to form, you will be so glad you had the courage to follow that rosy dream.

Liz Druitt

(For sources turn to pages 234–235.)

Note: Planting depth can vary depending on your growing conditions. Ask a local American Rose Society consulting rosarian if you have any questions on planting or caring for roses in your area. To find a nearby rosarian, contact the ARS at 1-800-637-6534. ◇

Starting Seeds

*Get your garden growing
early with these easy tips.*

Small pots of emerging stems, leaves, and roots, sprouting on the kitchen counter, are a daily reminder of a new garden's promise. It's also an opportunity to experiment—and learn a new plant's personality from the start.

The methods are easy, and the amount of equipment involved depends on the desired results. If you enjoy starting a few favorites for the simple pleasure of watching them grow, the supplies you need are minimal. If your interest is in production on a larger scale, there are ways to accomplish this with little fuss.

Most seeds germinate in anything that holds soil and drains well. For maximum success, use a lightweight seed-starting mix that provides good air circulation and stays evenly moist. Using heavy garden soil often causes seedlings to rot or fall victim to diseases.

An eggshell is a perfect place for a single seedling. As you use eggs, save the shells to make tiny seed pots. Break the egg toward the narrow top end, leaving a large portion of the shell intact. Rinse it with water, and carefully poke a drainage hole in the bottom with a sharp knife. Fill it with moist soil, and plant your seed. An egg carton keeps the shells upright and serves as a tray to catch water. When seedlings are ready, gently crush each shell, and plant. Roots grow through the cracks, and the shells add a small amount of calcium to the soil.

Another convenient container is a newspaper pot. A tool called a Paper Pot Maker aids in folding a strip of paper into a small vessel perfectly sized for one large seed or several small ones. The pot drains easily, and the newspaper does not deteriorate when damp. When seedlings are ready to set out, simply loosen the bottom folds, and plant—pot and all.

These seedlings can be planted container and all. Below: *A minigreenhouse provides humidity and moisture control.*

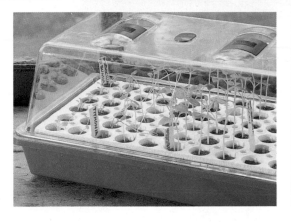

BOB HICKS'S TIPS FOR SUCCESSFUL SEEDS

For Germination:
- Keep humidity high and soil moisture consistent.

When Seeds Have Sprouted:
- Decrease humidity.
- Increase light gradually.
- Don't overwater.
- Handle seedlings gently.

If you choose to start a lot of seeds, a small greenhouse keeps the project contained and easy to regulate. Bob Hicks, of Park Seed in Greenwood, South Carolina, cites the best conditions, "A vented plastic dome allows all available light to come in and keeps drafts off the plants.

"Where a lot of homeowners fail is in the early stages of germination," Bob continues. "Problems arise when they start to overwater and expose the new seedlings to cool air right away. Once they sprout, open the vents on the plastic top so there is air exchange and the humidity level begins to drop. The air is still more moist than the rest of the house, but the seedlings are not exposed to drafts."

Once the new plants have several sets of leaves, remove the top, and place the tray in brighter light. Gradually get them ready to move outdoors by increasing the amount of light slowly. "Remember, plants are just like people. I lived in Florida for many years, and you could always tell people who had just arrived. They were totally red and blistered, and that's the same thing that happens to a plant when you move it into sunlight without acclimating it to the environment."

A seed is a miraculous thing. Give it water, soil, and light, and things begin to happen. Treat yourself to a gardening wonder, and get a jump on spring.

Ellen Riley
(For sources turn to pages 234–235.)

PHOTOGRAPHS: RALPH ANDERSON

PHOTOGRAPHS: EMILY MINTON

This adaptation of a Seaside arbor looks and feels at home in New Orleans. INSET: *Bobby Wozniak says his garden becomes like a jungle by summer's end.*

pretty. Because Bobby's home is in a historic neighborhood of New Orleans known as Bayou St. John, the 7-foot-tall fence provides much-needed privacy. It also serves as a backdrop for Bobby's many tropical plants.

"Like the rest of my house, the garden is very eclectic," Bobby admits. "It's not a large garden—this is midcity—so I take advantage of every available space." As guests enter through the arbor, they are greeted by a small carpet of grass surrounded by the lush foliage and bright flowers of Texas star hibiscus *(Hibiscus coccineus),* ginger lilies, spider flower *(Cleome hasslerana),* blood bananas, and angel's trumpet.

An Arbor Sets a Garden's Mood

Down along the Gulf Coast, and around New Orleans in particular, the word "lagniappe" pops up quite often. It refers to that little something extra given for good measure, usually between a merchant and a customer. It's going that extra mile—a thirteenth beignet the baker throws into a bag of a dozen.

In the case of New Orleans resident Bobby Wozniak, the lagniappe turned out to be the new fence and arbor that enclose his backyard garden. He had asked friend and landscape architect Blayney Fox Myers to come up with a design. She gave him all he asked for and then some.

"We're good friends, and he had seen a gate at my house and liked it a lot,"

Blayney recalls. "So he asked me to design a similar one for him." The idea for her own arbor came from a working vacation to the community of Seaside, Florida. "Visiting years ago was what originally got me going on my Victorian-esque arbor. Seaside is a great place to get inspiration for fences, arbors, pergolas, and all sorts of structures."

Because Bobby is a landscape photographer with a flourishing garden and a keen eye for details, Blayney designed a fence and arbor befitting his tastes—something that she knew he would be satisfied with in the long run.

Her custom-designed fence and arbor do more than just stand there and look

The fence and arbor, now seven years old, have weathered nicely and truly look at home in the garden. Bobby plans to brush on a clear sealer soon, but intends to keep that gray-green patina to complement his garden's casual style.

"It ended up a little more expensive than I first expected because the carpenters even took it a bit further than Blayney had drawn it," Bobby says. "They mitered some of the frame, and it took forever. But now I'm so glad they did because it turned out great. I see people stop their cars and point all of the time. And it's just so nice when you drive up, and it's there to greet you and welcome you to the garden."

Glenn R. DiNella

Colorful Pansy Pots

Selecting a great-looking container takes careful planning. First, choose the best pot for your home. Take a good look at its future location, and consider the surroundings—house and trim paint, stone, brickwork, existing landscape, and outdoor furniture all play a part in developing the proper combination of color and texture. The planter's tone and material should relate to these things. Choose a pot that looks comfortable in the location, and the plants will enhance its appearance.

Next, determine your pansy color scheme using the same principles. Choose one color flower for a dressy appearance and several shades for a more casual look. When adding other plants, as we have, make sure they all belong to the same color family.

TERRA-COTTA THREESOME

Our clay trio builds a collection around a central color theme. Yellow, orange, and red—all color cousins—establish a range of shades that includes the pots. (In parts of the South where clay may suffer freeze damage, use terra-cotta-colored plastic.) In the yellow pansy pot, we added an aucuba with golden variegation to mirror the flowers, plus a leatherleaf mahonia with lemon-colored blooms.

The pot to its left, filled with orange and red pansies, has a redtwig dogwood for height and color. The container below repeats the same flower combination with 'Bright Lights' chard,

Colors in the same family make a good choice for this brick landing.
Left: *Older pots have a less formal side that works well on hard surfaces.*

adding vibrant texture. In this arrangement, the plants and containers work together to create a fun and cohesive mix.

VIOLAS AND COMPANY

An old square planter with aged, peeling paint is a good choice for this landing where the brick meets the stone. The pot and the mortar share the same color, forming a common bond between the location and the container.

Purple violas billow over the front of the pot, their color tying together the red brick and bluestone. In back, shades of violet are continued with leafy purple sage, while dusty miller adds a silver surprise and gently

SUCCESSFUL CONTAINERS

Follow our suggestions and your pots will flourish.
- A large drainage hole is essential.
- Use good-quality potting soil.
- Thoroughly moisten the soil before planting.
- Mix a granular timed-release fertilizer, such as 14-14-14, into the soil when planting.
- Place the container in sufficient light for the plants you have selected.
- Continually monitor the soil, keeping it slightly moist at all times.

relates to the shade of the door frame and bluestone.

Containers are the finishing touch to any landscape, and pansies warm the winter with colorful blooms. Make them work in harmony, and you'll have perfect pansy planters.

Ellen Riley

Foxgloves tower over sweet William (See pages 52–53.)

March

Checklist
for
March

EDITOR'S NOTEBOOK

I have a singular relationship with mail-order nurseries. They love me to list them as sources for hard-to-find plants. Each mention generates hundreds of letters, phone calls, and frantic pleas. (I swear, you readers read EVERYTHING!) And, selfless to a fault, I ask nothing in return, except for a new house in the Bahamas. I'm up to it again. Ever grow a winter hazel (*Corylopsis* sp.)? Tsk, tsk—you should. It's only one of the finest flowering shrubs for late winter and early spring. There are several suitable species for the South, ranging in height from 6 to 15 feet. In late winter, they sport showy, pendulous chains of yellow, sweet-smelling blossoms even while the forsythia sleeps. Fall color isn't a sure bet, but I've seen these pest-free shrubs turn a nice yellow and even yellow-orange. Where can you get a winter hazel if your local nursery or home center doesn't have it? Give the folks at Carroll Gardens (1-800-638-6334) or Fairweather Gardens ([856] 451-6261) a call. While you're placing your order, ask them what the heck is holding up my blueprints.

Steve Bender

TIPS

□ **Annuals**—When it comes to buying transplants, bigger isn't always better. Choose the branched plant that is well-proportioned, not the tall one that has become rootbound. The transplant without flowers will perform better, and a young, healthy plant is a better bet than an older, stressed one.

□ **Birdhouses**—Get birdhouses and feeders out now so early arrivals will choose your garden for their nesting sites. Even if migrating birds don't stay around, you'll have an interesting parade of species to observe through the spring months.

□ **Division**—It's still time to divide deciduous clump-forming shrubs, such as forsythia, Japanese kerria, and winter honeysuckle. Just make sure this is done before they flower or foliage appears. To divide, prune shrubs back to within 4 inches of the ground, and dig up the plant. Separate the shrub into pieces, and replant the divisions in another part of your garden or give them to gardening friends.

□ **Spring bulbs**—As petite bulbs, such as crocus, Siberian iris, squill, and miniature daffodils, come into flower, a simple way to display them is in a nosegay. Cut the flowers in bud, and then attach a rubber band around the base of the blooms before putting them into a water-filled vase. This display is easy to arrange and gives the flowers support. ▶

PLANT

□ **Azaleas**—As this Southern classic comes into bloom, be sure to mark the color of each plant if you haven't planted them by color. For maximum impact, group azaleas in masses of one color or in layers of color. It is okay to move them while they are blooming. But if you wait until they finish, they can be rearranged, pruned, and shaped for a better show next year.

□ **Citrus**—This is a good time to add grapefruit, lemon, and sweet orange trees to gardens in the Coastal and Tropical South. 'Duncan' grapefruit, 'Navel' or 'Valencia' oranges, and 'Meyer' lemon are good choices. Fertilize existing trees with a citrus fertilizer, such as 8-2-8, early in the month to aid in fruit production. Scatter fertilizer under the tree, and water in well. Remove suckers on the bottom of the tree, and prune out any dead or weak limbs. Certain orange selections, such as 'Valencia,' are ready for harvest now.

□ **Ground covers**—'Needlepoint' English ivy, ajuga, liriope, monkey grass, vinca, perennial violets, and low-growing junipers are all good permanent ground covers. Perennials to use for ground covers in sunny areas include daylilies, thrift *(Phlox subulata),* dianthus, sedums, bouncing bets *(Saponaria officinalis),* and candytuft *(Iberis sempervirens).*

□ **Snap peas**—If you plan to plant sugar snap peas, do so as soon as possible. Because these are vines, it's a good idea to provide a trellis or other support when you plant. By doing this you will avoid injuring young seedlings and won't have to worry about when to add support.

Perennials—Plant perennials such as purple coneflower, 'Indigo Spires' salvia, and lantana. Also try gaura, 'Baby Sun' coreopsis, and hardy hibiscus such as 'Flare' and 'Disco Belle.' For texture and color include 'Powis Castle' artemesia and some of the colorful striped-foliage cannas.

Salad greens—As soon as the ground is workable, sow leaf lettuce and spinach seeds directly into the garden. Also when the danger of a hard freeze has passed, set out transplants of head lettuce. You can continue planting weekly throughout this month and the next to stagger harvest times.

☐ **Transplants**—Set out tomatoes, peppers, and eggplant, taking care to provide temporary protection from cold snaps in the Middle and Lower South. Okra, beans, squash, cucumbers, and melons can be planted from seed now. Mulch centers of rows with leaves, grass clippings, or coastal Bermuda grass hay applied over sections of newspaper to conserve moisture and reduce weed competition.

☐ **Tropicals**—Add tropicals to your garden this year in the Lower, Coastal, and Tropical South. The bold texture of dwarf bananas, crotons, gingers, elephant's ears (black, green, or variegated), and castor beans adds exotic interest to the summer garden. Brugmansia (angel's trumpets), night-blooming jasmine, bougainvillea, esperanza, and vines, such as mandevilla and allamanda, add color, fragrance, and texture from now until frost.

☐ **Vegetables**—In the Lower and Coastal South, start seeds for transplants of warm-weather crops, such as cucumbers, melons, squash, Spanish peanuts, and tomatoes. Stagger planting dates for continuous harvest. Try the supersweet corn types. These are especially good for weekend gardeners, as ears can stay on the plant a couple of days past ripening without becoming starchy. Potatoes can be planted directly into the ground. ▶

FERTILIZE

Daylilies—Looking to add color to your garden? Daylilies begin blooming this month and continue throughout the summer. Now is the time to select some of the many colors available for your perennial garden.

☐ **Lawns**—As warm-season turf begins to green, it's time to think about liming your grass. If your soil is acid, you need to do this every couple of years. A soil test will let you know exactly how much lime to apply. But if you're not able to get your soil tested, use the general guideline of 15 to 20 pounds of lime per 100 square feet of lawn area. Pelletized lime is less messy and easier to apply than the white-powdered kind.

☐ **Roses**—Rake old leaves and flowers from beneath your roses, and remulch the beds. Check your irrigation system, and make sure it is working properly. Avoid overhead irrigation that wets the foliage, as this can cause disease problems. A drip or 'leaky hose' system works better for roses. Fertilize with a timed-release granular rose fertilizer such as 15-5-13.

☐ **Trees**—Get trees ready for spring by fertilizing those not located in lawn areas. Sprinkle 12-6-6 fertilizer atop the ground around the tree, starting at 6 inches and extending to the dripline. At the middle of the month, prune branches damaged by cold weather. Scratch the bark with your fingernail to see if there is a green cambium layer underneath. Green indicates live wood. Cut injured branches back to the point at which you start to find green.

March notes:

❧

TIP OF THE MONTH

A tomato cage is excellent cover for small plants in cold weather. Place the cage over the plant, and slip a pillowcase over that. The pillowcase covers the cage, which keeps the cloth from touching the leaves.

A. WILLIS
HUDSON, FLORIDA

$\mathscr{S}cent$
OF THE SOUTH

*No wonder Carolina jessamine is a Southern favorite.
It's fragrant, evergreen, and easy to grow.*

O n an early spring trip to Savannah, as I strolled along brick-paved sidewalks beneath the canopy of venerable live oaks veiled in Spanish moss, I caught a whiff of a heavenly scent. I turned to see if I was being followed by some perfumed Southern belle. No such luck. I continued on a block or two and suddenly my nose detected it again. Trying desperately to place the fragrance, my mind conjured up images of powdery fresh babies, elderly ladies who sat near me in my childhood church, or perhaps some mom-and-pop flower shop.

Then I spotted it. Draped over an imposing black wrought iron fence was a twining vine adorned with thousands of sweet-smelling, buttery-yellow blooms—Carolina jessamine. I began noticing it everywhere—gently winding along picket fences, festooning arbors, trellises, and gazebos, even sprawling down steep slopes. It seemed this vine had been invited to take up residence at every home, from the smallest shotgun shack to the most elegant Italianate mansion.

This vine has certainly found a home in Savannah, but Carolina jessamine *(Gelsemium sempervirens)* should be invited to drape itself throughout the rest

of the South as well. It thrives from the hot Southern coasts of Texas and Florida to the milder areas of Maryland and Kentucky. Although jessamine bursts into bloom anytime from late winter to midspring (whenever the weather warms up), it surprises gardeners with sporadic light blooms during summer and fall. It flowers best in full to partial sun but also produces plenty of fragrant trumpet-shaped blooms in partial shade.

As the common name indicates, Carolina jessamine is a Southern native. South Carolina has even officially adopted it as the state flower. Being the Southern belle that it is, jessamine is very

BY GLENN R. DiNELLA / PHOTOGRAPHY VAN CHAPLIN

Carolina jessamine thrives above a bay window. Once planted, it takes only a few years for this graceful Southern vine to surround a window or door.

well-mannered and accommodating—never brash or pushy. It might be accused of being tenacious, but not usually invasive. Planted in good soil and watered well, a 1-gallon container of jessamine can cloak a mailbox in one or two growing seasons. Given an extra year or two, it can surround a door.

Once established, a little pruning every second or third year should keep the vine confined. Left unattended, it has been known to clamber across open fields, up tall pines, and envelop abandoned farmhouses. You can prune virtually any time of the year, but if you want to avoid cutting off the streamers of yellow blooms, the best time to prune is during spring or summer after the spring flush of flowers. You also might want to cut a few stems to use as sprays of yellow in a spring arrangement. When brought into a warm house just as the flowerbuds begin to open, they will soon unfurl to release their sweet perfume.

Because its foliage is so handsome, the vine would be well worth growing even if it never bloomed. Its small, glossy leaves are medium green in summer, but take on a deep reddish cast during winter. For most areas of the South, jessamine is evergreen, making it an effective screen. In the Upper South, it's better described as semievergreen, which means it loses many of its leaves in late winter, but leafs out again in early spring. In colder climes, it appreciates the

Jessamine doesn't have clingy aerial roots like English ivy, so it needs the assistance of a lattice to climb up and over this doorway. The lattice keeps the vine away from the siding for better air circulation and easier maintenance.

warmth of a south- or southwest-facing wall. Because jessamine's native habitat is either in or on the edge of woodland areas, it thrives in moist, well-drained soil amended with lots of organic matter. Planted in dry, infertile clay soil, it does fine but grows a bit slower.

Although Carolina jessamine looks great adorning doorways, fences, and trellises, it can also be useful elsewhere in the garden. It needs a little assistance from twist ties, fishing line, lattice, or masonry nails and wire to get started, but it can climb an arbor and help shade a bench, deck, or patio underneath. As jessamine twines upward, it has a tendency to get heavy at the top and leggy at the bottom. If you don't care for this look, try pruning some of the stems at the base to encourage new growth or plant low-growing shrubs or perennials to act as a

skirt around its knobby knees. You can always just let the vine tumble over until the stems sweep the ground. Without the help of a trellis or other support, this vine is perfectly content to form a thick blanket, putting down roots as it slithers along the ground.

Like most vines, jessamine is easy to pass along to others. Take stem cuttings anytime in summer, dip them in rooting powder, and then place them in potting soil. Keep cuttings slightly moist and protect them from hard freezes. The following spring you'll have lots of new plants to present to gardening friends.

Just invite Carolina jessamine over to your home, and offer it a seat beside your arbor or out by the gazebo; or simply let the vine spread out on that steep, un-mowable slope. Attend to its needs cordially as you would any refined Southern

CAROLINA JESSAMINE
At a Glance

Flowers: funnel-shaped yellow blooms in midspring; 'Pride of Augusta' is double-flowering form
Habit: twining stems need structure to climb but can also form 3-foot-high mounded ground cover; very tenacious
Zones: all but Tropical South
Light: best in full sun but does well in light shade
Soil: moist, fertile, well drained
Pests: none serious

belle visiting your home—a canapé of slow-release fertilizer such as Osmocote in spring and fall, an occasional generous libation of water through the heat of summer—and chances are it will make itself right at home. If you treat it hospitably, Carolina jessamine will grace your garden for years to come. ◇

Tips for Daffodil Care

20 EASY
DAFFODILS

Early
- 'Rijnvelds Early Sensation'
- 'Barrett Browning'
- 'February Gold'
- *Narcissus odorus*
  (a.k.a. 'Campernelle')
- 'Tête à Tête'
- 'Saint Keverne'

Midseason
- 'Carlton'
- 'Ceylon'
- 'Erlicheer'
- 'Ice Follies'
- 'Trevithian'
- 'Accent'
- 'Avalanche'
- 'Flower Record'
- *N. jonquilla* (a.k.a. 'Simplex')
- 'Quail'
- 'Sweetness'
- 'Geranium'

Late
- 'Hawera'
- 'Thalia'

Brent and Becky Heath know daffodils. They grow fields of them at their bulb farm, Brent and Becky's Bulbs, in Gloucester, Virginia. Here are some of their tried-and-true tips for success. For more on daffodils and additional advice from Brent, see "Naturalizing Daffodils," page 58.

"If you want to create a natural, graceful planting," suggests Brent, "try to lay out the bulbs in large, fluid sweeps of just a few kinds of daffodils. The initial investment for several hundreds or even thousands of daffodil bulbs may seem high, but it will be one of your least expensive landscape improvements because of their longevity and minimal maintenance."

Most daffodils will perennialize better when planted at a depth that equals at least three times their height. That's 6 to 8 inches deep for large bulbs, 3 to 6 inches for medium-size bulbs, and 2 to 3 inches for bulbs that are 1 inch in diameter or smaller. The reason for this, Brent explains, is that the soil pressure actually helps keep the bulb from splitting up too readily. Plant too shallowly, he says, "and bulbs tend to split up too quickly. You end up with bigger clumps, but smaller bulbs and fewer, smaller flowers."

When it's time to feed your daffodil bulbs in the fall, there won't be any foliage showing to help you remember where you planted them. Brent cleverly suggests outlining the drifts of daffodils with smaller bulbs, such grape hyacinth (*Muscari* sp.) or star flower (*Ipheion* sp.), whose leaves do come up in the fall. Or, he says, "Golf tees work well. Set them at the edges of the planting in late spring before the foliage dies down. They don't get pulled up accidentally because they're too low to the ground for a mower, and they're colorful enough to find later on." ◇

A Breath Of Spring

This time of year, a dose of spring is a good thing. Unfortunately, the weather is rarely ready to cooperate, and flowers are not always forthcoming. The solution is as simple as a trip to the grocery store or nearest plant shop.

Forced bulbs take center stage. Daffodils in all sizes and shapes bring sunshine indoors. Choose big-blossomed selections, such as 'Dutch Master' or 'King Alfred,' for a large display. On a smaller scale, miniature 'Tête à Tête' narcissus are laden with blooms.

Hyacinths spread their heady perfume from room to room, and usually, one bulb is plenty. If the container you chose has more, gently divide them and replant in smaller pots. The bulbs and blooms won't suffer from being disturbed. Spread them throughout the house, or share with a friend. You may also enjoy another relative: the petite grape hyacinth. This blue-flowered bulb looks lovely in a basket with tiny daffodils and does not have a strong hyacinth scent.

For the longest bloom time, purchase plants with buds and healthy, dark green foliage. Care for these springtime flowers is easy. Most containers are packed with bulbs, and the planting medium dries out quickly. Keep soil moist; small pots may require water every day. Soak them thoroughly, and drain well.

There is a bonus to buying forced bulbs. Enjoy their flowers indoors, and when the danger of frost has passed, plant them in your garden for future

ABOVE: Miniature daffodils, hyacinths, and primroses come together in a splashy seasonal celebration.
ABOVE, LEFT: Simplicity is never out of place. One perfect primrose in a large teacup reminds us that spring is here.

blooms. To store bulbs, remove faded flowers, and leave all foliage intact. Put the pots in a cool, out-of-the-way place, and water the bulbs occasionally to prevent them from dehydrating. When the weather and soil warm, plant in the garden, and allow the foliage to die before removing.

COOL AND COLORFUL

The jewel-tone blossoms of primroses can brighten a windowsill or illuminate a basket on the breakfast table. Pair them with blooming bulbs for a burst of spring, or place one fabulous flowering plant in an oversize teacup for a simple statement.

Purchase plants with a few open blooms to determine color, and look down into the rosette for additional buds. Choose plants with healthy, lush

green foliage, avoiding those with yellow leaves.

Care is simple, and primroses are forgiving. Soil must be kept moist, or the plant will wilt and the leaves will yellow. If you forget to water and discover a badly wilted plant, don't despair. Place the primrose in the sink in a saucer of tepid water. Allow the soil to rehydrate from the bottom, and then place the plant in a very cool place to recover. (I've gone so far as to revive a badly wilted plant in the refrigerator.)

Not unlike forced bulbs, a primrose's place is usually in the crisp spring garden. When used indoors, it will last longest if kept cool. Consider moving these flowers to an unheated garage or storage area at night or during the day when you're not at home. Primroses love a sunny spot and will bloom for weeks on end outdoors. A proper environment reduces the need for watering, and maintenance becomes less demanding.

Reasonably priced and full of color, these plants are a breath of fresh air, guaranteed to give you a lift.

Ellen Riley

Secrets of a Successful Relandscape

What happens to a yard when a one-story ranch house is upgraded to a two-story Tudor? Well, it isn't pretty. This remodeled home's old landscape was completely destroyed by backhoes, loaders, and other heavy machinery. But the following pages demonstrate that a good plan and new plants can make a house look great. So whether you are starting from scratch or have an established yard, there is something here for your.

Southern Living®
SPECIAL SECTION

Plan Before Planting

As construction was winding down on this remodeled house, it was evident we would need to completely relandscape. We considered trees, shrubs, flowers, and grass. A design plan helped us decide what we wanted—we're sure it can do the same for you. Choosing your yard's new look is the most important decision you'll make.

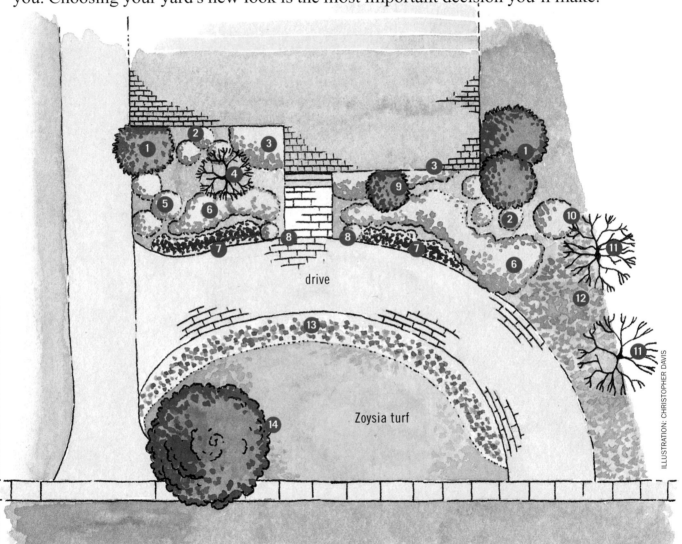

drive

Zoysia turf

ABOVE: *A well thought-out landscape plan helped make this yard both beautiful and functional.* RIGHT: *Construction of the newly remodeled house left the front yard a mess. In just weeks, our landscape plan started to take shape.*

The first thing we did was draw up a plan. For information on selecting someone to assist you, see the box at right. Once the plan was done, the brick landing and drive were installed. We completed the hardscape prior to planting because the additional construction would further compact the soil. We wanted all heavy machinery off the site before preparing the soil or setting out plants.

When the front landing and parking were finished, we used a large rear-tine tiller to break up the existing rock-hard soil. Then we spread topsoil, finely shredded bark, and sand over all the planting beds and tilled it in. The resulting soil was loose, fluffy, and ready for planting.

We wanted lots of color and only a small area of lawn. Not having to slave over a large area of grass would allow more time for tending annuals and perennials. Adding a tree, shrubs, flowers, and a touch of turf gave the landscape an established look in keeping with the home's new face and the well-groomed neighborhood.

The curb appeal is so strong, yet comfortable, that people who walk around the neighborhood for exercise casually stroll through the circular drive just to see what's in bloom. Though the remodeled house looks great by itself, the garden really complements the new facade. Look through the following pages to get ideas for your landscape. See how plantings dress up this house, giving it different looks throughout the seasons. ◇

The Southern Gardener Special Section was written and coordinated by Charlie Thigpen; installed by Scott Glenn, David Hicks, and John Merrill; photographed by Van Chaplin; with graphic design by Amy Kathryn R. Merk.

The Plants We Used

1. Weeping yaupon hollies
2. Nandina
3. Autumn ferns and cast-iron plants
4. Japanese maple
5. Spiraea
6. 'Carissa' hollies
7. Annual color beds
8. Dwarf Alberta spruces
9. Sasanqua camellia
10. Existing holly
11. Existing dogwoods
12. Existing ivy
13. Mixed flower border
14. Existing sweet gum

THE DISH ON DESIGNERS

A very important part of the landscaping process is choosing the right design professional. Landscape architects can draw up plans and make suggestions. They are also licensed to solve site problems, design plantings, pavings, and exterior structures. You can expect a higher fee from landscape architects, but they are capable of dealing with complex issues, such as high retaining walls, deck structures, extreme slopes, and drainage. A garden designer, horticulturist, or a reputable landscape contractor can also assist you with a plan. For information about our Custom Landscape Plan service, visit southernliving.com (AOL Keyword: Southern Living).

Choose a designer who will listen to your needs. Look at their finished products and check references from former clients. Prepare a list in advance of wishes and problems that need to be addressed in the design. Is there plenty of parking? Will you need more for guests? How about an irrigation system? Ask for a timeline so you will know the sequence of steps taken to complete the job and about how long it should take. Think about how much time you will have to tend your landscape. Work closely with whomever you choose, making sure you're comfortable with the plan and total cost before work begins.

Know your budget. If you need to install plants in stages because of cost, focus on the critical and visible areas first. Be patient. Landscape installation is very weather related. When it's spring and the weather's good, everyone wants yardwork done. Don't "cheap out" on your landscape. Nice plantings with a good design always enhance your home and increase its value.

Parking on the Loop

A new landing and parking area were the last hurdles to face before plantings could begin. We designed a half circular loop for off-street parking to complement the main driveway that runs along the side of the house. The front loop gives homeowners and guests a place to park their cars for a quick entry to the front door.

ABOVE: *Guests can now drive right up to the front door.* RIGHT: *We used a loader to grade the parking. Several curved 1 x 4s secured with wooden stakes form a guide for the brick edging.*

Although the new parking area takes up a lot of the front yard, it's not visually overwhelming. In fact, the finished look has a cottage feel and resembles a wide garden path. Using spray paint, we began by drawing the dimensions of the landing and parking area across the front yard, allowing us to easily visualize the space. For a driveway to be useful, it has to have maneuver room. A half circle like ours needs to be 10 feet wide or larger for

RIGHT: *After the parking area, the brick landing went in.* BELOW: *A single course of bricks, held tight with mortar, trims the parking area.*

DO IT MYSELF?

Be realistic with do-it-yourself projects. Let the pros handle the detailed work, and don't take on projects beyond your limits. Here, we let a brick mason do such work as the mortared edging and the brick landing, but we were able to do the gravel and brick patches ourselves.

LEFT: *We placed salvaged bricks to create irregular shapes in the gravel. The gravel packs firmly and holds the bricks in place.*

easy navigation and parking. If the new driveway is straight, about 12 feet is the minimum width you need.

Using salvaged brick left over from construction and two pickup truckloads of gravel, we achieved a great look on a budget. We used crushed limestone for the surface because it's inexpensive and looks good with the house. When using gravel for a driving surface, you need some type of edging to keep it in bounds. To make it, we selected bricks that matched those of the house. Our brick mason turned them vertically and set them on end in mortar. This edging easily holds 3 to 4 inches of crushed stone securely in place. We spread the gravel, wet it down, and then tamped it to make sure it would be the right level. Then we dug out a few areas in the gravel and set in patches of brick for some nice detailing. We leveled up the bricks and spaced them about an inch apart. We then poured gravel over and around the bricks and used a broom to sweep the gravel into all the gaps, stabilizing the bricks. The random patches look like remnants of an old brick roadbed, giving the surface an aged look.

Of course, you don't have to use limestone. In some regions, aggregates, such as pea gravel, crushed bricks, granite, and even oyster shells, may be more readily available. Concrete and asphalt are the most popular surfaces for driveways. Although concrete is usually more expensive than asphalt, it's more durable and can be dyed or stained. Before installing a driveway or parking court, look at the different materials available, and make sure they fit the style of your house. ◇

New Sod, New Look

In most everyone's thinking, no yard is complete without grass. So, we designed a small, tidy patch of turf. Just a single pallet of sod went into creating this half-circle lawn. If this looks too difficult, don't worry. Laying a small amount of sod yourself isn't that tough, and we teach you exactly what you need to know.

Soil preparation is the key to having a nice lawn. We installed this one in a couple of hours, but getting the soil ready took about twice as long. Never buy sod until your soil is prepared and weed free, because it should not be allowed to sit on the pallet for more than one to two days. Three weeks prior to laying our sod, we sprayed the site with Roundup to kill any weeds. A few days before starting to lay the sod, we thoroughly tilled a pickup truckload each of topsoil and coarse sand into the existing soil. Adding the extra topsoil and sand allowed us to raise the center of the lawn to ensure excellent drainage.

We selected 'Emerald' Zoysia for turf because its narrow leaf blades mesh together making a thick, cushiony carpet. It also grows well in sunny locations. Other warm-season turf grasses that work in these conditions are Bahia, Bermuda, buffalo grass, carpet grass, centipede, and St. Augustine. Bahia and St. Augustine are common in Florida, while buffalo grass is mostly grown in Texas.

If you live in the Upper South or upper Middle South, you may prefer a cool-season grass such as perennial

ABOVE: *These young neighbors like the looks of the new, cushiony-soft Zoysia lawn.* INSET (1): *Before sodding, prepare your soil. Remove weeds, and till 6 to 8 inches deep. Add organic matter and sand or topsoil as needed.*

BELOW (2): *Use a hard rake to remove tree roots, rocks, or other debris. Smooth the soil, and remove all dips and humps.* RIGHT (3): *Begin laying sod along a straight edge, such as the road, driveway, or sidewalk. Push pieces tightly together so they will quickly mesh.*

FAR LEFT (4): *Stagger the joints so they don't line up. This is critical on slopes where running water can cause washouts.* LEFT (5): *Cut sod with an ax or a sturdy knife. Then water thoroughly. Roll over the lawn in both directions with a partially weighted roller to help eliminate air pockets. Spread coarse sand in the joints.*

ryegrass, Kentucky bluegrass, or tall fescue that stays green all winter. Tall fescue also grows well in the upper half of the Lower South, provided it's watered regularly and grown with some shade. Centipede and Bermuda are common across the Middle South, as well as the upper part of the Lower South.

If you don't know what type of turf you need, check with your local county Extension agent. Drive around neighborhoods in your area, and don't hesitate to ask homeowners what kind of grass they have. Most people with nice lawns are proudly willing to share information.

Laying sod is hard work, but homeowners who don't mind getting dirty can do small areas. Just remember after the sod has been set out, you'll need to water, water, water.

During the first few weeks after sodding, the top 1 to 2 inches of ground should not be allowed to dry out. This is when the grass roots need to grow into the topsoil. Light daily waterings the first couple of weeks may be necessary to keep the soil damp. (Avoid sodding during dry periods.) Sod placed next to paved areas may need to be spot watered because these areas tend to dry out faster. As the turf roots in, you should water less frequently, but for longer periods. Lengthy waterings encourage the roots to grow deep into the soil. It's important to try to keep people and pets off new turf. Walking across damp sod causes it to be lumpy.

Don't cut the grass until it has grown a couple of inches. Then set your mower on its highest setting, and cut a strip to make sure you're not scalping the turf. Adjust your mower so that you remove only the top one-third of the grass blades. Plan to cut your grass often or on a weekly basis while it's actively growing. For a manicured golf course look, invest in a reel-type mower.

Most grasses are heavy feeders and need steady doses of fertilizer. Use a timed-release lawn fertilizer that feeds over a period of weeks or months. Most grasses need a fertilizer formula that's high in nitrogen and lower in phosphorus and potassium; however, the necessary ratio varies according to the type of grass and the time of year. Look for a fertilizer specifically labeled for your type of grass, and apply according to directions on the bag. Never overfertilize. Too much nitrogen and too little water can burn a lawn and kill it.

To keep your lawn neat looking and in bounds, use a string trimmer once a week during the growing season to edge along sidewalks, driveways, and flowerbeds. Cut a trench around flowerbeds with a flat shovel once a year.

Choose a turf that's right for you. To minimize maintenance, limit the amount of grass in your yard. A small attractive lawn can make a big impact. ◇

Easy Spring Flowers

How easy? Only seven flats of annuals and a few choice perennials went into this bursting flower border. Given the span of just a few months, the front yard looked like a cottage garden. The plants added appeal and charm. It hardly resembled the barren earth that surrounded the house not long ago. If you want a colorful spring garden like ours, you have to realize that the real work starts in the fall.

This curved flowerbed, which runs along the edge of the gravel parking area, is 4½ feet wide and 66 feet long. A small bed of Zoysia grass sweeps across the front edge of the border, making the flowerbed accessible from both sides of the border. Weeding and planting can be done without having to step all over plants or compact the loose, freshly tilled, and amended soil.

The area receives lots of direct light, so we used sun-loving plants. We put in

a few die-hard perennials, such as two ornamental grasses *(Miscanthus* sp.), one butterfly bush *(Buddleia* sp.), one Rose-of-Sharon *(Hibiscus syriacus),* and some 'Homestead Purple' verbena *(Verbena canadensis* 'Homestead Purple'). The plan is to install a few perennials each year and keep the open spaces covered with seasonal flowers.

To fill in the open areas, we used foxgloves, pansies, violas, snapdragons, and sweet Williams. We wanted lots of

ABOVE: *In the foreground, white violas, purple verbena, and sweet Williams mingle for a carefree look. Tall foxgloves give the border height and dimension.*

pink, yellow, purple, and white bloomers in the border because these colors blend well together. On a cool autumn day, we planted seven flats to produce a colorful April and May border. Each flat contained 36 little plants. When setting

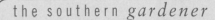

ABOVE, LEFT: *Foxgloves' bell-shaped blooms line stately stems.* TOP, RIGHT: *Creamy white snapdragons rise above pink geraniums.* BOTTOM, RIGHT: *The colorfully laced blooms of sweet William cluster atop 10- to 20-inch stems.*

them out, we worked a little timed-release fertilizer into each hole.

After the fall planting, little maintenance was needed. A blanket of pine straw mulch covered the ground, keeping most weeds out and helping to protect the new plants. We checked the border once a week and quickly pulled any weeds. Little watering is needed in winter, unless you're experiencing extended dry spells. The pansies were groomed occasionally by removing spent blooms. We did have to cut back the snapdragons after a few subfreezing nights turned their foliage brown, but cutting them back actually made them fuller in the spring. The tall foxgloves were supported using twine and a bamboo stake for each plant.

Why plant in the fall? The plants actually grew little in the fall and winter months, but underground roots began to spread, creating good anchorage and a strong growing base. The spring sun warmed the soil, and the tops of the plants began to flush with new growth. The foxgloves that were about 6 inches in March quickly grew to 4- and 5-foot-tall, multicolored spikes by May. Don't forget to set out plants in the fall for lots of spring blooms.

PLANTS TO MAKE YOUR YARD SPARKLE IN THE SPRING

Foxglove *(Digitalis purpurea)*—This is the most common foxglove. It's a biennial and sometimes a short-lived perennial in most of the region; in the Lower and Coastal South, treat it as an annual.

The flowers are 2 to 3 inches long and look like clusters of bells dangling from the sturdy stalks. Blooms vary in color from creamy white to dark pink and purple with spotted throats. Common foxglove grows 3 to 5 feet tall. It may need to be staked to withstand the beating of heavy rains. Plant foxgloves in protected areas next to walls or fences and away from windy locations. You get a lot of bang for your buck with foxgloves. They're easy to grow, and they add height and charm to any garden.

Pansy and viola *(Viola* sp.)—These compact annuals provide sporadic color in winter and then a carpet of blooms in the spring. Their cheery-cheeked flowers look like children's faces. Violas, also known as Johnny-jump-ups, are a compact version of pansies. Many violas will reseed freely in the garden.

Both pansies and violas come in a variety of colors ranging from white to blue, red, orange, yellow, and purple. Petals are often striped or blotched, but 'Crystal Bowl' pansies are a selection without the blotch. 'Crystal Bowl True Blue' and 'Crystal Bowl Yellow' are two reliable performers, and the yellow is also extremely fragrant. In the Upper South, plant them in the early spring; elsewhere, plant in the fall. To prolong bloom time, remove faded flowers regularly before they go to seed.

Snapdragon *(Antirrhinum majus)*—These are great flowers for sunny borders. They grow 6 to 36 inches tall, and come in many colors, including white, pink, red, yellow, and orange. Medium and tall snapdragons work well in the middle or back of a border underplanted with pansies. When planted in fall, they bloom on and off in winter and heavily in spring, except in the Upper South where they may be planted in spring for summer blooms. Or they can be grown as short-lived perennials in the Upper South. Elsewhere, snapdragons are discarded after spring and replanted in fall.

Sweet William *(Dianthus barbatus)*—These vigorous, old-fashioned biennials are often grown as annuals. Small plants set out in the fall garden quickly spread to form a mass of foliage. The plentiful leaves keep the garden green throughout winter. In spring, dense clusters of white, pink, rose, purple, or bicolored flowers appear. The blooms look like small clouds on top of tall stems. ◇

Selecting Shrubs and Trees

Annual and perennial flowers tend to get all the glory, but shrubs and trees hold the garden together through the seasons. Think of them as the bones of your yard. Here are some of our favorites that we're certain you'll want to bone up on.

LEFT: *Lined with white blooms in early spring, spiraea's stems look snow covered.* ABOVE AND RIGHT: *'Carissa' holly will grow spiny leaves if it reverts to its parent, Chinese holly. Clip these limbs when you see them growing.*

Common shrubs and a tree contribute to the new landscape by adding texture, form, and height. Some of the shrubs produce berries or seasonal blooms for an added bonus. The selection and placement of these plants at the remodeled house were critical because we didn't want them to cover windows or block walkways in a year or two.

A 10-foot-tall green Japanese maple *(Acer palmatum)* became a great specimen in the front yard, planted next to the landing. It was the most expensive plant in the whole project (around $250), but when fully leafed out in the summer, it shades the large front window. This tree will, in time, grow to about 20 feet tall, making it an excellent choice for the small lot. Japanese maples perform best in a slightly shady

location. If planted in full sun, they can suffer from leaf burn.

'Carissa' hollies *(Ilex cornuta* 'Carissa') planted across the front of the house create a low sweep of green. We placed 13 on one side of the walk and 23 on the other. These evergreen shrubs will grow 3 to 4 feet high in time. They don't produce berries like many hollies, but their durability and size make them a nice choice for the foundation plantings. Their leaves have one soft spine, so they aren't difficult to work with, like some of the spiky hollies. They need full to partial sun to maintain a full shape.

Baby's breath spiraea *(Spiraea thunbergii)* provides lots of early-spring color. A group of three produces sprays of tiny white blooms; the flowers look like lace lining the long, slender stems.

This old-fashioned shrub isn't evergreen but can have nice fall color, turning yellow to reddish brown. It grows around 5 feet tall and wide and likes sunny sites but will take a little shade.

Nandina *(Nandina domestica)* is another old-fashioned shrub used in this front yard. It usually grows 5 to 6 feet tall, but old, established plants can stretch up to 8 feet in height. An upright growth habit makes it a nice choice for a narrow spot. This durable landscape shrub produces clusters of red berries in autumn and winter. It will grow in either sun or shade.

Before you buy shrubs or trees for your yard, know what you're growing and the plants' ultimate sizes. A 2-foot-tall plant you buy now may reach 20 feet someday. ◇

Blooms To Beat the Heat

Spring blooms are easy for us all. The temperatures are nice, and there's usually adequate rainfall to keep flowers healthy and happy. Then summer rolls in like a sauna, the heat can be suffocating, and watering becomes a daily affair. Nobody wants to spend hours in the baking sun slaving over a garden. Let us show you which plants need little attention through the warm weather.

ABOVE: *Narrow-leaf zinnia* (Zinnia angustifolia) *frame the front door; lantana mixes with ivy geraniums.* INSET: *Purple heart, variegated ivy, ferns, and striped ornamental grasses add color, interest, and texture to the border.*

Most people have a hard time pulling up flowering plants. In late May, spring bloomers, such as pansies, still provide a little color in the garden; however, they begin to grow leggy and their bloom size decreases. Don't wait for cool-weather plants to totally decline, pull them out, and start planting for summer.

Most summer-blooming bedding plants do best when they're put out in May and June before summer becomes unbearable. This gives them a chance to root in, get established, and endure late-summer droughts.

Take a look at some of the plants that performed well for us in the landscape. Texas sage *(Salvia coccinea)*, purple heart, lantana, and narrow-leaf zinnia *(Zinnia angustifolia)* are favorite summer beauties that beat the heat. It's a good thing we used these tough plants, because part of the summer we were unable to water due to drought-imposed watering restrictions.

TIPS FOR YOUR SUMMER GARDEN

When adding color to your garden, don't forget about foliage plants. Purple heart, sweet potato vine, ornamental grasses, elephant's ears, ferns, coleus, and caladiums add bold colors and wonderful textures to the garden. And don't limit yourself—try colorful, tropical plants that thrive in the heat.

Avoid too many hot colors, such as red or orange. Instead, mix in cooling whites and blues. Using too many hues makes your garden look chaotic.

When your plants do need a drink, water them well. Try to soak the first couple of inches of soil, watering as little as possible and letting your soil dry a bit between waterings. Twice a week waterings are usually sufficient. Don't water daily, and remember frequent overhead waterings can cause plants to become infected with fungus or other disease. When possible, use drip irrigation systems and soaker hoses to minimize runoff. Make sure plants have a thick mat of mulch around them to help retain moisture, keep out weeds, and dress up beds.

Every few years you should add some organic matter, such as finely shredded pine bark, sphagnum peat moss, mushroom compost, or leaf mold to beds. Use a tiller or turning fork to mix the organic material thoroughly, loosening the soil and making it easy to dig and plant. ◇

TIMING IS CRITICAL

■ In late spring, pansies grow leggy and begin to melt in the heat. As they decline, pull them out, and weed and mulch beds. Then replace them with summer-blooming annuals.

■ Mulch beds before you plant. We put out a couple of inches of pine straw, and then planted through the mulch (below, left).

■ Space plants according to planting directions. These narrow-leaf zinnias (below, right) spaced about a foot apart looked sparse at first, but quickly grew together for a full-flowered look.

naturalizing
daffodils

BY LIZ DRUITT / PHOTOGRAPHY VAN CHAPLIN

*Sunny symbols of spring, these flowers are pest free, low maintenance,
and easy to establish in your garden or landscape.*

"We can't help being partial to daffodils," explains Brent Heath. "Yellow is a wonderful color, and daffodils put up these big yellow flowers to attract early spring pollinators, so they grab our attention and win our admiration at the same time." Brent would know. His family has been growing daffodils in Gloucester, Virginia, for more than 100 years. The fields of yellow, brilliant now in early spring, are part of Brent's heritage as well as the backbone of Brent and Becky's Bulbs, the business he runs with his wife.

Daffodils are among the easiest plants to grow. "You don't have to do anything if you just want a one-time spring display," says Brent. "Bulbs, daffodils in particular, are pretty resilient and typically adapt to whatever situation you give them." For your daffodils to come back year after year, however, Brent has a few suggestions that will increase your success.

First, be sure of the sunlight. Choose a site that gets at least six hours of sunlight after the leaves are on the trees. It can be morning, afternoon, or constant dappled light, but the daffodils must have light for their leaves. Otherwise, they can't replenish the nutrients in their bulbs for the next blooming season.

Floods of golden flowers wash across these sunny gardens and reliably return year after year in greater beauty.

The third requirement for happy daffodils is to fertilize your bulbs every fall with a time-release organic or encapsulated product (such as Holland Bulb Booster or Brent and Becky's Daffodil Fertilizer), broadcasting it over the bulb beds according to instructions on the bag. "The ideal fertilizer for daffodils would have an N-P-K balance of 10-10-20," Brent says. "We recommend feeding in the fall when roots begin to form, but it's actually never too late to make a difference unless you wait until after they bloom. In early spring, you can't count on the nutrients leaching down to the roots quickly enough, so if you wait till then, use a fast, water-soluble fertilizer."

If you follow Brent's advice, you not only get beautiful drifts of daffodils every spring, but also you get a much better looking landscape after the burst of bloom is over. "You're left with nice, healthy foliage that normally stands upright and remains green as long as it's still actively supporting the bulbs underneath through photosynthesis," says Brent. He goes on to add that it's only if there's a shortage of three critical elements—sunlight, moisture, or nutrients—that the foliage weakens, flops over, and becomes unattractive. "Then gardeners want to tie it in knots, braid it, or fold it over and pin it to the ground, all of which suffocate the leaves and starve the bulbs."

After the foliage begins to turn yellow, you can cut, mow, or cover it with mulch if it isn't neatly hidden by companion perennials growing around the daffodils. That's also the time to dig, divide, and transplant bulbs. Until then, leave your daffodils alone. They need to gather all the sunlight they can, blending it with moisture and nutrients to make starches and sugars, stored in their bulbs for next year's joyful yellow blooms.

Secondly, plant so your bulbs have water during their growing season and good drainage all the time. Brent points out that most of the South has less than ideal soil for bulbs, which need to stay especially well drained during the summer so they don't rot. Daffodils would prefer sandy loam, but Southern gardeners are more likely to be wrestling with thick, sticky clay.

The easiest way to deal with heavy soil, Brent says, is to build your beds on top of it. "Improve just the top layer of soil by turning or tilling in well-composted organic material. Plant the bulbs shallowly; then add several inches of clay, or even coarse builder's sand, on top. Bulbs grow up through the clay or sand just fine, put out their roots in good soil, and get all the drainage benefits of a raised bed."

For more tips on growing daffodils, turn to page 43. ◇

(For sources turn to pages 234–235.)

*A terrace garden
(See pages 74–79.)*

April

Checklist for April

EDITOR'S NOTEBOOK

I've always said that dogs and gardens don't go together. But that was before I planted Florida anise *(Illicium floridanum)*. This large native shrub, which grows 6 to 12 feet tall, is an anchor of my shade garden. In summer and fall, it sits peacefully beneath tall trees at the woods' edge, calling no attention to itself. But when the oaks, hickories, and gums drop their leaves in winter, its handsome evergreen leaves give the garden welcome color and form. Another thing I like about this plant is that it has no pest problems. This is all highly enlightening, you say, but what does it have to do with dogs? Well, in spring the shrub bears showy flowers, ranging from red to maroon to white. Some blooms smell sweet. Others, for some strange reason, smell like a wet dog. This leads some folks to call this shrub "stinking anise." I don't think that's a very nice name for a plant—but it's a perfect name for a dog.

Steve Bender

☐ **Lawns**—It's time to start cutting warm-season turf, such as Bermuda, St. Augustine, and centipede. Be careful not to scalp your lawn. Adjust the blade height so that the turf looks cut when finished, but you can't see spots of soil. A good general rule of thumb for spring cutting: Remove only about the top third of the grass blades each cutting. During periods of fast growth, try to cut your lawn at least once a week. ▶

☐ **Mulch**—Now that winter is gone, remove and replace mulch around such plants as azaleas, roses, and camellias because disease spores and insects may have overwintered in this material. If you think disease or insects are not a problem, just freshen your mulch.

☐ **Caladiums**—The foliage of dormant caladiums will begin pushing up this month in the Coastal and Tropical South. Plant new tubers 2 to 3 inches deep in sunny to lightly shaded locations now too. Feed with a 6-6-6 or other complete fertilizer, and keep tubers moist for best growth. When planted in full sun, make sure to supply adequate moisture. 'Red Flash,' 'White Christmas,' and 'Pink Beauty' fancy-leaved caladiums will grow taller in the shade; 'Pink Gem' or 'Red Frill' produce abundant leaves and are perfect ground covers. For sunnier locations, choose dwarf selections, such as 'Little Miss Muffet' and 'Gingerland.'

☐ **Easter lilies**—For a temporary indoor treat, look for Easter lilies in your garden center this month. Select medium to compact lilies with dark green foliage and buds just beginning to open. Cut off flowers as they start to shrivel. Place the pot in bright, indirect light. Water when the soil feels dry; pour excess water from the saucer. When the bulb finishes blooming, plant it about 3 inches below the ground in a sunny location outdoors. Cut the stem to the ground, and water thoroughly. Expect blooms in early summer next year.

☐ **Herbs**—Once the frost period has passed, it's time to plant herbs. Culinary herbs are easy to grow, but be sure that you've planted enough of the ones you frequently use. As a general rule, it takes twice as many fresh herbs as it does dried ones to equal the same amount of flavor in cooking.

☐ **Perennials**—Set out perennials now in the Middle, Lower, and Coastal South for extended seasons of garden color. Favorites include lantana, cannas, cape plumbago, *Salvia greggii,* 'Indigo Spires' salvia, gaura, and turk's cap hibiscus *(Malvaviscus arboreus drummondii).*

☐ **Shade trees**—Select containerized trees that are easily transplanted and in ample supply at local nurseries and garden centers. Among the good choices are lacebark elm *(Ulmus parvifolia),* bur oak *(Quercus macrocarpa),* cedar elm *(U. crassifolia),* Bradford pear, and bald cypress. Protect their trunks against frost damage and sunscald by applying a tree wrap for the first year or two. Be sure to stake newly planted trees

Daisies—You may want to cut the bloom stalks off when Shasta daisies finish blooming to prevent them from reseeding around the parent plant. Or if you want them to reseed, wait to cut until the seedheads are dry and crisp and the seeds have already scattered naturally.

Zinnias—In the Coastal and Tropical South, direct sow large cutting selections of zinnias. Cut the flowers often to encourage more blooms. For a denser, lower-growing plant, consider hybrid bedding types such as 'Profusion,' which will last all summer.

to keep them upright and stable while new roots are forming.

☐ **Summer annuals**—In the Middle, Lower, and Coastal South, continue plantings of small- and large-flowered zinnias, portulaca, bedding begonias, geraniums, coleus, angelonias, Philippine violets *(Barleria cristata),* impatiens, and marigolds. Wait a few weeks until the soil is warmer to plant cleome, bachelor's buttons (globe amaranth), crested- or spike-flowering celosias, and Madagascar periwinkle.

☐ **Tropical vines**—Add a new dimension to your garden. Vines require little space at the ground level but can create splendid displays of foliage and flowers, while providing screening and welcome shade during the summer. Good choices include bleeding heart vine *(Clerodendrum thomsoniae),* butterfly vine, hyacinth bean*,* rangoon creeper *(Quisqualis indica),* and air potato vine *(Dioscorea bulbifera).* Plant after your last frost.

☐ **Vegetables and herbs**—In the Lower South, it's the last chance for planting snap peas, broccoli, and potatoes. Chives, dill, and rosemary can also be added to the garden. Water only when soil is dry to encourage deep root growth.

PRUNE

☐ **Azaleas**—If your azaleas need pruning, do so immediately after their flowers fade. Make sure you remove stray branches and shape the plants to look good for the summer. Apply 16-4-8 or similar fertilizer at the rate recommended on the label. Sprinkle around the dripline of the plant to avoid letting the fertilizer touch the branches.

☐ **Snapdragons**—As the stalks of snapdragons elongate and the blooms finish, cut the stalks off deep in the plant. This extends the blooming season several weeks, allowing a second set of bloom stalks that will be smaller but more abundant.

FERTILIZE

☐ **Tropicals**—Once night temperatures are above 50 degrees, move your tropical plants that have been stored indoors to the outside into shade, and water well. After they adjust, an application of fertilizer would be beneficial. Liquid fertilizers such as 20-20-20 or a similar formulation will encourage them to flush with new growth.

CONTROL

☐ **Pests**—Aphids, mites, and thrips are making an appearance this time of year. Check new growth for aphids, undersides of leaves for mites, and opening flower-buds for thrips. Aphids and mites can be controlled by removing the affected part or by applying insecticidal soap or horticultural oil, available at your garden center. To control thrips, spray with a product such as acephate (Orthene).

Coleus in Containers— Plan eye-catching combinations for summer container displays. Mound several tall-growing plants, such as coleus, scented geraniums, or ornamental peppers, near the pot centers. For the rims of the pots, place such trailing foliage plants as ornamental sweet potato vine or English ivy.

April notes:

TIP OF THE MONTH

Now that tomato season has arrived, get empty gallon-size food cans, and cut out the bottoms. Bury them halfway into the ground, and then plant tomatoes inside the cans. This prevents cutworm problems. Also, when it's hot and dry in summer, you can fill up the cans with water, and they will direct water to the roots.

J.L. EWING
SHREVEPORT, LOUISIANA

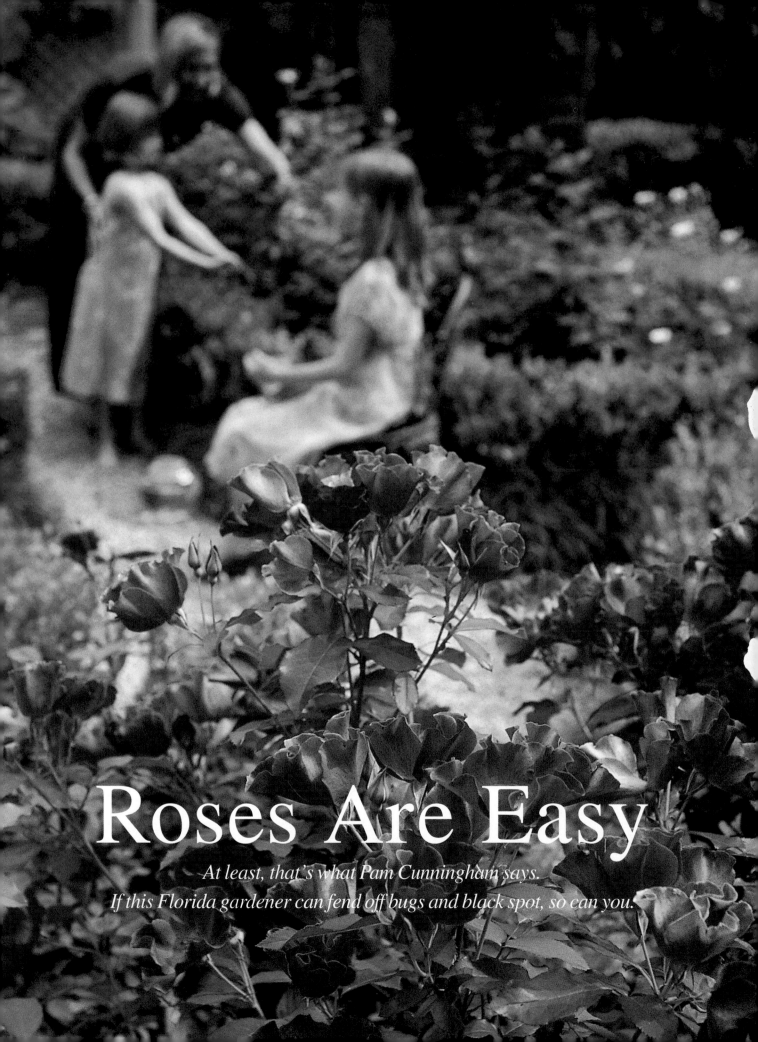

Roses Are Easy

At least, that's what Pam Cunningham says.
If this Florida gardener can fend off bugs and black spot, so can you.

GARDENING
PLANTS AND DESIGN

Japanese boxwoods edge formal beds linked by paths of brick and gravel. Drip irrigation lines keep thirsty roses watered. LEFT: *Pam tends roses with daughters Ellison and Kelli.*

I may be older than King Tut's underwear, but that doesn't mean I can't learn something new. Case in point: Until I met Pam Cunningham, I never knew roses were low-maintenance plants.

"Madness!" you cry, having heard horror stories about incessant spraying, grooming, feeding, and weeding of roses. But Pam swears she gets beautiful flowers year-round with little effort.

Her garden in Ocala, Florida, was originally designed by a local landscape architect as a home for vegetables and herbs. But she quickly found the upkeep to be overwhelming. "We had to completely replant the garden every season," Pam explains. "And our plants were getting killed by insects. Then I had the idea that I should garden organically, so my

daughter and I would go out and remove caterpillars from broccoli by hand and fill paper cups. It was disgusting."

Out went the vexing vegetables and herbs. Then, aided by a local horticulturist, Pam rededicated her garden using the original design. "We dug up the beds; amended the clay soil with sand, peat moss, and manure; and edged the beds with Japanese boxwoods," she recalls. "Then we planted roses. And they were so much easier."

Several factors determined the kinds of roses. "I wanted great color and a lot of variety," she says, "some antique-looking roses, some long-stemmed ones like 'Mr. Lincoln' and 'Tropicana,' others like 'Playgirl' that have just a few petals, and small-flowered ones like

'Summer Snow.' When 'Summer Snow' is in bloom, you can cut it and make huge bouquets of flowers."

But what of the unending toil and high anxiety we all know beautiful roses demand? It's a myth, insists Pam. She simultaneously feeds her roses and fends off insects by sprinkling RosePride Systemic Rose & Flower Care 8-12-4 around the base of her plants every six weeks. She doesn't bother spraying for black spot or mildew. Instead, she simply picks off any diseased leaves she spots. To retain soil moisture and inhibit weeds, she mulches with pine bark chips several times a year. Finally, a drip irrigation system supplies necessary water without wetting the foliage, which would promote disease.

BY STEVE BENDER / PHOTOGRAPHY VAN CHAPLIN

'Tropicana'

'Playgirl'

'Peace'

TOP: *Running beside the house, the garden contains about two dozen kinds of roses, as well as a variety of perennials. Its modest size makes for easy maintenance.*

"What I like most about the garden is the continuous flowers," Pam states. "I cut the roses back around Valentine's Day, they grow back, and I have flowers all year long." Her daughters, Ellison and Kelli, enjoy the roses too. "They've taken a real interest," she notes. "They'll cut a rose and call it theirs. I think they'll grow into an even greater appreciation of gardening than I have myself."

And they won't have to stick with just the selections Pam grows now. Other easy-to-grow roses include 'Souvenir de la Malmaison Rouge,' 'Hansa,' 'Heritage,' 'La Marne,' 'Pet Pink,' 'St Patrick,' 'Moonstone,' and 'Cecile Brunner.'

"Gardening isn't a big secret," Pam concludes, admiring multitudinous blossoms. "Maybe it seems easier because I have good soil and an irrigation system. But I think that plants require very little

GETTING STARTED WITH ROSES

For success in the South, follow these tips.

■ Plant in full sun. The more sun your rose gets, the more flowers you'll get.

■ Roses prefer fertile, well-drained soil that contains lots of organic matter, such as sphagnum peat moss, garden compost, ground bark, chopped leaves, and composted manure. Organic matter is especially important in sand or clay soils.

■ Water roses deeply once a week, thoroughly soaking the soil. Do not wet the foliage.

■ If you don't like spraying, try the roses mentioned at the bottom of this page, as well as 'Louis Philippe,' 'Mrs. B.R. Cant,' 'Bonica,' 'Carefree Beauty,' and 'Carefree Wonder.'

care, other than food and water. And if you give them that, they'll thrive."

For more on roses, see "Bare Facts for Planting Bare-root Roses," page 32. ◇

Divide
And
Conquer

BEFORE

PHOTOGRAPHS: VAN CHAPLIN

TOP: *A new parking court, circular drive, and fresh plantings solved a couple of problems while bringing a lot of curb appeal to this residence.*
ABOVE, LEFT: *The hard angles of the new brick planters and fountain are tempered by plantings that will fill in but not outgrow the space too quickly.*
ABOVE, RIGHT: *Brick expansion joints and edging help visually break up the large concrete parking area and courtyard.*

When Lee Churchill called on landscape architect Tom Keith at Arbor Engineering, Inc., she knew she didn't like her front entrance but couldn't quite put her finger on the problem. She just wanted to create a more inviting look to her Greenville, South Carolina, home. Tom was able to draw up a plan that would have made any military tactician proud.

On his initial visit to the property, Tom realized that it would take more than a simple planting plan to make the home present its best face to the public. "Lee was looking to upgrade the front, but she was just thinking of redoing the plantings," Tom says.

After talking things over with Lee, Tom saw that she also had some concerns about the dead-end drive. "With a single-lane driveway it only takes one car to block up the whole thing," he says. He also noticed that the home had a recessed front door, so a visitor's first impression was of the garage door.

Tom targeted a substantial open area to the right of the existing driveway where he proposed a circular drive wide enough to allow two cars to pass. The entire old driveway was torn out, and Tom suggested mixing a dark gray color into the concrete to help the new drive blend with the shaded surroundings.

With that problem solved, he turned to improving the transition between the front door and the driveway. "We devised a planter and fountain area that presents a miniplaza," he says. Using

brick matched to the home, he designed low walls for the planter and fountain that also serve as seating. A small bubbler in the fountain sends out a subliminal message to visitors. "The sound of the water helps pull people into the space," Tom says. "It really echoes nicely in the courtyard and just reinforces the natural tendency to move in that direction."

Although the new courtyard does step out from the front of the home, Tom wanted to enclose it to provide a little separation between the public area of the driveway and the more intimate space, which includes the courtyard and family parking in the garage. Brick columns connected by a 2-foot-high wall, which is topped by a 4-foot wrought iron fence, provide the dividing

line. Between the columns, there is a wide gate that allows Lee easy access and a pedestrian gate where guests enter.

With the hardscape in place, Tom turned to the plants. In the courtyard, 'Gumpo' azaleas, a cutleaf Japanese maple (*Acer palmatum* 'Dissectum'), variegated English ivy, and mondo grass billow from the planters. Iris, pickerel weed (*Pontederia* sp.), and water lilies stock the water garden. Adorning the drive, natural plantings of azaleas, oakleaf hydrangeas, red maple (*A. rubrum*), and a ground cover of English ivy look at home under the tall pines.

By dividing Lee's landscape into two distinct domains and attacking them separately, Tom achieved one smooth-flowing design that welcomes cars and people. *Glenn R. DiNella*

Hanging Gardens

Suspending plants from porches and porticos is a part of the gardening ritual. Fabulous ferns and masses of brilliant impatiens, dripping over the edges of hanging baskets, have long been favorites to place color in difficult spaces.

This year, look at the hanging container as a potential garden—just as you would a flowerbed. A variety of colors, textures, and shapes will become a focal point, sure to enhance your landscape.

SELECTING BASKETS

Have fun shopping for your hanging container. Only one of our planters (right) was designed for that purpose. The others—a small miner's basket (below, far right) and a cone-shaped fire bucket (below, left)—were found at a flea market and antiques shop, and then put to garden use. Choose a container that can be suspended easily and is strong enough to hold the weight of soil and plants.

When deciding on the basket, think about the plants to go in it. If it does not hold much soil, like the miner's basket, the plants need to be shallow-rooted to flourish. Consider this when choosing the basket, and purchase the appropriate one for the plant requirements.

PLANTING AND PLACEMENT

Plan color and texture carefully for your hanging garden. If you prefer a single flower color, vary the shades for interest. Instead of planting all pink impatiens in our shady basket (top), we added a few light blush and a few deeper rose-hued plants for depth.

Variegated spider plants contribute a long, lance-shaped leaf to the mix. Angel-wing begonias have large leaves with colorful markings, as well as cascading blooms. Ferns and ivy, which thrive outdoors, also bring texture.

Our miner's basket, designed for full sun, is planted with sculptural succulents. Their water needs aren't demanding, and they adapt easily to the shallow container. Hens and chicks provide a round flowerlike shape, and creeping

sedums offer several different leaf shapes. This tiny garden, without a flower, illustrates how effective green can be.

The conical fire bucket is planted for dappled light—a little sun and a little shade. A cascading red ivy-leaf geranium highlights the bucket's lettering, and white petunias add lush blossoms for contrast and brightness.

Place your hanging garden where you would love color, but can't find a

way to get it there. Loop chain or rope around a sturdy tree limb, placing an old piece of hose between them to prevent damage. Hang the garden, ensuring the branch can support the weight.

Turn your hanging baskets into something special with a creative container and a garden approach to planting. You will enjoy hanging them around.

Ellen Riley

PHOTOGRAPHS: VAN CHAPLIN

LEFT: *Richard and Beth Melton didn't realize when they bought their first house that they had also purchased a champion tree. The largest dogwood in the state of Alabama—and one of the largest in the nation—creates a wonderful canopy over their deck.*

BELOW: *The massive trunk of this dogwood rises up through the deck, which helps protect the tree's shallow root system.*

Champion Dogwood

The University of Alabama's Crimson Tide has brought plenty of football championships home to Tuscaloosa. Recently, though, another champion was discovered in this college town. This champ is a large dogwood that doesn't produce victories but thousands of starry white blooms instead.

The sprawling tree, with its armlike limbs, reaches out and greets spring each year. For several days, clouds of flowers hover over this large deck. Then the petals grow tired, lose their grip, and drift to the ground like a gentle snow.

Soon after Richard Melton—garden designer and owner of Gardens on Main in Northport—and his wife, Beth, bought their first home, they began to marvel over the size of the overgrown dogwood in the backyard. Richard called an arborist in to inspect the tree and make sure it was in good health. Not only was the tree healthy, but after measurements were taken, it was declared a champion tree by the Alabama Forestry Commission. This means it's the largest of its species to be found in the state. It also ranks as one of the largest in the nation, with just two other trees surpassing it. According to the arborist's measurements, the dogwood stands 41 feet tall and 45½ feet wide.

This living legend is in good hands. Richard expanded the back deck to help cover and protect the roots of the tree. It has its own irrigation system misting it on hot, dry summer days.

A stone column was even constructed to help support one of the large sagging limbs. The deck has become an extension of the house, functioning as an outdoor room for the Meltons. It's a favorite place to dine in nice weather. Several outdoor speakers surround the area and pipe in music to help set the mood. In summer, foliage covers the tree and shades the deck from the hot sun. As the leaves begin to drop in the fall, red berries are exposed on the tips of branches, supplying food for migrating birds.

The tree serves as the centerpiece of the backyard. Its owners spend many days gathered under its wide canopy. The spring blooms are truly special. In fact, the Meltons hosted a large wedding last spring. During the ceremony, the tree's creamy petals sprinkled down on the bride and groom.

Now, under this venerable old tree, a young couple goes about their daily activities. They nurse the tree, fertilizing and watering it, making sure it stays healthy. This dogwood also takes care of the couple, shading their back deck and allowing them to witness one of spring's most impressive shows.

Charlie Thigpen

If you would like to visit Tuscaloosa and see this champion, please call Gardens on Main at (205) 752-8161 and arrange a time to visit. ◇

'Heritage' river birch features beautiful bark; thrives in hot, humid climates; and isn't plagued by borers.

The Right Plants for the South

Alien beings have moved in next door. My family is justifiably concerned. We know they're not from around here because of all the weird plants they've brought with them—lilac, paper birch, blue spruce, delphinium. Word has it our new neighbors come from a planet named Wisconsin.

Alien plants from the North look nice when first set out. But they usually can't hack the South's hot, humid summers and short, mild winters. So they either fail to bloom, fail to thrive, or simply croak. Why, then, do aliens keep trying?

For an answer, I consulted several admitted aliens. Kathy Foster, who grew up in wintry Northern Kentucky and Ohio before moving south to Fort Walton Beach, Florida, told me, "We try because we have

pass-along plants from grandparents, family, friends, and deceased loved ones that we don't want to lose. These plants evoke pleasant memories." Other aliens said they just like to buck advice and plant something people living here say

won't do. And if they succeed, native Southerners often copy them.

Of course, the ultimate fate of such plants depends largely on where in the South you live. Many of them do okay in the Upper South but struggle elsewhere.

You could make them feel more at home by refrigerating the soil or dressing your kids in stripes and plaids, but this is a lot of trouble. It's easier to simply substitute plants better adapted to the South that possess similar qualities.

For example, you love lilac, the favorite plant of the planet Wisconsin, but you now live in New Orleans. Lilacs won't bloom in the Big Easy, due to the lack of winter chill. So, instead, plant chaste tree *(Vitex agnus-castus)*. It has beautiful blue flowers like lilac, grows 15 to 20 feet tall, tolerates heat

BETTER PLANTS, BETTER CHOICES

If You Can't Grow This:	Try This:
lilac	chaste tree, crepe myrtle
rhododendron	French hydrangea, camellia
English holly	lusterleaf holly
delphinium	larkspur
tuberous begonia	angel-wing begonia
bearded iris	Louisiana iris
lupine	foxglove
tulip	amaryllis
Colorado blue spruce	'Carolina Sapphire' Arizona cypress
paper birch or European white birch	'Heritage' river birch

INSET: *Northerners grieving for lilacs should try crepe myrtle.* ABOVE: *Angel-wing begonias combine showy flowers with striking foliage.*

and drought, and resists pests. Or plant a crepe myrtle. Its flowers are just as striking as a lilac's. Crepe myrtle also features colorful autumn foliage and handsome winter bark, where lilac is ornamental only when blooming.

Want a few more examples? Okay. Rather than planting the paper birch *(Betula papyrifera)* or European white birch *(B. pendula)* you remember from your home world, try 'Heritage' river birch *(B. nigra* 'Heritage'). Its bark is just as lovely, but it doesn't get the borers that plague the other two down here. Do rhododendrons wilt and die before your eyes? Substitute French hydrangea *(Hydrangea macrophylla).* It loves our climate and flaunts gorgeous flowers of blue, purple, pink, rose, or white for many more weeks than a rhodie does. Can't grow delphinium? Try larkspur. This reseeding annual gives you the same shape and flower colors, but it's much easier to grow. And instead of maintaining tuberous begonias on life support throughout the hot summer, grow the lovely and carefree angel-wing begonias. Lots of blooms, little fuss.

My new neighbors from Wisconsin desperately need this advice, but we don't know how to approach them. We saw them having brats and beer for breakfast, and we're very much afraid.   *Steve Bender*

Atamasco Lily

Among the most charming of wildflowers is our little, wild rain lily *(Zephyranthes atamasco).* Its clustered, white-petaled trumpets brighten boggy meadows and roadside ditches for about six weeks every spring, from late March through April and sometimes into May.

Atamasco lilies are the earliest of all the *Zephyranthes* species to bloom, and they also have the distinction of being one of the largest flowered and most fragrant. Country gardeners long ago christened them "wild Easter lilies" for their appearance and time of bloom, and many woodland gardens in the Southeastern states include flourishing patches of these lovely lilies in their shady beds.

Atamasco bulbs can be planted anytime from February to November, but one of the easiest times to get a start is after their blooming season is finished and the foliage is going dormant. That's the perfect time to divide and transplant them, so in April keep an eye out for neighbors who are growing them. Be ready to swap a horticultural goody of your own for a start of atamasco bulbs soon after the flowers are gone. The bulbs can also be found at some mail-order nurseries, so don't despair if you can't find a friendly source in your own neighborhood. Whatever you do, definitely don't dig them from the wild.

When you get your bulbs, set them in rich, damp, slightly acid soil in a shady place, perhaps as an underplanting for azaleas or for mingling with Louisiana phlox. Atamasco lilies will also be happy under the leaf mold around deciduous trees at the edge of a yard or along a woodland path. Those locations offer them acid soil, a little shade in summer while they're dormant, and sunlight on their short, grassy foliage when it comes up in early winter.

If you don't have naturally acid soil, these lilies can be grown very successfully in containers and even brought inside as houseplants. Use a good-quality potting soil, and never let the bulbs dry out completely, even during their summer dormancy. Atamasco lilies are easy to grow and even easier to love, especially when their white trumpets lift up again to herald the return of the Southern spring. ◇

(For sources turn to pages 234–235.)

ATAMASCO LILIES
At a Glance

Size: grassy foliage to 8 inches, blooms can be 15 inches tall
Bloom season: six weeks or more in spring
Propagation: divide clumps of bulbs, or start from seed
Light: shade to partial sun
Soil: moist, slightly acid
Water: keep moist all year
Range: all but Tropical South

Queen of The Road

You usually notice this queen standing along the roadside. She originally came from Europe but has set deep roots in the South. The name implies royalty, yet she's often seen mingling with the commoners. This well-postured lady stands straight and proud on the shoulders of even the most rural roadways. Her distinguished cottony-white hair is always neatly groomed atop her head. Delicate, green foliage clothes her long, lean body.

Queen Anne's lace *(Daucus carota)* is one of the most recognized Southern flowers, but we are more likely to see it while taking a leisurely Sunday drive, rather than strolling through gardens. This annual or biennial is an ancestor of cultivated carrots. It produces small, yellow, carrotlike roots that are edible. Some refer to this plant as "wild carrot."

But don't grow Queen Anne's lace to eat; grow it to grace your garden with lacy blooms. Few companies still sell the seeds because they're so easy to collect from wild patches. If you know someone who grows this prolific plant, ask if you can have a handful of seeds.

You can collect the seeds in late summer or fall, as soon as they have dried completely. Spent flowers curl up and form a dry, gobletlike ball. Inside the goblet are hundreds of tiny seeds that resemble little spiders.

Seeds may be sown in the early spring or in the fall. You can seed them directly in the garden in any sunny spot. The white blooms look at home scattered along a fencerow or in meadowlike settings. You can also start them in flats and later transplant them into your flower border.

These plants are tough and will survive in poor soil, but they prosper where the earth is loose, fertile, and well drained. Under ideal conditions, they can grow 4 feet tall. Plants that struggle due to droughts or poor soil may not do so well, reaching only 2 feet in height.

When seedlings first appear, they look like small sprigs of parsley. Plants

The delicate flowers of Queen Anne's lace are a common sight on the shoulders of most Southern roadways, yet few gardeners incorporate them into their plantings. The broad flower heads are made up of hundreds of tiny blooms that cluster atop long, narrow stems.

usually flower their second year, but some act as annuals and bloom the first year. The species *D. pusillus* is an annual that is most often found around the Lower and Coastal South. It is a smaller version of Queen Anne's lace and the blooms aren't quite as showy.

Many consider Queen Anne's lace a weed, but it can be controlled in your garden by cutting off the seedpods before they dry and drop seeds. You'll enjoy these long-stemmed, lacy blooms in your yard. They also make nice cut flowers and can be brought into your home for a summery arrangement. Their white blooms mix well with almost any flower.

This queen isn't fussy and doesn't need a formal setting. Just give her a sunny spot, and watch her add a little royalty to your garden.   *Charlie Thigpen*
(For sources turn to pages 234–235.)

Upping the Stakes

Few things are prettier than a flower-bed chock-full of zinnias or cosmos. Seeded directly into the soil, those annuals become a blooming carpet. But with summer's first shower, their heads become heavy with rainwater, and the blooms end up facedown in the dirt.

Staking each stem is impractical, but support is a must to keep these flowers standing tall. With bamboo garden stakes and twine, you can create an attractive web to hold stems in place.

After preparing the soil for planting, install the support system. Arrange the garden stakes throughout the bed in a grid pattern or randomly if the bed is irregular. Allow only a foot between stakes, and push them deeply into the soil.

Tie one end of the garden twine to a bamboo stake, about a foot above the soil surface. Wrap it once around the pole to secure, and move on to the next. Weave between the supports, crisscrossing to create a web. Keep the string fairly taut, but avoid making it too tight as this will pull the stakes over. Repeat the process, starting about 2 feet above the soil surface. When you are finished, plant your flowers. Reach between the webbing to sprinkle and cover seeds, taking care not to poke yourself on the stakes. As the new flowers emerge, they will work themselves into the web.

Use the maze of bamboo stakes to add a whimsical dimension to your garden. In the photo above, colorful glazed ceramic spheres, found at a flea market, were placed on some of the stakes. They bobbed gracefully above the blooms, adding another shape as well as more colors to the bed. They were also a constant reminder to be careful of the pole ends when bending over to cut flowers.

The same effect can be achieved using plastic foam balls and spray paint. Use only one size with a single paint color, or go all out varying both the sizes and hues. The foam spheres should last through the summer season.

When the flowers reach their full summer stature, it's time to assess the height of the stakes. If the blooms do not come

ABOVE: *The second layer of twine provides support to flowers.* INSET: *Wrap twine around each stake; then move on to the next.*

above the tops of the bamboo, use heavy-duty pruners to cut the stakes to the desired height.

Summer showers are rarely gentle, and the strongest stems can't stand a watery beating. Staking keeps flowers on their feet.   *Ellen Riley*

(For sources turn to pages 234–235.)

LOVE IS A
garden

BY LINDA C. ASKEY
PHOTOGRAPHY VAN CHAPLIN

An Eden cannot be set out and just left to grow. Season after season it must be nurtured. Indeed a garden is never done. It is an unending fascination that is nothing short of romance.

LEFT: *Simple panels of grass and green hedges give order to the abundant flowers and foliage.* INSET: *Inside the gate lies the playground of garden designer Ryan Gainey.*

At first glance, 129 Emerson Avenue seems like any other house in the early 20th-century-bungalow neighborhood of Decatur, Georgia. But one glimpse under the canopy of linden trees that line the sidewalk outside Ryan Gainey's garden will make you do a double take. You've happened upon a treasure, one man's fantasy in flower and leaf.

"My dream is real," says Ryan. After 20 years of cultivating, building, experimenting, and playing, the garden that surrounds his home has matured as he has as a gardener. While there was a time when it needed much from him, it now gives back. A stroll down its paths brings him peace, pleases him, and makes him feel thankful.

Known as a gifted designer, lecturer, and author, Ryan has always sought opportunity, and the opportunities have multiplied with his success, growing into a demanding career and making him a public persona. But in this personal paradise,

ABOVE: *Ryan calls his terrace garden "a place of solace with shadows from the trees, trickling water, and simple plantings."*
LEFT: *Ryan with companions Joe and Cracker Jack*

BELOW AND INSET: *Bearded iris grows with a bright pink climber at the entrance to the temple garden, which was named for the stylized temple made of Eastern red cedar.*

a different side emerges, a quiet honesty that is disarming. "It's not what I've done, but what's been given to me," he says.

Like an author with a well-developed character, Ryan sees the garden as having a life of its own. The mischievous squirrel that scampers down the ridge of the greenhouse with one of Ryan's peaches is a welcome sight. Likewise, the pond that is part of the terrace garden embraces other elements of life—fish and aquatic plants—that would not be here without it. This garden is the natural world distilled and guided by his vision, and he embraces the whole of it.

Although the garden has been refined in bits and pieces over the years, Ryan surprisingly dug up about 60% of his long borders a little over a year ago and added strips of turf between the paving and plantings. He realized that the carefully arranged compositions within the beds needed "breathing room."

Such change is ongoing in any landscape. Gardens are places transformed by nature, as well as by whim of the gardener. But changes here have not been sweeping in recent years. The structure is well established. To be honest, much of the layout was inherited. The Holcombe family lived in the house, where Mrs. Holcombe grew cut flowers and potted plants to sell.

The pleasure garden that it is today is a remarkable change from the property's utilitarian beginning. But in many ways, the transition is seamless; it is simply a matter of growing horticultural sophistication. Where former greenhouses stood, gardens have been built in their footprints. Plantings have evolved from Mrs. Holcolmbe's rows of seedlings into carefully orchestrated harmonies of flower and foliage.

Essential to the free-flowing nature of the borders is the frame Ryan has placed around each of his garden pictures. The garden is not one, but many rooms. Paths form the central axis in most of the rooms, as well as the cross axes between rooms. Each area is surrounded by trellises, hedges, or house walls to create enclosure, what Ryan calls "the holiness of the place."

In addition, Ryan has drawn hard lines within the individual gardens with hedges and shrubs, providing a firm counterpoint to the effervescence of the beds. These forms contain and punctuate the abundance with order and simplicity. They define, creating pattern and structure. As he explains, "They become the architecture of the garden.

"All the rooms are expressions of my love for classical garden design, but they are expressed in a cottage-garden setting," says Ryan, an avid student of garden history. And everywhere you see his affinity for pattern—in the fences, arbors, paths, and the sheared and espaliered forms.

FAR LEFT: *This playful parterre features sweet William and forget-me-nots in spring.* ABOVE: *A black locust tower provides a treetop getaway and an overlook into the garden.* INSET: *Foliage and flowers are equal players in Ryan's plant compositions.*

Within the structure lies evidence of keen plantsmanship. In Ryan's garden, color and flowers are not necessarily the same thing or the only feature. "For me it has a lot more to do with foliage and texture than just mere flowers," he explains. "To me the flowers are there, but they are not the answer to the question. They are a piece of the puzzle."

Ryan's plant compositions speak for themselves. "In order for plants to work for you, you have to know them and understand how they grow," he explains. Colors and textures resonate between leaf and petal, brick and stone, bark and glass. Putting such knowledge to work has produced a garden beyond seasonal peaks; it is a garden that lives year-round.

From the early-morning coffee walk to his anticipated return at day's end, this garden echoes with Ryan's footsteps. It is rare to have an opportunity to look through another's eyes, but in a garden such as this, you can stand alone in the quiet and see what he has done, what his eyes longed to see, and what his hands have created.

And in this place a visitor learns quickly that Ryan's daily ration is beauty in equal or greater portion to calories or even water. He is complex and demanding, as is his garden. And in the stillness there is a peaceful spirit, a place that this man loves and loves to share. ◇

Hardy, carefree chestnut rose *(See page 93.)*

May

Checklist for May

EDITOR'S NOTEBOOK

My good friends Bill and Margaret Sanders of Columbus, Mississippi, always struck me as compassionate. So it came as no surprise to discover that they'd used an old crutch to prop up a venerable but infirm oakleaf hydrangea. Like many gardeners, they faced the dilemma of how to care for an aging shrub that couldn't care for itself. When old trunks can't support new foliage, storms often snap the wood. Feeding the shrub eggs and cheese for calcium does no good and smells bad. No, the answer lies in one of two things. First, use cables or a stake (or an old crutch) to prop up the leaning trunk. Or reduce the weight of the trunk by cutting it back to a lower crotch, which promotes firm growth below the cut. But if you choose the latter operation, take my advice: Don't go to your HMO. You will never get a referral.

Steve Bender

□ **Daffodils**—As the foliage of daffodils begins to die, right now is the perfect time to divide clumps that did not bloom well. An application of bulb booster encourages good root growth.

□ **Irrigation**—Now is the time to water container-grown plants several times a week when rainfall is scarce and the soil is dry to the touch. Irrigating your landscape depends on your plants' needs. Check them for drooping leaves or signs of distress. Older trees and shrubs can go longer without water. When watering, an early morning drink that thoroughly wets the soil is best.

□ **Lilies**—While it's late to plant hybrid lilies unless you buy them already potted, it is important that the tall-flowering types get support. A loose staking method is best. Position the stake 3 to 4 inches away from the base to prevent injuring the bulb. Tie the stalk to the stake loosely in several places so that it can move but will not break on windy days.

Water gardens—When you see new growth in the Coastal and Tropical South, feed lilies and lotus plants fertilizer tablets formulated for water gardens. Add tablets once a month while temperatures are between 60 and 70 degrees; feed twice a month when temperatures rise above 75 degrees. Use tablets according to directions.

PLANT

◀ **Annuals**—It's time for planting your summer annuals, such as petunias, marigolds, salvia, and impatiens. If the plants are in pots or trays, make sure the roots are not so matted that they can't expand outward into the soil easily. If they are matted, gently pull the roots apart.

□ **Coleus**—Plant for quick color and textural contrasts. Most selections prefer shade or partial shade, but certain coleus, such as 'Solar Flair' and 'Alabama Sunset,' thrive in the sun, provided they receive sufficient water. Consider drifts of similar shades of coleus in areas where spring bulbs are past their prime.

□ **Perennials**—Set out perennials now. Good choices for the warm months ahead include the salvias. 'Indigo Spires' salvia forms a 4-foot mound of purplish-blue flower spikes that bloom until frost. Red, white, pink, lavender, or bicolored *Salvia greggii* is another trouble-free plant. *S. guaranitica* comes in several shades of blue and can reach 5 feet in height. Mexican bush sage *(S. leucantha)* makes a spectacular show in the late summer and fall and comes in a purple-and-white form as well as solid purple. ▶

□ **Turf**—Plug bare spots in St. Augustine, and seed bare areas in Bahia lawns in the Coastal and Tropical South. Loosen the soil with a rake, and plant St. Augustine plugs about 10 inches apart. Keep moist until new runners appear; then reduce watering. For Bahia, spread seeds evenly in prepared ground; cover with a ¼-inch layer of soil. Keep the soil moist until the grass seeds sprout and begin growing.

□ **Vegetables**—In the Upper and Middle South, plant tomatoes, peppers, beans, cucumbers, squash, okra, and Southern peas. Tomatoes benefit from planting inside wire cages surrounded with plastic to minimize effects of wind and cool temperatures.

☐ **Warm-season turf grasses**—For sunny areas in the Middle, Lower, and Coastal South, St. Augustine, Zoysia, Bermuda grass, and buffalo grass are well adapted. In shaded places, consider ground covers such as Asian star jasmine, periwinkle, ajuga, English ivy, or liriope.

PRUNE

☐ **Blooming shrubs**—Prune azaleas and gardenias when they finish blooming. Trim the main stem to encourage side shoots, a bushier plant, and a shrub with more possible blooms. Apply a sulfur-coated fertilizer such as 14-14-12, following label directions. Check the undersides of your camellia leaves for scale and red spider mites. Use Safer Insecticidal Soap or horticultural oil if either is present.

☐ **Climbing roses**—Now is a good time to prune climbing roses back to 4 to 5 feet after they finish blooming. Train new growth to twist and turn around supports to double the number of flowers.

Caladiums—In the Middle and Lower South, plant caladium tubers now. Choose the largest tubers for maximum impact. Prepare the soil by adding 3 to 5 inches of organic matter. Spade or till the material into the top 6 to 8 inches of soil, adding 4 to 5 pounds of slow-release fertilizer per 100 square feet of bed area.

FERTILIZE

☐ **Lawns**—Once your brown turf has turned green, it is time to fertilize on a regular basis. Some warm-season grasses, such as hybrid Bermuda and Zoysia types, like high nitrogen-based lawn fertilizers. Some turf, such as centipede, needs little or no fertilizer and minimal amounts of nitrogen. Remember high-nitrogen fertilizers always have a large first number in the ratio listed on the bag. For example, 16-4-8 is a high-nitrogen fertilizer. Be sure to apply according to label directions to prevent burning your lawn. ▶

CONTROL

☐ **Poison ivy**—"Leaflets three, let it be" is true as these plants unfold their leaves and begin to grow. Control poison ivy vines early by applying glyphosate (Roundup) or triclopyr (Brush Killer) according to label directions. Protective clothing and rubber gloves are a must when spraying this plant.

☐ **Roses**—Scout your rosebushes for both black spot and powdery mildew. Treat any infected plants with a fungicide such as chlorothalonil (Daconil) or triforine (Funginex). The best way to help control these diseases is to water in the morning so leaves will stay dry throughout the day, and to remove dropped leaves from the surrounding ground.

☐ **Seedlings**—Directly seeded plants that have their first true leaves need to be thinned this month for proper spacing. Instead of pulling, you may want simply to snip at ground level. This generally will kill the plant and not disturb others you want to keep.

TIP OF THE MONTH

We have three wooden window boxes outside our breakfast area. In order to keep nice seasonal flowers in them, I have two sets of plastic liners. I plant the first set with pansies for early spring. Before they begin to decline, I plant the second set with geraniums. Nearing the end of summer, I replant the first set with chrysanthemums to replace the geraniums in fall. This keeps the boxes nice and full, and we really enjoy the changes.

NANCY OGLESBY
ROEBUCK, SOUTH CAROLINA

Quick Color
For Summer

When creating a flower border, a little toil in the soil yields a bounty of blooms.

We installed this 36-foot-long x 15-foot-deep informal flower border just last spring, but by summer's end it was full of color and life. The layers of vibrant blooms attracted bees, butterflies, and hummingbirds, which made frequent air raids on the numerous flowers. The companion foliage plants also helped add texture and form to this magical garden spot.

Before we purchased any plants, we had to choose the proper site. We selected a location that received lots of sun throughout the day. This gave us the opportunity to try many different sun-loving plants. If your yard is shady, don't be discouraged—you can still have a great border. Plants such as caladiums, coleus, impatiens, hostas, and ferns put on a show even in low-light conditions.

Soil preparation was the hardest part of the entire project, but nothing promotes healthy plant growth better than loose, cultivated soil. First, we sprayed

BY CHARLIE THIGPEN
PHOTOGRAPHY VAN CHAPLIN

MAY

ABOVE: *Newly planted, this border is still in its infancy.* LEFT: *In just one summer, it quickly grew together, creating a kaleidoscope of colors.*

RIGHT: *This variegated lantana didn't bloom heavily, but its marbled foliage adds a splash of color to the bed.*

the area with a nonselective herbicide. Ten days later, a rear-tine tiller was used to mix the dead plant matter into the compacted existing red clay. Then we mixed two pickup truckloads of leaf mold and 25 bags of a clay soil conditioner into the existing soil. If you have clay soil, use Perma Till or Profile to help improve drainage and reduce compaction.

After we spent a few hours tilling, raking, and removing rocks, the earth was finally loose. Using a hard rake, we pushed soil toward the center of the bed, crowning it in the middle to force rainwater to drain to the outside edges. Then we covered the entire area with a couple of inches of pine straw.

Next, we evenly spaced three 8-foot-tall cedar posts in the border. We put flower-filled hanging baskets on two of them and placed colorful bottles on the limbs of the third post to make a bottle tree; its glassy ornaments gleam in the garden throughout the seasons. The hanging baskets and bottle tree give the border much needed vertical interest.

We installed a few tall perennials and annuals in the center and back of the border and sprinkled a little controlled-release fertilizer under each plant. Ornamental maiden grass *(Miscanthus* sp.) and fountain grass *(Pennisetum* sp.) add attractive mounding forms to the border. We also included three 'Tropicanna' cannas for their striking foliage and bright flowers.

Don't think you have to use only flowers in a border. Trees and shrubs give year-round structure. We opted for bridal wreath spiraea *(Spiraea prunifolia)* and a dwarf chartreuse barberry *(Berberis thunbergii)*. We chose the spiraea for its white, early-spring blooms and the barberry for its glowing green leaves. A small chaste tree *(Vitex agnus-castus)* placed on the back side will produce blue summer flowers.

Once the taller plants were in place, it was time to pick a few flowering annuals. We set out two flats of orange cosmos and white narrow-leaf zinnias on the front side of the border. We used seven 'Gold Mound' lantana plants in the middle. We also set out three variegated lantanas. They didn't bloom quite as well, but the yellow- and green-marbled foliage was quite attractive.

Friends gave us plenty of gift plants, including sprigs of white coneflower, yellow columbine, Louisiana iris, and some hot pink dianthus for open areas. After each planting, we watered the garden thoroughly. Always water bedding

KEY PLAYERS

Background
maiden grass
fountain grass
'Tropicanna' canna

Middle Ground
'Gold Mound' lantana
white coneflower

Foreground
orange cosmos
narrow-leaf zinnia
hot pink dianthus

LEFT: *We added lots of organic matter and a clay soil conditioner to our planting bed.*

plants immediately after setting them out. We soaked the border three or four times a week the first two weeks, and then reduced watering to twice a week.

We spent every other day observing the new plantings and hand weeding. As summer heated up and the plants became established, we fed the border with a water-soluble liquid fertilizer, and the plants quickly grew together.

All the hard work and soil preparation paid off in this over-the-summer success. Many of the plants were showy well into the fall, and each year the border will take on different looks as the seasonal plantings change. ◇

New Arbor, Big Impact

BEFORE

Offering fragrant flowers and evergreen foliage, Confederate jasmine shades the terrace and makes it a pleasant place to sit.

Think it takes big bucks to make a big improvement? Bob and Susan Wilson of Ocala, Florida, don't think so. And the new arbor and side entry to their house prove it.

The project began when they replaced a window on the side of their house with French doors to improve access. They immediately discovered two problems. "The doors faced west, so the entrance was really hot in the afternoon," recalls Susan. "And when it rained, the water came shooting right off the roof and rotted out the doors." That's when the Wilsons called local landscape architect John Adams for help.

John designed a new side entry consisting of two facets. The first is a brick walk and terrace that take you quickly from the driveway to the door. The second is an arbor, attached to the roof, that shelters the terrace. Made of rough-sawn cedar and painted to match the house trim, the arbor supports a glorious bower of Confederate jasmine. This vigorous, evergreen vine shades the terrace and doors. It also supplies fragrant, white flowers in spring. To solve the water problem, John added an 18-inch copper gutter at the roofline to collect rainwater and shunt it to a nearby downspout.

The arbor creates a natural transition between the garden and house and emphasizes the entry, giving it impact. Susan appreciates this latter point. "We didn't do it for looks. We did it to solve problems," she says. "But it ended up looking great." *Steve Bender*

PHOTOGRAPHS: VAN CHAPLIN

Don't Let Wet Soil Bog You Down

Japanese primrose puts on a colorful display in the wet soil bordering a pond. This perennial dislikes long, steamy summers and is best suited to the Upper South.

It just makes you want to scream. You read the description of a coveted plant and it inevitably states "needs well-drained soil."

Providing the proper drainage is easy if you live near the sand dunes of Daytona Beach or the arid rock piles of Southwest Texas. But what if your soil consists of sticky red clay that clutches water molecules in a death grip? What if your garden sits in a low spot that fills with water from runoff and seepage? Are there any desirable plants you can grow without constructing raised beds or putting your entire garden up on stilts?

Of course there are. We've listed them for you in the box at right. There you'll find a whole slew of trees, shrubs, bulbs, and perennials that thrive in wet soil.

Keep in mind, though, that some plants like it wetter than others. For example, some will grow with their roots completely underwater for months at a time. Bald cypress, winterberry, cardinal flower, yellow flag iris, royal fern, and canna are good examples. Other plants prefer soil that's constantly moist, but not flooded for long stretches. These include red maple, sweet bay, Texas star, Virginia sweetspire, Japanese primrose, cinnamon fern, and weeping willow.

Those of you already blessed with good drainage will find useful information in these plant lists too. Although all of them tolerate poorly drained, oxygen-starved soil, most grow just fine in average, well-drained conditions. To help you determine the needs of plants, look for the letters "S," "M," or "WD" after the name. "S" means the plant tolerates saturated or inundated soil; "M" means it tolerates constantly moist, but not soaked, soil; and "WD" means it thrives in drier, well-drained soil. *Steve Bender*

PLANTS FOR SOGGY SOIL

TREES
bald cypress
(Taxodium distichum)—S, M, WD

black gum
(Nyssa sylvatica)—M, WD

loblolly bay
(Gordonia lasianthus)—M, WD

red maple
(Acer rubrum)—M, WD

sweet bay
(Magnolia virginiana)—M, WD

sweet gum
(Liquidambar styraciflua)—M, WD

water oak
(Quercus nigra)—M, WD

weeping willow
(Salix babylonica)—M

SHRUBS
bottlebrush buckeye
(Aesculus parviflora)—M, WD

buttonbush
(Cephalanthus occidentalis)—S, M

dwarf palmetto
(Sabal minor)—M, WD

inkberry
(Ilex glabra)—M, WD

red chokeberry
(Aronia arbutifolia)—M, WD

sweet pepperbush
(Clethra alnifolia)—M, WD

sweetshrub
(Calycanthus floridus)—M, WD

Virginia sweetspire
(Itea virginica)—M, WD

winterberry
(Ilex verticillata)—S, M, WD

BULBS
calla lily
(Zantedeschia sp.)—M

canna
(Canna sp.)—S, M, WD

elephant's ear
(Colocasia esculenta)—S, M, WD

Japanese iris
(Iris ensata)—S, M

Louisiana iris
(Iris hybrida)—S, M, WD

yellow flag iris
(Iris pseudacorus)—S, M

PERENNIALS
cardinal flower
(Lobelia cardinalis)—S, M

cinnamon fern
(Osmunda cinnamomea)—M

Japanese primrose
(Primula japonica)—M

royal fern
(Osmunda regalis)—S, M

Texas star
(Hibiscus coccineus)—M, WD

Pretty And Painless

Golden groundsel looks beautiful all on its own.

There are few things that gardeners despise more than a plant that's too easy to grow, which may explain why so few people try golden groundsel. "It's tough, grows in sun or shade and also in damp or very dry places," says Andrea Sessions of Sunlight Gardens, a mail-order supplier of native plants in Andersonville, Tennessee. "When I show it to people, their first reaction often is, 'Why, I thought that was a weed!'"

In fact, golden groundsel *(Senecio aureus)* is an attractive wildflower that is native to eastern North America. Yes, it spreads but not usually aggressively. And its mounds of rounded evergreen leaves are always handsome. Bright green on top and purplish underneath, the leaves turn burgundy-green in winter. The foliage makes this plant worth growing even if it never bloomed.

But, of course, it does bloom, and magnificently too. Bright yellow, daisy-like blossoms stand tall atop 1- to 2-foot stems in late spring. And unlike some other wildflowers, whose blooms drop faster than you can blink, this one often stays in bloom for up to four weeks.

Golden groundsel's accommodating nature makes it a choice plant for all sorts of situations, including bog gardens, woodland gardens, mixed borders, and even containers. Andrea suggests combining it with fire pink *(Silene virginica)* and blue phlox *(Phlox divaricata)* in a natural area. Although

ABOVE: *Its yellow flowers standing tall, golden groundsel butters the wood's edge in Greenville, Delaware.* RIGHT: *Its blossoms pair well with those of many native plants, including the fruity-scented blooms of sweetshrub* (Calycanthus floridus).

golden groundsel tolerates poor, dry, rocky soil, it grows most luxuriantly in moist, fertile, slightly acid soil and light shade. Be aware, however, that the more fertile and moist the soil, the faster this thing spreads. So don't plant it next to a pond or stream thinking golden groundsel will stay at home.

I can't end this story without including an interesting pharmaceutical footnote: It seems that long before it made it to the garden, golden groundsel (also know as golden ragwort and squaw weed) earned a spot in the pioneer medicine cabinet. Taking a cue from their native American counterparts, female settlers used an extract from the root to chase away troublesome "women's problems." Unfortunately, this remedy seldom worked, as most women who took it reported afterwards that their husbands were still there. *Steve Bender*

GOLDEN GROUNDSEL
At a Glance

Height: 1 to 2 feet
Light: sun or shade
Soil: sightly acid to neutral, preferably fertile
Pests: none serious
Propagation: seed or division
Range: Upper, Middle, Lower, Coastal South

A Minor Miracle

Make an old garden come to life again using resourcefulness rather than resources.

"All I wanted were two sets of French doors and a nice garden," says Kay Minor of the 1929 bungalow she and husband Peter bought 10 years ago. Like many young couples, they had moved into an older house with a garden in desperate need of rejuvenation. Kay and Peter knew there was potential hiding under all those weeds and volunteer trees.

"We had just moved in, there were unpacked boxes still standing in the kitchen, but I had all my bulbs planted," confesses Kay, who comes from a farming background. "I feel like I'm not grounded when I'm not digging." With bulbs safely in the ground, the couple began the deliberate process of planning their garden.

WATCH, PLAN, AND PLANT

Kay advises that you "take time to observe the plants and conditions before you start removing and pruning." One of the benefits of moving into an older home is that there are often established trees that provide shade and a framework on which to build. There

was a huge oak tree in the front yard of their Charlotte home, plus a magnificent Yoshino cherry and a few dogwoods in the back. They pulled up volunteer trees so they could plant choice ones such as Japanese maples and more evergreens such as boxwoods for winter structure. Kay and Peter planned for their favorite activities—bird watching, eating outside, napping in the shade, and gardening.

PUT YOUR PERSONALITY IN IT

Kay's resourcefulness and creativity are apparent throughout the garden. Her use of found art from antiques shops and flea markets reflects a whimsical style that is perfect for a cottage garden. She dressed up an old storage building in the backyard with window boxes and salvaged shutters, and she put a large mirror between the windows to reflect the garden. Sap buckets and a folk-art piece add bright color. With the addition of a rustic table and chairs, this shady spot is now a sitting area.

A narrow space between their house and the neighbor's called for a creative solution.

BY ORENE STROUD HORTON / PHOTOGRAPHY VAN CHAPLIN

"I didn't want a wall, but I did want something pretty to look at," says Kay. An open fence of arched metal trellises between cedar posts supports clematis vines and Confederate jasmine that twine around the posts and through the trellises. Anchored by the new fence, the side garden is filled with perennials, annuals, bulbs, and miniature roses. In winter, she plants colorful salad greens and cool-weather annuals, so the garden provides year-round enjoyment for Kay and her neighbors. Birdhouses hang all along the fence. She has even found tiny nests made from pieces of rosemary and lavender that the birds gathered from the garden.

One captivating feature is the water garden, made from an old bathtub Kay rescued from the back of Peter's nephew's truck on its way to a secondhand store. Her first thought was to sink it into the ground as a pool. "But everyone has an in-ground pool," explains Kay, so they left it on top of the soil.

Peter wired and plumbed a showerhead for the fountain, and they placed the tub

ABOVE: *A colorful flowerbed planted beside a see-through fence marks the property line between the Minors and their appreciative neighbors.* TOP LEFT, FROM LEFT TO RIGHT: *A shady garden nook, a bathtub turned fountain, and The Cleaning Fairy* LEFT: *Kay in her garden*

along the path to the back garden. Kay filled the pool with plants and fish, and then placed stepping-stones and plants around the base. It quickly became an attraction for neighborhood children, who loved to stand on the stones and peer into the pool. One night an enterprising raccoon unplugged the tub's stopper, drained the water, and then helped itself to a fish buffet. Undaunted, Kay placed the pump housing and several heavy stones over the plug to prevent a recurrence. Last year, a huge bullfrog took up residence in the pond, much to Kay's delight.

Kay knows change is the essence of gardening and keeps thinking of new things to try. For example, she and Peter decided that the back lawn looked like a dance floor. When they spotted a rusty metal sculpture with two figures that seemed to be dancing, they bought it. They then covered the small lawn to make a flagstone patio and installed the sculpture in the center. "I spent so much time trying to get grass to grow in the shade and tiptoeing around," reasons Kay. "A hard surface I could walk on made more sense."

The garden is filled with interesting artwork that the couple has collected, much of it metal sculpture, such as the airplane that marks the beginning of the side fence. Its propeller spins gently when the wind blows. A fantastic concrete container decorated with broken bits of colorful pottery is another favorite piece. But the most interesting work of art is a large metal figure Kay calls "The Cleaning Fairy." It lives on the back porch and, as Kay related to her 4-year-old niece, "while we're asleep she comes in and cleans the house." When her niece expressed concern about the fairy coming into her room, she had to admit it was just make-believe.

The front yard presented Kay with a challenge. Huge oak trees towered over it, so she made a welcoming shade garden with water for birds and benches for people. At the street entrance, she installed a small section of fencing on each side of the walk, just enough to discourage dogs from ruining her boxwoods. The fence is now covered with small-leaved ivy. "When people come by walking their dogs, I just smile," says Kay.

Passing neighbors soon noticed Kay's flair and requested help with their own gardens.

TOP: *An inviting setting with beautiful benches and shade-loving plants beckons.* ABOVE: *Birds and people both are invited to the Minors' garden.* LEFT: *Tan pebbles and the colorful foliage of Persian shield brighten the front garden.*

Now she does garden consulting as a part-time job. Kay's imaginative concepts are an inspiration to others. Her yard is frequently featured on local garden tours. Recently she has taken on a new project: She is enthusiastically searching for a spot in the neighborhood to start a community vegetable garden. "I think it would be wonderful to get older people and children involved," proposes Kay, always seeking hidden potential in everyday things and spaces. ◇

KAY'S ADVICE FOR GARDEN REDOS

■ Take your time. Resist the urge to start digging and cutting until you know what you have—you might remove a treasure. A year is not too long to observe the soil, sun, weather, and existing plant material.

■ Make a plan and a list. Decide how you want to use your garden and what you want to grow. Then organize your space accordingly.

■ Think long term. Don't be sentimental. Remove plants you don't like so you can plant what you really want.

■ Make it yours. Find your look. Choose a style that suits your lifestyle and taste, and be consistent.

■ Check out sources such as farmers market bulletins for old-fashioned plants or building materials such as cedar posts. Resourcefulness is a great substitute for resources. Most of all, have fun.

One Tough, Showy Rose

It doesn't need spraying. It doesn't need watering. It doesn't need fertilizing. Frankly, it's beginning to sound like chestnut rose isn't a rose at all.

But, of course, it is. A large, gangly shrub growing 5 to 7 feet high and wide, chestnut rose *(Rosa roxburghii)* bears plump, showy blossoms of bright pink. The bush blooms heavily in spring, and then off and on throughout summer and fall. Pretty as they are, the flowers don't set this rose apart. That honor goes to curious prickles, reminiscent of spiny chestnut burrs. They cover both hips and buds, giving the plant its name. Chestnut rose's leathery green foliage is also noteworthy as it is immune to black spot and powdery mildew.

Once established, this rose is tougher than Grade D beef. It can easily live in a garden for a century or more with absolutely no care. Many years ago, Liz Tedder of Newnan, Georgia, received one from an old friend, Julia Blackburn. Julia had gotten her start from her mother years before. Liz says chestnut rose sends up suckers periodically, so it's easy to pass along.

Nice as it is, chestnut rose isn't perfect. For one thing, Japanese beetles love to eat the blooms, even though they aren't the least bit fragrant. Moreover, it's one of the spiniest roses around.

Despite these failings, it deserves a place in your garden. If you hate spraying, watering, and fertilizing, this is the rose for you.   *Steve Bender*

(For sources turn to pages 234–235.)

CHESTNUT ROSE
At a Glance

Size: 5 to 7 feet tall and wide
Light: full sun
Soil: well drained
Blooms: heavily in spring, sporadically thereafter
Fragrance: none to speak of
Pests: Japanese beetles
Propagation: separate suckers, root cuttings, or pin long canes to the ground until rooted
Range: all but Tropical South

A Dream Blossoms

At first glance you might think it's just another rustic, out-in-the-country, 1930s farmhouse. The flower-laden porch wraps lazily around the old home, and the front-yard fence drips with a profusion of old-fashioned roses and perennials that would make grandma proud. But up near the road, a sign invites you to stop, welcoming you to Petals from the Past, a garden shop and nursery in Jemison, Alabama.

Jason and Shelley Powell, the energetic young owners of this vintage site, have filled the place with heirloom flowers, and they've given the farmhouse new life as the focal point of their blossoming business.

"I was trying to decide what to do when I finished school," Jason says. "I liked the idea of a nursery, but it's hard to get excited about rows and rows of the same old things. I wanted to do something that would not only be different, but also educational." After graduating from Texas A&M, Jason and Shelley moved to Jemison to build that dream.

"I grew up in an Extension Service family," Jason says. "My dad would travel all over the place when I was little, and I got to go along. We would meet the researchers at their field stations, and from there we would go to visit different groups of farmers. Dad could communicate with the researchers on a scientific level and the farmers in layman's terms. I thought that was so cool and the way you should do things. He took valuable information and gave people what they needed to know to grow their crops. I wanted to use the same philosophy with Petals from the Past."

While still in school, the Powells began collecting seed catalogs and took rose starts from Mike Shoup at The Antique Rose Emporium. Before they left Texas, a college professor gave them a grand gift to get them started. "Dr. Bill Welch let me raid all of his gardens and propagate the plant material we knew people would love," Jason says.

As the nursery and gardens developed, friends began sharing hard-to-find plants. "With permission, we were collecting from private gardens. People also began sharing plants with us from old homesites," Jason says. The demonstration beds were planted and have

The farmhouse is home base for the nursery and display gardens of Petals from the Past in Jemison, Alabama. Browse the grounds, and then retire to a rocker on the porch.

wanted to honor the garden style appropriate to the house, so we designed the gardens as you would have found them, out in the country, in the 1930s," Jason explains. "Range laws were not in effect yet, so every garden had to be fenced to keep out the neighbors' cows."

Among the displays, a cutting garden boasts the season's bouquet, which includes flowers you may not have seen in years. You can even cut a few stems to take home for a simple country arrangement. Their vegetable garden offers inspiration and a delicious look at tried-and-true forgotten selections—all with an easygoing emphasis on education.

Whether you plan a special trip or just stop by on your way elsewhere, a visit to these lovely gardens will remind you how new and refreshing the past can be.   *Ellen Riley*

Petals from the Past: 16034 County Road 29, Jemison, AL 35085; (205) 646-0069. **Directions:** Petals from the Past is located only a few miles west of I-65, at Exit 219 (the Jemison/ Thorsby exit), about 40 miles south of Birmingham. ◇

become mature over the last few years. "It's so much more effective to see plants full grown, instead of in 4-inch pots," he says. "I love to use the garden as a teaching tool and to get people really excited about their own gardens."

While the gardens provide a glimpse of what your border can become, the real treat waits out back. Here, neatly arranged rows of heirloom roses perfume the summer air, and pots of perennials and annuals line up, tempting you to take them home. Browse among the flowers, filling a wagon with your colorful treasures, and then move on to the herbs and water plants. If you have questions, there are plenty of answers from the gracious and knowledgeable staff. Jason's commitment to educate carries through to his willing and able crew.

The gardens around the old house's gift shop complement the setting. "We

Jason Powell's enthusiasm for gardening flavors his workshops and tours.

fiesta
In Lucinda's Garden

A gracious invitation to wonderful food and an extraordinary place

It may be the purple house that stops traffic. Or perhaps it's the explosion of flowers that fills the tiny urban yard, tumbling over the curb, forgetting where to stop. Then again, it may just be the old-world charm that oozes from every square inch of this Technicolor Eden, enticing you to sneak a peek.

Lucinda Hutson's garden is something of a legend in Austin. An invitation from Lucinda, an authority on ethnic herbs and an accomplished cook, to sample a new dish or special punch in her flamboyant setting is a guaranteed fiesta. You may be encouraged to garnish your salad from the kitchen bed or add a splash of color to your sangría from any number of flowering herbs. "You can browse through the garden and add different flavors to your meal. I like people to interact with the garden," Lucinda says. One thing is certain—your hostess will welcome you with a gracious mix of Southern charm and Hispanic culture.

"My passion for gardening comes from my trips to Mexico," she says. "I grew up in El Paso, with only gravel and cactus in the yard. In Mexico, even in the countryside, everyone has something blooming—at the very least, a flower-filled jalapeño tin on the doorstep. These trips inspired my garden. I've gone from growing up in a home that looked like The Alamo to a screaming purple house, with every imaginable space planted."

This artful landscape is a study in the expert use of

Lucinda's whimsical purple house boldly invites you into her world.

space, color, and style. The entrance to the side and back gardens, through a tall gate at the corner of the house, bisects the original driveway. Lucinda shortened the drive into a graveled pull-off and built a stacked Texas limestone wall to separate the public front yard from private spaces to the rear. Behind the wall, the former driveway has been transformed into a series of small garden rooms, with every space breathing its own personality.

"It's kind of like walking through different rooms of the house, with each being its own vignette," she says. "Because my home is small, my goal was to have more entertaining areas outdoors and to extend the living space. And I try to use native Texas elements in a Mexican style."

BY SCOTT JONES AND ELLEN RILEY / PHOTOGRAPHY RALPH ANDERSON

Color is a celebration in Lucinda's garden. The untraditional house color and garage-turned-garden-shed are a throwback to Mexican culture and family. "In Mexico, houses are painted bright colors—many times they're turquoise, hot pink, or canary yellow. I wanted a strong color, and purple was my grandmother's favorite. She wore purple, and everything she owned was purple. So in a funny way, it's in homage to Grandmother," she tells us.

With this vibrant backdrop, strong shades balance the color palette. "I use mostly purple, pink, blue, and white flowers. I also like a bit of yellow and orange, but I'm not a red person," she says. Silvery herbs weave through the brilliant blooms, and succulent foliage from cactus and agave tones down the mix with cooling shades of green.

Style is Lucinda's forte, along with an easygoing flair for detail. Each garden room is furnished with folk art collected from south-of-the-border trips and gifts from local artist friends. A joyful mix of Mexican terra-cotta ornaments, mosaics, and folk art makes each space unique. "My garden is such a personal place,

filled with special things my friends have made and memories of my travels," she says. "They are as important to the garden as the flowers and herbs."

GARDEN AND KITCHEN IN ONE FESTIVE WORLD

Growing up in El Paso, Lucinda was exposed to food and culture with a decidedly "border" flair. "We ate in a style very similar to that of North Mexico—grilled meats and wild game and chili con queso made with true *queso blanco,* a wonderful Mexican-style white cheese. In other words, real Tex-Mex," says Lucinda. "But perhaps my greatest childhood memory is of enchiladas, flavored with the most delicious, locally grown red and green chiles."

By her late teens, Lucinda, now fluent in Spanish, regularly traveled through rural Mexican towns, soaking up culture and exploring indigenous foods. "I gravitated toward the kitchen, talking and eating with locals who always shared what little food they had," she says.

However, a college term paper in an anthropology class changed the course of her life. For Lucinda, a "simultaneous explosion" of interest in both food and gardening emerged. "My paper explored the medicinal use of herbs by Mexican women. I immersed myself in the project and again wound up in kitchens chatting with local women who shared gardening secrets and recipes. It was during this time that I learned the importance of cooking with fresh herbs and

Top: *Artist friends have shared their talents, making the garden a personal gallery of remembrances.* Above: *Lucinda's unique take on the Latin wine-cooler sangría makes a refreshing treat on a summer afternoon.* Right: *Preparing for fiesta, sunflowers are tied to a trellis and a few blossoms float in the birdbath.*

how herbs enliven even the most simple of recipes," remembers Lucinda.

Today, her kitchen comes alive with the smells, flavors, and spirit of the Southwestern and Mexican cultures she holds dear. "Don't be surprised to find garlic and chile peppers in many of my recipes," says Lucinda. "After all, they are as inherent to the Southwest as sunshine." Her gusto for entertaining and cooking is exemplified in her recipes, adapted from her book, *The Herb Garden Cookbook: The Complete Gardening and Gourmet Guide.* "I don't want people to be in the kitchen all day. When I entertain, it's usually in the garden, so I keep things simple, relying on bold flavors and garnishes to be festive, colorful, and fun," she explains.

When it's time to go, you reluctantly leave a world of boisterous color, exquisite food, and gracious ambience. But you'll probably go with something in hand. "I've shared so many parts of my garden with people who just stop or walk by. My garden is starting to stretch down the street, and that's really fun. Everyone takes something with them."

GARLIC-AND-ROSEMARY SHRIMP

Use this recipe to make either an appetizer or a main dish with pasta.

1 pound unpeeled, medium-size fresh shrimp
2 tablespoons butter or margarine
¼ cup extra virgin olive oil
1 large garlic bulb
½ cup dry white wine
2 tablespoons white wine vinegar
1 tablespoon lemon juice
3 dried red chile peppers
3 bay leaves
1 teaspoon salt
2 tablespoons chopped fresh rosemary
1 teaspoon dried oregano
½ teaspoon dried crushed red pepper
Garnishes: lemon slices, red chile peppers, fresh rosemary sprigs

PEEL shrimp, leaving tails on; devein, if desired, and set aside.
MELT butter with oil in a skillet over medium-high heat. Cut garlic bulb in half crosswise; separate and peel cloves. Add to butter mixture; sauté 2 minutes.
STIR in wine and next 8 ingredients;

cook, stirring constantly, 1 minute or until thoroughly heated.
ADD shrimp; cook 5 to 6 minutes or just until shrimp turn pink. Garnish, if desired. **Yield:** 4 servings.
Prep: 20 min., Cook: 10 min.
NOTE: If serving over pasta, remove bay leaves.

TOP: *Lucinda uses color to enhance the garden's Mexican atmosphere. Bold and inviting, the flower shades complement the purple house and garden shed.* TOP, RIGHT: *Spice up your next get-together with the bold Southwest flavors of Garlic-and-Rosemary Shrimp.* ABOVE: *Festively display this colorful Basil-Cheese Torta for a beautiful presentation and delicious garden-party treat.*

(For sources turn to pages 234–235.)

ROASTED RED PEPPER SALSA:

4 red bell peppers
1 tablespoon olive oil
½ cup dried tomatoes*
3 tablespoons chopped fresh basil
1 tablespoon balsamic vinegar
2 to 3 garlic cloves, minced
½ teaspoon salt
½ teaspoon fresh rosemary, finely chopped
¼ teaspoon ground red pepper

BAKE peppers on aluminum foil-lined baking sheet at 500° for 12 minutes or until peppers blister, turning once.
PLACE peppers in a heavy-duty zip-top plastic bag; seal and let stand 10 minutes to loosen skins. Peel peppers; remove and discard seeds. Coarsely chop peppers. Drizzle with 1 tablespoon olive oil; set aside.
POUR boiling water to cover over dried tomatoes. Let stand 3 minutes; drain and coarsely chop.
STIR together bell pepper, tomato, basil, and remaining ingredients. Cover and chill salsa up to 2 days, if desired. **Yield:** 2 cups.
Prep: 20 min., Bake: 12 min.
* ⅓ cup dried tomatoes in oil may be substituted for dried tomatoes. Drain tomatoes well, pressing between layers of paper towels.

GARDEN SANGRÍA

1 gallon dry white wine
2 cups brandy
1 cup orange liqueur
4 oranges, sliced
1 bunch fresh mint leaves
1 (1-liter) bottle club soda, chilled*
1 quart whole strawberries
2 lemons, thinly sliced
2 limes, thinly sliced
Garnishes: fresh mint sprigs, strawberries, red seedless grapes, orange and lime wedges

COMBINE first 5 ingredients in a large container; cover and chill 8 hours.
ADD club soda and next 3 ingredients just before serving; serve sangría over ice, if desired. Garnish, if desired. **Yield:** 1½ gallons.
Prep: 10 min., Chill: 8 hrs.
* Ginger ale may be substituted for club soda. ◇

BASIL-CHEESE TORTA

1 (8-ounce) package cream cheese, softened
1 (4-ounce) package feta cheese
2 tablespoons butter or margarine, softened
Lucinda's Garden Pesto
2 (6-ounce) packages provolone cheese slices
Roasted Red Pepper Salsa, divided
¼ cup chopped pine nuts, toasted
Garnishes: chopped fresh basil, fresh basil sprigs, pine nuts

PROCESS first 3 ingredients in a blender or food processor until smooth, stopping to scrape down sides. Stir in Lucinda's Garden Pesto, blending well.
LINE an 8- x 4-inch loafpan with plastic wrap, allowing 1 inch to hang over on each side.
ARRANGE one-third of cheese slices on bottom and up sides of pan. Layer evenly with half of pesto mixture, ⅓ cup Roasted Red Pepper Salsa, 2 tablespoons pine nuts, and half of remaining cheese slices. Repeat layers, ending with cheese slices, gently pressing each layer. Fold cheese slices toward center. Cover and chill 8 hours.
INVERT torta onto a serving platter. Top with ⅓ cup salsa; garnish, if desired. Serve with remaining salsa and toasted French baguette slices. **Yield:** 12 servings.
Prep: 40 min., Chill: 8 hrs.

LUCINDA'S GARDEN PESTO:

3 cups fresh basil leaves
4 to 6 garlic cloves
½ cup pine nuts, walnuts, or pecans
¾ cup shredded Parmesan cheese
2 to 3 tablespoons shredded Romano cheese
⅔ cup olive oil

PROCESS basil and garlic in a food processor until chopped. Add pine nuts and cheeses, and process until blended, stopping to scrape down sides. With processor running, pour oil through food chute in a slow, steady stream; process until smooth. Chill up to 5 days, if desired. **Yield:** 1 cup.
Prep: 10 min.

Airy blue lilies-of-the-Nile (See page 115.)

June

Checklist for June

EDITOR'S NOTEBOOK

E.L. and Mary Boteler's vibrant pink hydrangeas on page 120 tell me one thing for sure—their soil is alkaline (that is, the pH is above 7.0). That's because French hydrangea *(Hydrangea macrophylla)* is nature's living litmus test. Blue flowers mean the soil is acid, pink flowers mean it's alkaline, and a mixture of blue and pink means the soil is near neutral. Here are a couple of tricks to turn hydrangea flowers the color you want. To turn blue flowers pink, sprinkle 3 to 4 cups of lime around the base of the plant. Do this again several months later. To turn pink flowers blue, add 4 tablespoons aluminum sulfate to a gallon of water, and drench around the base. Do this again three weeks later. The color change takes about a year in either case, so be patient. What about altering a white hydrangea? Some people claim there is no way to change the color, but I disagree. Just stop watering it for a few months at the height of summer and watch what happens.

Steve Bender

TIPS

☐ **Irrigation**—Plan now for efficient summer irrigation. Place soaker hoses under heavy mulches to reduce water use. Drip emitters are useful for watering your trees and shrubs. Operate sprinkler irrigation systems early in the morning to reduce loss through evaporation. Thorough, deep watering is better than frequent, shallow applications. Collect and store rainwater for use on indoor and other container plants. Also pay close attention to your hanging baskets. As you make additions to your garden, you will need to water them more than plants that are already established and containers, because they dry out more quickly with the warmer temperatures. ▶

☐ **Vegetables**—Pick tomatoes, squash, okra, beans, and cucumbers regularly this month, because production drops if vegetables are allowed to become too mature. Picking every other day in either the early morning or the late afternoon will ensure a steady supply of tasty, high-quality vegetables.

PLANT

☐ **Herbs**—Various types of mints are excellent choices for moist areas where other plants may not thrive. Mexican mint marigold *(Tagetes lucida),* rosemary, artemisias, basil, stevia, and lemongrass may all be planted now for continuous use during the warm seasons.

☐ **Mulch**—Now is the time to apply extra pine straw or shredded bark mulch around newly planted trees and shrubs to better transition these plants into your garden. The extra mulch will reduce water loss and heat stress to the new roots.

◀ **Plant**—Gourds, Southern peas, and pumpkins are all useful to fill empty spaces in the summer garden. Gourds are more productive and will have better shapes if allowed to grow on trellises or other supports.

☐ **Summer bulbs and tubers**—Cannas, elephant's ears, dahlias, caladiums, and blackberry lilies are available in containers this month at your local garden center. Use these plants to add brightly colored flowers or bold textures in your garden. ▶

☐ **Summer containers**—Soft-leaf yuccas, hesperaloes (red yucca), and yellow bells *(Tecoma stans)* are all heat-, drought-, and insect-resistant choices that provide weeks of color in the garden. Goldmoss sedum *(Sedum acre)* or other small succulents will add contrasting texture and color. Also consider such ornamental grasses as Lindheimer's muhly *(Muhlenbergia lindheimeri),* Mexican feather grass *(Stipa tenuissima),* or pennisetum.

☐ **Vegetables**—Plant eggplant, peppers, okra, and black-eyed peas in the garden. Sweet potatoes can be planted now for fall harvest.

PRUNE

☐ **Shrubs**—Continue to prune flowering shrubs, such as gardenias, Indian hawthorn, and azaleas, as they finish blooming. Hand-prune them for a natural look. After trimming, add fertilizer per label directions. ▶

FERTILIZE

☐ **Crepe myrtles**—An application of fertilizer at bloom time should give you a longer flowering period. A granular 6-6-6 around the drip line works well. Apply according to label directions, and water in thoroughly afterwards. As soon as trees finish blooming, remove the seedpods to encourage a second bloom and possibly a third. If mildew is visible, spray with a fungicide. Black sooty mold may indicate an aphid infestation that can be treated with an insecticidal soap.

☐ **Fertilizer**—It's time to feed your warm-season lawn again with a slow-release fertilizer high in nitrogen and low in phosphorous. (Do not use a high-nitrogen fertilizer on centipede.) Check the bag for recommended rate of application, or ask your garden center or Extension office for help to determine the right amount. If you are getting heavy summer rains, fertilize your annuals, vegetables, trees, shrubs, and citrus with an application of a granular 6-6-6, as most nutrients are probably getting leached out of the soil.

☐ **Roses**—Spread about half a cup of 12-6-8 or similar fertilizer beneath each plant. Scratch the fertilizer lightly into the soil with a hand cultivator, and water gently to wash the nutrients down to the roots.

CONTROL

☐ **Houseplants**—Place houseplants outside in a shady location so that they can enjoy the fresh air and rejuvenate. Remember to water the plants regularly; to encourage abundant new growth, feed them with an all-purpose (20-20-20) water-soluble fertilizer.

☐ **Insects**—Check plants for aphids, usually noticed by sooty mold on new growth, and treat with insecticidal soap. Pick off caterpillars and grasshoppers by hand, and combat scale found on the undersides of leaves by scraping it off or treating with oils found at your garden center. Here's an important precaution: When using horticultural oil, apply when the air is cool to avoid burning the foliage.

☐ **Weeds**—Pull weeds out of your garden before they bloom or set seed. Removing a few weeds as you see them now will save you from having to deal with many later in the season.

Cut flowers—Zinnias are plentiful in cell packs now, and if cut regularly, they will supply flowers until fall. The 'State Fair' hybrids or other large-flowering types are ideal for cutting. Open, sunny locations are best for zinnias as well as for bachelor's buttons (globe amaranth), cockscomb, coreopsis, and annual sunflowers.

TIP OF THE MONTH

We have many thorny shrubs around our home that can be a real pain to trim, but I discovered a good solution. I shove an open umbrella upside down under the bush and proceed to trim. The thorny branches fall into the umbrella. I just pick up the umbrella by the end of the handle and haul the trimmings off to the brush pile.

CATHY MITCHELL
LAVONIA, GEORGIA

*Enjoy these easygoing plants
that pack a punch of fragrance.*

scented
Geraniums

Brush against the mounds of lacy leaves, and get a whiff of lemon or maybe the essence of a rose. The fragrance is distinct and definite, but the origin, elusive. Look no further than the scented geraniums, where an aromatic surprise awaits in every pot. "I love to grow them for their fragrance," says Bobbie Cyphers, owner of The Herb of Grace in Hot Springs, North Carolina. "They all flower, and the blooms are extremely beautiful, but it's their fragrance that gives you a lot of joy."

Scented geraniums claim kinship with the boldly flowering geraniums *(Pelargonium* sp.) common in summer gardens. The difference lies in their demure flowers and leaves packed with a redolent punch. "Rub their leaves gently between your fingers to release the essential oils and get their full effect," Bobbie recommends.

The diversity of these geraniums is enormous. "They're like a whole garden in one type of plant. The leaves go from the little tiny smooth ones of the nutmeg spice up to the huge grape-leaved ones with a musky scent," Bobbie says.

Choose any number of rose, citrus, fruit, or spicy selections, each wearing its own unique perfume. "The 'Attar of Roses,' an old-fashioned rose-scented geranium, is probably the first that people pick, because it really does have that whiff of rose when you rub the leaves," she explains.

GET GROWING
Bobbie recommends growing these geraniums in containers. The secret to success lies within the pot. The container must have a drainage hole and be filled with a porous, fast-draining

potting soil. "While scented geraniums need moisture, overwatering will kill them quickly," she says. "I have seen my plants recover from too little water, but they die very quickly from too much."

Provide a bright location, with early-morning sunshine and protection from hot afternoon rays. As light increases, the need for moisture will also grow. Keep the soil evenly damp, but never allow the pot to sit in water. Brown, crispy leaves are the telltale sign of dryness. If they appear, remove them, and increase the amount of water. ▶

BY ELLEN RILEY / PHOTOGRAPHY RALPH ANDERSON

Perfectly at home in pots, scented geraniums need to stay where you can touch them often and enjoy their special fragrances. ABOVE, FAR LEFT: *Rub the leaves gently to release the essential oils.*

During summer months, scented geraniums grow vigorously. Trim them regularly to maintain full, lush plants. "Keep them nice and shrubby," Bobbie says. "I prune mine quite a bit to keep them from becoming leggy. Pinching them back gets the fragrance all over your fingers, and it smells wonderful all day."

THE MORE, THE MERRIER

These plants have been collected and shared since Victorian times. One reason is their easy rooting habits. After pruning scented geraniums, save a few cuttings to propagate. Fill pots no larger than 3 inches in diameter with soil. "For rooting, I like

BOBBIE'S FAVORITES

We asked Bobbie to choose her top five.
- 'Apple Cider'
- 'Nutmeg'
- 'Cinnamon Rose'
- 'Old-Fashioned Rose'
- 'Lemon Crispum'

to use potting mix with a lot of sphagnum peat moss," Bobbie says. "I mix it half and half with perlite to increase air circulation around the new roots."

Clip a stem, 3 to 4 inches from the tip, right above a leaf. Remove the lower

ABOVE, LEFT: *To propagate more plants from the cuttings, remove the stem right above a leaf.* ABOVE: *A collection of scented geraniums makes a colorful, fragrant bouquet.*

leaves, dip the cut end into rooting hormone, and push the stem securely into the soil. Place the new plant in bright light, and keep the potting medium moist until the cutting has established roots.

COME ON IN

When summer ends and frost is imminent, bring your favorite scented geraniums indoors. "Place them in a cool room with high light, and they'll thrive beautifully," says Bobbie. Water requirements remain the same, with the geranium needing moist soil. Indoors, the plant may dry more slowly, so adjust your watering schedule accordingly.

Scented geraniums may be the ultimate plant for all seasons. With dainty flowers and fragrant leaves, these sturdy plants grace the garden in summer, and then move willingly indoors for winter. A word of caution—once you have one, you'll be hooked on all the perfumed possibilities. ◇

(For sources turn to pages 234–235.)

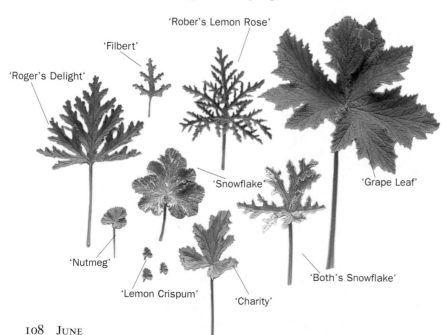

'Rober's Lemon Rose'
'Filbert'
'Roger's Delight'
'Snowflake'
'Grape Leaf'
'Nutmeg'
'Lemon Crispum'
'Charity'
'Both's Snowflake'

ABOVE: *Attractive in any setting, mealy-cup sage is one of the best blue flowers for the hottest part of summer.* INSET: *The blooms have a dusting of fine hairs that insulate them from heat and give them a deliciously frosted appearance.*

Ice Blue Salvia

Imagine a typical, sweltering summer day. Then imagine a light frost descending through the blistering heat and humidity. Ice blue mealy-cup sage *(Salvia farinacea)* in a sunburnt border works like a floral plunge into cool water.

The flowers and stems are densely covered with tiny hairs that make them look as if they are dusted with a coat of frost. For practical purposes, these little hairs insulate the plant's surfaces from heat and slow water loss. Visually, the effect is restful in the daytime and luminous in moonlight.

Whether grown as an annual or a perennial, mealy-cup sage stands out as an individual performer, but it's also a great team player. The silver and blue colors make nearby flowers of orange, red, and yellow burn hotter. The same icy shades blend beautifully with pastel blossoms.

MEALY-CUP SAGE
At a Glance

Height: 2 to 3 feet
Width: 1 to 2 feet
Light: full sun to partial shade
Soil: any, well drained
Pests: none serious
Propagation: seed, cuttings, or division
Range: annual throughout the South; hardy to 25 degrees

Care is simple. Plant it from seed in early spring, or transplant it at any time during the year. It enjoys sun, needs minimal water and fertilizer, and doesn't care about the soil as long as there's decent drainage. In a large border, this plant can be left alone to bloom from midspring until frost. Then either replace it, or prune it to the ground early in the following spring, before the new foliage pushes through.

If you can't get the species form of *S. farinacea*, look for a selection called 'Strata' to get the same effect. There are also white selections ('Porcelain,' 'Silver,' and 'Cirrus') and the darker blue 'Victoria' or 'Blue Bedder.'

(For sources turn to pages 234–235.)

PHOTOGRAPHS: RALPH ANDERSON

For Goodness' Sake

Southerners are all about family and history. Our perennials are no exception—each comes with a story and a bit of advice.

It had always been presumed that perennials wouldn't grow in the South. Visions of the quintessential border were merely a dream, with summers considered too hot and winters not cold enough. But Marc Richardson and Rick Berry knew there were plants that would come back faithfully every year. These were the flowers from childhood, those grown in grandmothers' gardens and colorful pastures along yawning country roads. After 24 years of triumphs and tribulations at their nursery, Goodness Grows, in Lexington, Georgia, the two men have proved that we certainly can

grow perennials in the South—we simply have our own plant palette.

"Driving between Athens and South Georgia, where Marc grew up, we noticed native wildflowers on the roadsides. At different times there were blackberry lilies, baptisias, and rudbeckias," Rick remembers. "We knew these were good candidates for Southern gardens." Thus began Goodness Grows—and a dedication to preserving the South's perennials.

Marc and Rick started by collecting plants and learning the personality and viability of each. "We would go see

Marc's grandmother and bring things back from her garden," Rick says. "Mama Claude's ginger lily is one we've tried to perpetuate all these years."

Another story comes along with Miss Huff's lantana. In 1979 Rick and Marc began a daily commute between Lexington and their nursery in Crawford. Every trip took them past Miss Huff's home, with a large orange-yellow lantana on the front lawn. "We did this for several years, watching the plant in each season. There was a big freeze during the Christmas of '83, and the whole winter was very cold," Rick recalls. "We

ABOVE AND FAR LEFT: *The colorful display beds teach gardeners how to create fabulous borders.* LEFT: *Red wagons do all of the work as visitors stroll the grounds picking out plants.*

decided if the lantana came back after those temperatures, we would go beg a piece from Miss Huff. Sure enough, it came back that spring."

"We went over to see Miss Huff and asked her for a piece of the plant," Rick recounts. "She wanted to barter. 'Well, I'll share some of this with you if you'll plant some hollies here in front of my porch,' she told us. So we did plant her hollies, and she gave us a big old chunk of lantana."

The coveted plant went home with the new owners and flourished. In the fall, after the first freeze, it lost all its leaves, as they expected. "We cut it back and cleaned up our garden like nice, tidy little gardeners would do," Rick says.

"The following year, our lantana didn't come back. Hers did."

A spring visit to Miss Huff yielded an important tidbit of information. "She explained about not cutting it back in fall but leaving the dead wood all winter. She showed us its hollow stem and explained that it would suck water down into the crown and rot if you cut it back in winter," Rick says. The next year, the lantana did exactly as Miss Huff had promised. "That same plant has been in our Crawford garden ever since. Miss Huff's lantana has been in her garden for more than 40 years. She's shared it with people from all over," he says.

From the beginning, the mission of Marc and Rick's nursery has stayed the

same. "We want the public to see what they can have," Rick says. "People get excited when they see things their grandmothers have grown, and they haven't seen them in years." Since those early days, Goodness Grows has blossomed from a few family favorites to a massive collection. Rick and Marc work tirelessly to offer plants that speak of times past and to find new introductions for our gardens—all with the charm and grace expected of old Southern friends.

Ellen Riley

Goodness Grows is located at 332 Elberton Road (State 77 North), P.O. Box 311, Lexington, GA 30648; (706) 743-5055. ◇

Simple Steps

The genius of this solution to an unfriendly entrance lies in its simplicity.

Before its redo, the entrance to Susan Shockley's home was not only unfriendly, it was unsafe. Awkward steps came with the new home when she purchased it in 1985, and she lived with the problem for many years before deciding something had to be done.

The narrow 4-foot, 4-inch-wide steps were further confined by handrails that took up precious space. Susan resented the fact that there was not enough room to sit on the stoop and visit with her Midlothian, Virginia, neighbors or watch the children play in the yard. Although these were really just inconveniences, the steps, composed of different heights, were an accident just waiting for an unsuspecting victim.

By widening the old steps and reducing the number of risers, the new entrance appears much more accessible.

"There were four risers on the original steps," recalls her landscape architect Preston Dalrymple. "The top one was 6¾ inches, the middle two steps were 7⅜ inches, and the bottom one was 4¾ inches. It was like they had a built-in tripping hazard. And unfortunately, this is not that unusual." This problem often is caused by the ground settling beneath the steps of a new home, creating a low first step and a high top step.

So out went the old steps and in went Preston's new design. By regrading the approach and replacing the existing walk with a new brick path that slopes up to the base of the steps, he was able to reduce the number of steps from four to three. All of the risers were made an even 7 inches, so there's less chance of anyone tripping. The new steps are also a foot wider than the old ones. "We only picked up a foot, but the illusion that's created by having three risers is that the steps are much longer," Preston says.

BEFORE

LEFT: *The old handrails were modified and reused with the new steps. A few colorful containers filled with geraniums and petunias extend a friendly greeting to visitors.*

To complete the project, he reconnected the old railings with a slight modification. To comfortably allow two people to use the steps at the same time, the two short sections of rails that ran between the main columns and the handrails were eliminated.

"Before we reworked it, you had this good-size structure with these narrow steps," Preston says. "Now the entrance is more in proportion with the rest of the home. It's such a simple thing but it made a big difference on the presentation of the house." *Glenn R. DiNella*

Shade, Summer's Blessing

When Bob Rossier and Eldred Hudson bought this Arts and Crafts-style bungalow in Charlotte, the narrow side yard had only two notable features. One was a large shade tree. The other was an air conditioner overflow pipe protruding from the house. With a little creativity and the right plants, the area saw a dramatic transformation.

The overflow pipe was an eyesore until it became part of a delightful fountain, now the focal point of the little garden. Bob and Eldred combined a Victorian fireback (a cast-iron plate used to line a fireplace) and the sculpted head of a mythological creature. After painting

both pieces to match, they mounted them on the wall so the pipe extends from the sculpture's mouth. A shallow, old birdbath now catches the overflow water for an array of birds to enjoy.

Filtered light lets in just enough morning sun to support the growth of a range of shade-loving plants. Two Japanese maples are part of the understory. Shrubs include fatsia, viburnum, sasanqua camellia, and a 10-year-old *Daphne odora*. "The daphne must have thrived on benign neglect," admits Bob.

Most of the garden is in fairly dry

Top: Steps lead from the front yard into a shady side garden. Above, left: An inviting bench faces the fountain and birdbath. Above, right: A mythological character and an antique fireback lend beauty to a utilitarian drainage pipe.

shade. Without irrigation, plants in this garden must be accommodating. "Only the fittest survive," says Eldred. In these conditions perennials such as lily of China *(Rohdea japonica),* trillium, bloodroot, Italian arum, variegated periwinkle, galax, hellebores, wild ginger, epimedium, and cyclamen are happy. "A wonderful thing about dry shade," says Bob, "is that weeds don't grow well."

Fragrance is also an important part of the garden's appeal. A gardenia's scent heralds the summer. Daphne and wintersweet saturate the late winter air. Spring brings the flowers of a 'Mohawk' viburnum, and an empress tree blooms in vanilla-scented violet panicles.

Nestled 8 feet below the front garden, this side garden is not only protected, but private as well. *Orene Stroud Horton*

LEFT: *Snapdragons, impatiens, rangoon creeper, and purple fountain grass brighten the pond's edge, while carex, parrot's-feather, and variegated iris offer texture.* BELOW: *Carefully shaped beds full of colorful plants soften the strong, formal lines of the house.*

The Liveliest Garden

This is Houston," Susan Howard says, "and our yards can have color all year round. As long as you're going to put something in the ground, why not choose something to see and smell and touch?"

Of course, for Susan, this wasn't anything new. She's a real estate broker who buys and remodels homes in order to sell them, including those she actually inhabits. "I don't do as much on the inside," Susan explains, "because my real pleasure is doing the gardens. You have to do both, but if it's pretty from the outside, it gets them in the front door."

Through the years, Susan has developed a workable system for creating a garden without breaking the bank or her back. Her current house had absolutely nothing in the yard when she started. "It was a clean palette," she says. "I took garden hoses and laid out shapes until I found a design that pleased my eyes. I like my garden beds to have natural lines, and I like to define them. I found stones that went with the color of the bricks and used them to edge the beds." Because Susan wants to keep her costs to a

This lively suburban garden was easy and economical to create.

minimum, she has developed a knack for filling her beds with plants that are on sale or discarded. "If I see somebody throw out a plant, I'll bring it home. If it grows and blooms okay, I'll find a place to put it. Alyssum, periwinkles [vinca], impatiens, coleus, violas, snapdragons, different colors of sweet-potato vine, I plant cell packs with some timed-release fertilizer such as Osmocote, and they catch up to the 1-gallon containers in no time." Once she has the basics in place, Susan adds an extra touch, the "lagniappe," by visiting specialty nurseries to get favorite roses or unusual plants to make each garden distinctive.

Susan's gardens, though, end up with even more life and color than most nurseries can provide. Mama Cat, a former stray, sunbathes while Sadie, the little black dog, keeps an eye on the rambunctious kittens. Even discounting the rabbit and parrots that live indoors, it's a lot of action for a small suburban garden.

Susan's fan-tail goldfish, swimming decoratively in her tiny pond garden, are also part of the interactive universe she creates wherever she goes. She's got them completely hand-tamed, swirling up like golden flowers in the water to take little pieces of carrot, sweet potato, and green bean from her fingers whenever she calls "fishie, fishie, fishie."

"I have time to play with that kind of thing because the garden really doesn't take much work," Susan says. "I go out with a cup of coffee and mess around, maybe an hour a week, pulling weeds, etc. About every three months I trim things back, especially along the driveway, so it doesn't hit the car."

It's hard to believe, looking at Susan's blooming, living garden, that she and her husband, Kermit, are planning to move again soon and leave it all behind. "I won't say it doesn't upset me to leave each garden," she says, "especially if I go back and it isn't kept up. But I know that not everyone is going to be as passionate about it as I am. But I take along anything that's in pots, and all my yard art, and the animals, even the fish. So you know I'll be ready to start the next garden wherever we go. I am always," says Susan, "ready to garden." *Liz Druitt*

PHOTOGRAPH: VAN CHAPLIN

LILY-OF-THE-NILE
At a Glance

Soil: rich, well-manured soil with excellent drainage
Water: well in spring and summer; lightly in fall and winter
Fertilizer: slow-release fertilizer or compost after blooming
Sun: full sun to light shade
Bloom season: six weeks or more in summer
Range: Lower, Coastal, and Tropical South in the ground; Upper and Middle South in contalners
Comments: Don't divide too often. *Agapanthus* will bloom best if left undisturbed and a little crowded.

Easy-Care Lilies

As Southern days stretch smoothly from spring into summer, increasing warmth brings stately blue lilies into bloom. Ann Donnelly, head gardener at Longue Vue House and Gardens in New Orleans, notes, "That first warm day, you'll see blue buds on the Nile lilies. Then they all start opening and put on a show for a month or more."

Lilies-of-the-Nile, also known by their botanical name, *Agapanthus,* are not true lilies and come from South Africa rather than Egypt. But Southern gardeners care much more about their elegance and ease of culture than about such minor details. These flowers are so useful in containers, borders, and vases, that it's impossible not to like them.

Fortunately they are easy to grow anywhere in the South. Some species are more cold hardy than others, and the different forms have mingled in the nursery trade, so the easiest way to sort them out is by winter foliage. If they have leaves in winter, they're evergreen and will prefer to occupy flower borders in the warmer zones. Deciduous lilies-of-the-Nile, whose straplike foliage dies back in winter, should be cold hardy in the ground through the Middle South.

PHOTOGRAPH: JEAN ALLSOPP

ABOVE: *Airy blue flowers of lily-of-the-Nile cool off the summer borders at Longue Vue House and Gardens in New Orleans.* LEFT: *'Peter Pan,' a popular dwarf selection, is only 18 inches high.*

Ann points out that the gorgeous blue border at Longue Vue needs only the most minimal care. These plants require good drainage and plenty of water during the early part of the growing season, but once established they'll keep blooming even through a drought. "The Nile lilies here have probably been in the ground about 15 years. They bloom reliably every year from late April or early May, whenever the temperature gets really warm, into June," Ann says. "They don't require much special attention."

Occasionally, according to Ann, the leaves can get a little fungus late in the summer, after the bloom season. Instead of spraying the plants, she just cuts them back. "It's easy, and they come back with foliage when it's cooler.

"Basically they do exactly what they're supposed to do every year, with almost no effort from me," Ann says. "They're really satisfying. *Agapanthus* is supposed to be Greek for 'flower of love.' I can see that."

Liz Druitt
(For sources turn to pages 234–235.)

LEFT AND BELOW: *Pink to please everyone, mandevilla's flowers change from pale to deep rose as they mature.*

OTHER TROPICAL VINES TO TRY

- queen's-wreath *(Petrea volubilis)*
- pink trumpet vine *(Podranea ricasoliana)*
- violet trumpet vine *(Clytostoma callistegioides)*
- chalice vine *(Solandra maxima)*
- cup-and-saucer vine *(Cobaea scandens)*
- black-eyed Susan vine *(Thunbergia alata)*
- Chilean jasmine *(Mandevilla laxa)*
- Mina lobata *(Ipomoea lobata)*
- Brazilian nightshade *(Solanum seaforthianum)*

Some Like It Hot

For vivid summer color and ease of care, you can't beat these showy vines.

Shocking. Gorgeous. The wild colors of tropical vines practically burn a trail across the eyes of admirers. They are all the colors your mother told you not to wear, all the forbidden and delicious perfumes. How brave are you? Do you dare bring home those same luscious colors—flaunting pinks, screaming yellows, flaming oranges?

Of course you do. Tropical vines are making their way into more and more garden centers, and their vivid flowers and easy care make an irresistible combination. If you can provide heat and sunlight, you're all set to grow yourself a brilliant little jungle. Here are some of our favorite tropical treasures, with ways to use them in your own yard.

Mandevilla *(Mandevilla* 'Alice du Pont'): Queen of all mailbox vines, mandevilla is a fast-growing twiner from Brazil with 2- to 4-inch floral trumpets that open pale pink and flush through shocking pink to deep rose. These exuberant flowers appear in great abundance all summer, but even in the off-season mandevilla will continue to bloom lightly.

To get the absolute best performance out of this vine, give it a rich, very well-drained soil, with weekly applications of liquid fertilizer and regular deep watering while it's actively growing. The tuberous roots are fairly tolerant of drought, but sensitive to overwatering, so be sure the soil never gets waterlogged. Mandevilla prefers temperatures of 65 degrees or more, and it will stop active growth if it gets too cool. That's the time to back off on both feeding and watering, or transfer container-grown plants to a warm indoor environment.

Everblooming allamanda shines in a tropical setting and will greatly reward gardeners.

Mandevilla's flashy blooms make a stunning hanging basket, as long as you regularly pinch off the vine's tips to keep it from getting too long. Within one summer season it can fill a moderate trellis with shiny green foliage and pink trumpets or curl around a mailbox or lamppost in eye-catching fashion. As a container plant for a balcony, mandevilla is an amazing success. Juliet herself couldn't compete for attention with a Southern belle leaning over a railing wrapped with this vine.

Allamanda *(Allamanda cathartica):* Golden trumpet is the common name for this gorgeous climber, and it has every reason to be blowing its own horn. Its fragrant yellow flowers, 5 inches wide, bloom year-round in frost-free areas on a vine with glossy, evergreen foliage.

Allamanda isn't as sensitive as mandevilla to soil moisture, so it's hard to make any mistakes when growing it. Regular watering and feeding during the hot months will keep it blooming freely. Pinching it back makes this vine bushier and even more full of blooms.

Mexican flame vine blooming with purple climbing aster

PHOTOGRAPH: SYLVIA MARTIN

Golden trumpet can serve a number of different uses, among them mailbox or lamppost enhancement. It also flourishes happily in a patio container as a clipped flowering bush, or it can drape itself over a balcony railing. If you're fortunate enough to live in a frost-free climate, you can let allamanda reach its full potential as a 20-foot vine. If you do this, either groom it carefully, or underplant with hibiscus or plumbago to cover up the leafless lower canes. Another plus—mandevilla and allamanda attract hummingbirds.

Mexican flame vine *(Senecio confusus):* Also known as orangeglow vine, this tropical beauty is almost too easy to grow. You can purchase the plant in full bloom at the nursery right now. Once established, this evergreen produces clusters of orange daisies with fluffy golden centers year-round in frost-free areas. Flame vine will die back with light frost, but it is root hardy through the Coastal South and will bloom year after year in this region.

Good drainage and plenty of sunshine are the only requirements for growing Mexican flame vine. It isn't particular about soil, is tolerant of dry conditions, doesn't need much fertilizer (though several applications of a balanced liquid fertilizer during the growing season will encourage heavier flowering), and basically thrives on neglect.

Flame vine is not only vivid but also versatile. It sprawls 8 to 10 feet as a ground cover, drapes beautifully from a hanging basket or window box, covers a small trellis, and spills over a railing or retaining wall. It's even fragrant (though the selection 'São Paolo' is not) and acts as an irresistible attractant for butterflies. For a glorious color experience, plant Mexican flame vine with other such rambling plants as blue plumbago, yellow butterfly vine, or purple climbing aster.

Tropical vines may not overwinter outdoors north of the Coastal South, but they grow and bloom so freely that they give more than a full measure of beauty before frost strikes them down. Should you grow them? Yes. Their intensity will light up your summer garden with passion, and, no matter what your mother said, a little passion is very good for the Southern soul.

Liz Druitt

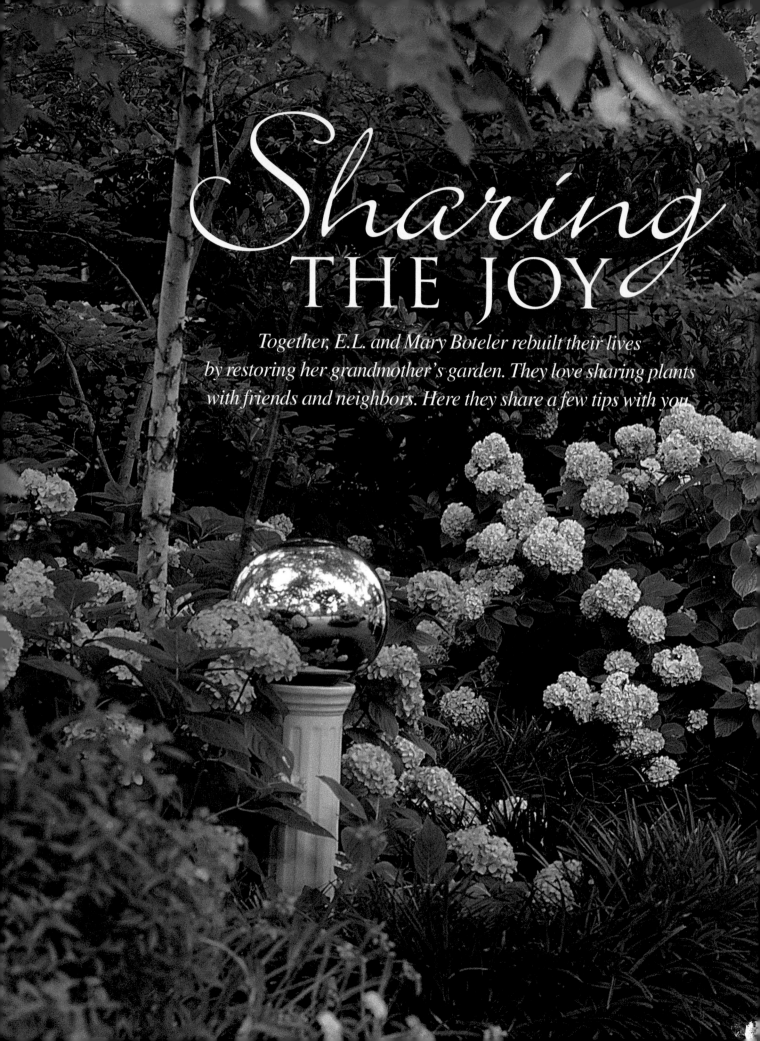

Sharing
THE JOY

*Together, E.L. and Mary Boteler rebuilt their lives
by restoring her grandmother's garden. They love sharing plants
with friends and neighbors. Here they share a few tips with you.*

by Steve Bender / photography Jean Allsopp

ABOVE: *E.L. and Mary Boteler*
RIGHT: *Flowering plants provide beautiful blooms for cutting.*

If roots run deep in Leland, Mississippi, give credit to the soil. Through the millennia, the surging Mississippi River has ladled so much alluvium over the area that in some places the topsoil is 30 feet thick. Give credit, too, to folks like Mary Boteler, who faithfully garden in the footsteps of their forebears—smelling the same summer-sweet flowers, turning over the same brown earth.

"Most all gardeners can trace their love of gardening to someone," says Mary. In her case, that someone was her grandmother Ruth Mathis who, with her husband, J.T., created the first garden here shortly after the house was built in 1925. "I have very fond memories of that magical place," Mary recalls. "I followed in her footsteps and learned a lot about plants. I still have her garden journals." Shrubs that Mrs. Mathis planted more than a half-century ago—Japanese kerria, mahonia, spiraea, flowering almond, forsythia, nandina, and sweetheart rose—thrive in the garden to this day.

In 1964, Mary and her first husband moved into Mrs. Mathis's house and raised a family. Eventually, she was widowed and in 1988, married E.L. Boteler, who was also widowed. The two decided to restore the rundown garden, but with one important change. No longer would it be the formal garden of rectangular beds that Mary's grandmother had laid out. Instead, it would feature a large central lawn ringed by curving beds and grass pathways, all edged in liriope. "We

wanted to loosen things up," says E.L.

Today, you'd be hard-pressed to find a single month when something isn't blooming in this garden. Hundreds of old-fashioned pass alongs—bulbs, perennials, shrubs, and vines—fill the beds, many destined to be shared with friends and neighbors. But if truth be told, the time to be here is in June. That's when E.L.'s hydrangeas bloom—hundreds of them.

Where did the plants come from? After they married, E.L. and Mary passed the garden of neighbor Katherine Fulgham. "E.L. said, 'Oh, look at those hydrangeas! My mother had hydrangeas, and I would love to have some,'" remembers Mary. "So I said, 'I know Katherine. She's in my garden club. Let's ask her if we can take cuttings.'" The couple left with six or eight and proceeded to root every one. Then E.L., Master Hydrangea

E.L.'S METHOD FOR PROPAGATING HYDRANGEAS

Step 1: First, take tip cuttings in summer and strip off the lowest pair of leaves.
Step 2: Next, wet the cut ends, and dip them in rooting powder.
Step 3: Stick each cutting into a container of moist potting soil. Keep the soil moist and the plant in the shade. The cutting should root in six to eight weeks. You can also stick cuttings directly into a garden bed.

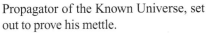

PHOTO STYLING: MISSIE NEVILLE CRAWFORD

Propagator of the Known Universe, set out to prove his mettle.

"The next year, I rooted about 200 cuttings," he says. "It's extremely easy. I take cuttings in summer and dip them in rooting powder. At first, I rooted them all in pots and transplanted them. Then I decided, why bother doing that? I'll root 'em right where I want 'em. So I fix the ground good, put a cutting in it, and just keep the dirt muddy. I get 80% to 90%

livability on 'em." Which explains why about 300 hydrangeas are blooming their heads off right now.

That's a lot of blooms. To enjoy their beauty throughout the year, Mary cuts some just as they begin to fade and turn green. Then she stretches a string between two chairs in her dining room and hangs the blooms upside-down to dry. It takes two to three days. She says the flowers dry much better in the air-conditioned house.

E.L. and Mary have learned a lot about successful gardening in the Mississippi Delta. One rule, they say, is to

stop trying plants that dislike the Delta's rich, alkaline soil. This means no dogwoods, azaleas, and rhododendrons. Notes Mary, "It's like [Mississippi garden writer] Felder Rushing says: 'If you want to see rhododendrons, go to North Carolina.'"

A second rule is to recognize what truly matters. The Botelers traveled quite a bit soon after they married. But as their garden grew, they found their greatest satisfaction came from simply being in it with each other. "The best thing about the garden," says Mary, "is that we share it together and also share it with other people. To me, that's the greatest joy." ◇

A pathway leads to beauty
(See pages 134–137.)

July

Checklist for July

EDITOR'S NOTEBOOK

Southern gardeners love to share. That's how a lot of quirky, time-honored plants like tater vine, touch-me-not, and kiss-me-over-the-garden-gate survive in modern gardens. You can't buy them in local nurseries. About the only way to get one is from a neighbor who has it. No self-respecting Southerner would turn you down. But always be wary of a plant that someone seems too eager to share. Case in point—the double, orange daylily you see here. Named 'Kwanso,' it's been around for more than 2,000 years. Know why? Because it spreads faster than you can dig it up. I think they should rename it "Ebola." Plant one outside your house, and a week later you'll find it in bed beside you. Of course, its prolific nature makes it the perfect plant to lift, divide, and share. It reminds me of the basket of loaves and fishes in the Bible. No matter how many you take out, you'll always find more.

Steve Bender

□ **Birdbaths**—Relocate birdbaths to a shaded spot to slow evaporation and keep water from becoming too hot. Placing the bath near a small tree or large shrub provides shelter for the birds and encourages use.

□ **Bulbs**—You should set out gladioli bulbs every couple of weeks this month to ensure blooms and provide cut flowers in the fall. Daylilies can be thinned and divided and the seedpods and stems removed to improve next year's blooms.

□ **Roses**—Well-tended roses should produce blooms throughout the month. Remove faded flowers and rose hips from hybrid tea roses. Cut off flowers just above a leaf node with five leaflets.

PLANT

□ **Cut flowers**—Be sure to plant seeds or transplants of tithonia (Mexican sunflower), coreopsis, zinnias, gomphrena, and sunflowers in a sunny location for a steady supply of cut flowers throughout the summer.

□ **Vegetables**—Remember that tomatoes and peppers can be rejuvenated for fall with only a light pruning and an all-purpose fertilizer. If you live in the Middle and Lower South, you should replant squash, beans, and cucumbers now to ensure late-summer harvests. If you prefer tender vegetables, harvest your current crop on a daily basis. You can plant pumpkins now, and they're be ready for decorating around Halloween; bear in mind that most selections need at least 90 to 110 days to mature. ▶

Mulch—Add mulch to help alleviate water loss and to cut down on weeds. Mulch also helps keep the roots cool during the hottest part of the summer. Pull weeds as they appear through the layer.

◀ **Palms**—This is a good time to add a palm tree to your landscape in the Coastal and Tropical South. Check the tag for the mature height, and plant accordingly, making sure not to plant too close to building eaves or under power lines. Select an area with good drainage; dig a hole twice the size of the root ball. Water daily for the first month. Stake large palms as their root systems are not large and the wind can cause new trees to fall over. As soon as the new fronds are visible, feed with a 16-4-8 fertilizer monthly through September.

PRUNE

☐ **Artemisia**—Choose 'Powis Castle' artemisia for its silvery accent and its ability to harmonize with different colors. This plant is relatively trouble free and needs only occasional cutting back to keep its mounding foliage in proportion. Purchase 6-inch pots or 1-gallon sizes, and place 2 feet apart for quick effect. Cuttings root easily if foliage is removed from the base of the cut stem and stuck into damp potting media. Keep cuttings moist and in bright but indirect light until rooted (about three to four weeks). ▶

☐ **Perennials**—Lightly cut back vigorous fall-blooming perennials such as chrysanthemums, Mexican bush sage and 'Indigo Spires' salvia, Mexican mint marigold *(Tagetes lucida),* and copper canyon daisies *(Tagetes lemmonii)* to keep them compact. To promote flowering, deadhead summer-blooming roses. Rose enthusiasts typically prune to just above the first five-part leaf in belief that these buds will be stimulated to form more flowers.

FERTILIZE

☐ **Azaleas and camellias**—Be sure not to prune azaleas as they are beginning to set buds for next spring's bloom. Apply a timed-release fertilizer with extra iron to the top of surrounding soil of the azalea or camellia, and water in.

☐ **Citrus**—In the Coastal and Tropical South, feed container-grown citrus trees this month with a granular fertilizer formulated for citrus or a slow-release fertilizer such as 12-5-8. Water in well. Remove suckers that are coming up from below the graft. Check leaves for mites, whiteflies, or scales, and visit your garden center for a recommended treatment.

Lantana—Add a purple or white trailing selection to sunny areas to provide color, attract butterflies, and soften edges of containers. Lantanas are among our most heat-, drought-, and pest-resistant perennials and bloom from spring until frost.

Basil—Cut plants back several inches as they begin to flower for a flush of new growth. Cuttings then can be rooted in jars of water in a kitchen window for new plants to add to your garden later. This is also a great way to keep fresh leaves handy for cooking.

☐ **Chrysanthemums**—Give mums a last trimming at the tips to promote a dense bloom before they start to set buds at month's end in the Coastal South. Feed them early in the month with a balanced fertilizer, and keep them well watered.

☐ **Shrubs**—Give shrubs the last fertilization of the season. Use a granular slow-release fertilizer spread around the dripline, and water well.

CONTROL

☐ **Lawns**—Raise the cutting height of your lawnmower 1 to 1½ inches to help your grass survive drought and heat. Tall turf shades the soil, slows evaporation, and reduces weeds.

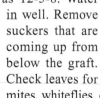

TIP OF THE MONTH

Here's a good way to protect ripening ears of corn from the birds. Just put a clear plastic sandwich bag over each ear and secure it. These bags are inexpensive, last for years, and really do the trick.

LOUIS KULPA
WHEELING, WEST VIRGINIA

*Blessed with bold foliage
and a sweet perfume, this easy
plant deserves a spot in every
Southerner's garden.*

fragrant
H O S T A S

The moon, round and silvery cool, floats above your summer garden, just as the fierce sun sets with a red blaze. You breathe deeply, letting the cares of a busy day vanish with the last of the sun's heat. Across your face, in an invisible caress, drifts the delicate scent of flowers. Their fragrance weaves in a perfumed tapestry through shafts of rising moonlight. It's hosta time in the garden.

Not just any hosta, but specifically *Hosta plantaginea*. It is called the autumn lily, fragrant plantain, or even August lily, though it blooms in July for the Lower and Coastal South. This species hosta carries the largest, loveliest flowers of all, the only ones to open in late afternoon rather than morning, and the only ones to be so outstandingly fragrant. Most of this hosta's sports (spontaneous mutations) and hybrids have a similar gift of perfume. But it's the grand old lady herself that is most beloved of Southern gardeners.

"August lily is one of the classic examples of a *good* introduced plant," says Tony Avent, proprietor of North Carolina's Plant Delights Nursery and a hosta breeder himself. "It has been here since the Civil War and is still a garden favorite. It's easy to grow, handsome, fragrant, and not at all invasive."

Tony adds that this species and its fragrant offspring have always been favored in his garden, not just because of their scent. "August lily is the southernmost native species in China, so it prefers a warmer climate," he explains. "This means it's actually a better hosta in the South than in the North, unlike all the others." He stresses, too, that it's the only hosta species that requires no winter chilling. "It never needs to rest, which means it can be grown all the way down into Central Florida, where temperatures never get cold enough to make a hosta go

dormant. Other hostas try to grow year-round in a situation like that," Tony says, "and they eventually get exhausted. This hosta and its hybrids are perfectly happy to go dormant if it's cold or keep on going with no break. They can also be grown in full sun or bright shade, anywhere but really deep shade. They're unquestionably more versatile."

On the down side, because it is so adapted to warm climates, *H. plantaginea* may try to come up earlier in spring than it sometimes should. "It's out of the ground as soon as it sees signs of warm weather," says Tony, "and can get frost nipped as a result." That applies just to the species itself though. Most of its hybrids, such as 'Honeybells,' 'Sugar and Cream,' or 'Guacamole,' benefit from mixed genes, so they are either more cold tolerant or are later to break dormancy. They rarely get hurt by late frosts that might affect their fragrant parent.

Should gardeners worry about possible frost damage? "No," answers Tony. "The great thing about this species is that it continues to produce new foliage all year. All the other species just produce one flush in the spring and that's it. So August lily can easily recover from something like frost, hail, or a slug attack when the others can't."

Tony suggests planting several clumps where you'll get full benefit of the perfume during the three or four week bloom season. "Near a pathway, near a door, anywhere you can enjoy the fragrance," he says. "It isn't picky about soils, as long as there's constant moisture and plenty of fertilizer. Just about anyone can grow it, and they obviously should. The thing that amazes me is that this really wonderful plant has been in this country for 150 years—why doesn't everybody have one?" ◇

(For sources, turn to pages 234–235.)

BY LIZ DRUITT / PHOTOGRAPHY VAN CHAPLIN

A Deck for RELAXING

Classic, cost-effective, and splendidly Southern, a new design transformed this backyard into an idyllic sanctuary.

I just wanted some garden space," says this Birmingham homeowner. "This area consisted of a steep slope broken up by nothing but a long wooden walk, like a fishing pier, out to the alley. There was basically no usable space at all in this backyard." Anyone looking now at the perfect, white, Tara-like columns of his deck, the smoothly graveled courts, stone walls, and exuberant flowerbeds would find it difficult to imagine both the former dreariness of the space and the tight budget that transformed it.

It took the owner, an engineer, a little time to figure out how to solve the problems his sloping yard created. But with the help of local architect Bob Burns, he arrived at a great solution. "It became clear to us in stages," the owner explains. "I wanted access to the outside, some gardening space, and a way to transition from the house to the garden. A brick patio would have been nice, but with the slope and the elevation, it was financially impractical to install. At the same time, I didn't want a deck that looked like an afterthought."

Bob suggested a simple, cost-effective, flat deck finished on all sides for a groomed look and fronted with elegant white columns. "It was the romantic feeling of the white columns that sold me on Bob's idea," the owner admits. "I love that kind of Southernness; I'm a traditional Southern gardener. But I also find it very attractive that you don't see the supports under the deck. That makes it look more solid and porchlike to me." The arbor was added last to protect the deck from sun. With the budget in mind, the arbor was carefully engineered so as not to interfere with the existing roofline of the house in any way.

The owner chose not to build a rail around his deck because he felt it was low enough to be safe. Plus, he likes the feeling of accessibility to the surrounding garden. As a result, broad steps connect the deck with the courtyards on two of its three sides.

The graveled areas and flowerbeds were the next stage of the backyard project. For the garden design, the owner worked with Landscape Services, Inc., of Birmingham, to help him get the kind of spaces he wanted. "What they came up with basically echoes the strong visual statement of the deck," he says. "There

LEFT: *The highlights of this project are two sets of broad steps, finishing boards for a groomed look, and careful planning so the arbor doesn't invade the roofline.*

BY LIZ DRUITT / PHOTOGRAPHY SYLVIA MARTIN

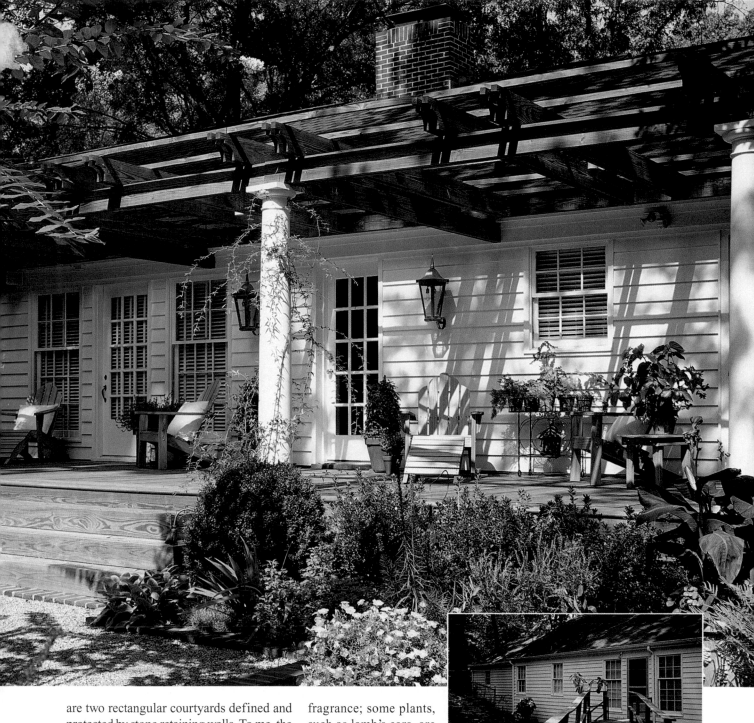

BEFORE

are two rectangular courtyards defined and protected by stone retaining walls. To me, the stone makes the space feel natural, like a garden carved into the living mountain.

"With the deck itself," he adds, "it's like having three individual rooms. The deck serves as a living room; the larger garden rectangle has the barbecue grill and functions as a sort of family room; and the smallest area is like my personal study, with flowers."

The gravel surface of the courtyards was chosen for practicality, but the owner found it added extra pleasure to his garden space. "The flower borders offer color and

fragrance; some plants, such as lamb's ears, are even pleasurable to the touch. The gravel appeals to one more sense when you add the *sound* of walking on it. It's easy to maintain too. Just a blower for leaves and a big metal rake to do some grooming, and it's ready for guests."

The entire backyard, in fact, is now ready for guests. The owner has transformed it from a featureless, slippery slope into the perfect outdoor space for a gardener to display his Southern hospitality. ◇

ABOVE: *The addition of the deck, with its white columns and an overhead arbor, was the most important part of this backyard makeover.* INSET: *Before the redo, this was not a place anyone would enjoy spending time.*

It's Okra Time

You may be harvesting or you may be planting—either way, warm weather comes with plenty of mouthwatering okra.

Okra, tender and succulent, with pearly seeds that burst in your mouth like vegetarian caviar, is the only good reason to wear a long-sleeved shirt in the summertime. Of course, okra-loving gardeners would don a hoopskirt and tiara if that's what was needed to get at those tasty pods. Nothing compares to the crisp delights of fresh okra or the soul-satisfying savor of steaming gumbo.

A cousin to cotton, okra *(Abelmoschus esculentus)* is an easy vegetable to raise as long as you live in a warm climate. In fact, there's no point planting the seeds until the soil temperature reaches about 75 degrees, and the hotter and more humid it gets, the better your okra will grow. In the Coastal South this means planting as early as April, but for most of us the usual time for planting okra seeds comes in late May or June through mid-July.

Soak the seeds overnight in warm water to aid germination, and sow them in the sunniest part of your garden. To shorten the soaking time, pour boiling water over them, and then plant them after they cool. Make sure you've worked plenty of organic material into the garden soil, especially if you live where nematodes are a problem. (This will encourage the development of beneficial soil fungi that attack nematodes.) Press the okra seeds into that warm soil ½ to 1 inch deep and 4 or 5 inches apart in raised rows that are about 3 feet apart.

When the seedlings are a few inches tall, thin them to 1 or 2 feet apart, giving the large-leaved plants plenty of room to grow. At this point you can feed with 10-10-10 or a similar formulation, using about ½ cup of fertilizer for every 10 feet of row. Plan on three to five plants per person; you;ll want to be able to keep up with requests for fried okra and gumbo all summer.

Okra is a naturally drought-tolerant plant, but if you expect a water shortage during the hot months, it's a good idea to add mulch once the plants are nearly mature. Even a 1-inch protective layer scattered over the

TOP, LEFT: *The flared flowers of 'Clemson Spineless' show their kinship with hibiscus.* TOP, RIGHT: *Most okra pods will be at their tender best when about 4 inches long, as with this one sliced open to show deliciously perfect seeds.* ABOVE: *Okra thrives in hot weather. Be sure to leave plenty of room in the garden for the large leaves to get their full share of sunshine.*

OKRA
At a Glance

Time To Plant: 4 to 12 weeks after last spring freeze, or when soil temperature reaches 75 degrees

Days to harvest: 48 to 60

Light: full sun

Soil: any organically enriched and well drained

Height: 3 to 8 feet, depending on selection

Pests: Japanese beetles in Upper and Middle South, nematodes where they are common

roots will help stabilize temperatures and moisture at the root zone, which means steadier production of those delicious pods.

Within 48 days of planting, you can expect to harvest the first pods from rich red 'Burgundy' and little 'Annie Oakley II,' a dwarf spineless selection. Another dwarf, 'Lee,' comes in a bit later, and 'Clemson Spineless' and 'Cajun Delight' will be ready after 55 to 60 days. 'Burgundy' and a few others have pods that stay tender even when mature, but the general rule for okra is to pick early and often. Young pods up to 4 inches long are the most tender and flavorful. The more you pick, the more you encourage new flowers and new pods to form.

Don't wait any longer to get those seeds in the ground. Put your long-sleeved shirt and your tiara where you can grab them in a hurry. It's okra time down South. *Liz Druitt*

PHOTOGRAPHS: SYLVIA MARTIN

ABOVE, LEFT: *The airy texture, arching form, and fiery flowers of firecracker plant make it a great garden accent.* INSET: *Like a mass of genuine little firecrackers, the vivid flowers burst from every branch.*

Patriotic Plant

Red hot, tubular flowers flare like firecrackers from the branches of this long-blooming favorite.

Want some fireworks for the Fourth of July that won't burst your eardrums or burn out after one glorious salvo? You can get that lively action in your garden with the explosive flowers of the well-named firecracker plant *(Russelia equisetiformis)*. Its slim, green, nearly leafless branches light up with a fiery barrage of tubular, scarlet-red blossoms. These are produced all through the growing season, but the major display happens during the hottest months of summer and will lift any Independence Day garden into the proper patriotic spirit.

Firecracker plant is also known as fountain or coral plant, and under one or another of these names, you'll find this traditional Southern favorite at nearly every nursery or garden center. It has been around for generations but remains popular because it's so easy to grow, so colorful, and so versatile. This plant loves hot weather, doesn't care about soil quality as long as there's drainage, and can be propagated by simple root division. It's also a favorite of hummingbirds.

In the Coastal and Tropical South, where it can be grown as a perennial and has essentially naturalized, firecracker plant mounds up to 4 feet high and blooms year-round. Treated as an annual, the trailing shape of this plant makes it perfect for hanging baskets in sunny places. It also looks great spilling over retaining walls or containers and mounding around garden features like statuary, gazing globes, or flags, of course.

In fact, firecracker plant will give you superior visual bang for your bucks. And the only noise involved will be the whir of wings, as hummingbirds feed at its brilliant flowers.   *Liz Druitt*

Off With Their Heads

It's hard to cut back blooming things, but this is a temporary sacrifice for long-term gain.

Mary Zahl

Right now if your garden is in full swing, all those impatiens you planted in spring are blooming themselves silly. They've probably grown a bit too tall, but the flowers still are amazing. So, what I'm about to tell you may seem outrageous, preposterous, or just plain cruel. It's time to cut off their heads.

Actually, you want to go even further than that and lop them off at the knees. What is the point of this inhumane treatment? The answer is quite simple: more flowers. Cutting back annuals such as impatiens gives them a new lease on life and ensures a pretty garden until frost.

"I started cutting back impatiens when I lived in Charleston, South Carolina," says Mary Zahl, a Birmingham gardener and landscape designer. "I needed everything to look good in September and October for fall garden tours. By July, the impatiens were already 2 feet tall, so I tried cutting them back." Mary discovered that about two weeks after a severe pruning, the impatiens began to fill out and look good again.

"This is also a great idea when people are going on vacation in July or August. If they cut back their impatiens radically before they leave, when they return they will have a whole new garden," Mary says. "It's hard to cut back blooming things, but this is a temporary sacrifice for long-term gain."

BITE THE BULLET

The first cut is the most difficult. After that, you're committed. Impatiens have nodes, or bumps, going up their bare stems. Prune about 4 inches up from the soil, directly above a node. New leaves and flowers will emerge from this point, and, after a few weeks, plants will once again be stocky and full.

ABOVE: *The first cut is always the hardest. Prune about 4 inches up from the soil, directly above a node.* RIGHT: *Within several weeks of pruning, the impatiens will fill out to become healthy, stocky plants again.*

PERFECT CANDIDATES

Cut back these annuals for sustained summer color.
- impatiens
- begonias
- lantana
- 'Lady in Red' and 'Coral Nymph' salvias
- star zinnias
- verbena

Fertilizer is another important part of this process. "Annuals are hungry, especially in the South, where they have such a long growing season," Mary says. Feed your impatiens every other week with a water-soluble fertilizer. A granular timed-release fertilizer will produce the same results, although it may take a little longer. "Sometimes I use fish emulsion and other times an all-purpose or blossom-boosting blend," she says. "It almost doesn't matter what you feed them, as long as you give them something."

FOR THE LONG HAUL

As the season winds down and the impatiens thrive, they beautifully fill in the gardening gap between summer and fall. With cooler temperatures, flower color improves, and they gain a second wind. "September and October are transition times throughout the South. You can't really plant much that is going to look good right away. Rejuvenated summer annuals give your garden better color than anything else you might find this time of year," Mary says.

The idea of cutting back also applies to other summer annuals. "I've had good luck cutting back begonias, star zinnias, lantana, and salvias, such as 'Lady in Red' and 'Coral Nymph,' " Mary says. She recommends these annuals as candidates for long-lasting color. "I haven't had success with periwinkle—it seems to give up by September."

Sometimes, garden tasks are difficult to perform. Although cutting back plants in full bloom does not feel like a natural thing to do, the benefits far outweigh any momentary pain. It ensures the promise of a fabulous, colorful garden well into fall.

Ellen Riley

planting surprises

Grab your imagination, and come along to Phillip's garden. You never know what might pop up.

When he bought his property in Irmo, South Carolina, Phillip Jenkins intended to cultivate only a small part of the wooded lot and leave the rest to nature, but childhood memories of gardening with his mother and grandmother flooded back. "I couldn't help myself, I suppose. I guess you'd have to call me an addict," he admits. "I'm passionate about gardening." Yet this is no ordinary garden. The palmetto tree sculpture, assembled from old garden rakes, leads you to suspect there just might be more to this place than meets the eye.

The front borders offer Phillip a place to indulge his love of hot colors. "My garden is an ever-changing palette, and I'm not one who thinks everything must match," he declares. An artist in combining hues, textures, and forms of plants, he keeps the color going from spring through fall in beds that are large enough to accommodate many kinds of plants. In spring dogwoods, cherries, snowball viburnum, mock orange, and various bulbs bloom. Summer brings a riot of lilies,

LEFT: *The area under a maple tree serves as an outdoor living room.* ABOVE: *Phillip with Miss Goldberg, one of his three cats* ABOVE, RIGHT: *A mulched path meanders among contrasting foliage.* RIGHT: *This urn houses a pop-up sprinkler head.*

BY ORENE STROUD HORTON / PHOTOGRAPHY JEAN ALLSOPP

crinums, rudbeckia, phlox, salvias, and echinacea, along with splashy annuals such as sun coleus, sunflowers, and pentas. Fall is fabulous with mature grasses, cannas, chrysanthemums, castor bean, and zinnias.

The garden also gives Phillip an outlet to express both his powers of imagination and his mechanical skill. The babbling sounds of water features echo through the woodland part of the garden. Using black pond liner and stones, Phillip constructed two small pump-fed ponds, one with a waterfall. He also formed a creative fountain using a birdbath. Shrubs and perennials, such as Virginia bluebells, complement the setting.

His whimsical sculpture of the South Carolina state tree was inspired by a local arts campaign in which artists built and decorated steel palmetto trees. Dominating his mailbox garden, the tree represents only one example of Phillip's sense of humor.

When he found he needed an irrigation system, he decided to have some fun with

> My garden is an ever-changing palette, and I'm not one who thinks everything must match.
>
> *Phillip Jenkins*

that too. Sprinkler heads, tucked inside birdhouses, urns, columns, and even a big moss-covered mound of soil, pop up, do their work, and then disappear. Phillip built everything in the system himself. The pop-up steeple atop one birdhouse is made from a piece of plastic foam glued to the top of a sprinkler head. Pinecone-scale shingles cover the roof, and when the water comes on, up shoots the steeple. To fashion his novel sprinklers, Phillip bought the irrigation equipment, plus the cedar wood and posts, from his local garden center.

Ingenious solutions to problems are Phillip's forte. A shady area, rendered inhospitable for plants by shallow-rooted maple trees, suggested to him the perfect place for a sitting area. Phillip tackled the problem of growing flowers by planting them in plastic pots sunk into the soil. Now, mulch forms an attractive floor, and colorful container plants surround a table and comfortable chairs.

The almost superhuman attention demanded by such a large and intricate garden makes one wonder how a mere mortal could find time for his day jobs as a real estate agent and a church musician. This riddle was solved by a neighbor, who often sees Phillip toiling outside in old clothes. "His pocket beeper sounds, and Phillip dashes inside. Then, like Clark Kent emerging from the telephone booth as Superman, he quickly steps out all clean, pressed, and khakied; and he's off to show a house to a client." Another creative solution to an everyday problem. ◇

TOP: *Contrasting shapes, forms, and colors provide eye-catching interest.*
ABOVE: *Phillip's lighthearted version of the Columbia Palmetto Tree Project.*
FAR LEFT: *A hot mix of sun coleus with bright yellow lantana* INSET: *Another of Phillip's discreetly hidden sprinklers*
LEFT: *A long view down one of the garden's spectacular mixed borders*

Flowers stretch as far as the eye can see (See pages 156–159.)

August

Checklist for August

EDITOR'S NOTEBOOK

Is there something big in your yard you'd like to hide—such as a cell tower, telephone pole, or Jesse Ventura's mouth? Plant a vine on it. Vines are literal growing machines. Most climb faster than the mercury on an August day in Dallas. And they never stop—as soon as they reach the top of something, they start down the other side. That's what happened here. The homeowner planted an evergreen vine, fiveleaf akebia *(Akebia quinata)*, at the base of a 100-foot TV antenna. I wonder what would happen if they planted akebia at the Eiffel Tower. My point is, vines can be beautiful, but rampant ones, such as akebia, trumpet vine, and wisteria, can get out of control. I'm concerned for the guy who owns this antenna. With that vine blocking the signal, will he still receive the Futon Channel? What about those exciting episodes of *This Old Sofa*?

Steve Bender

☐ **Dahlias**—Tall, large-flowered selections will need support stakes as they begin to bloom this month. When placing the stakes, take care not to damage the tubers. Tie the stems to the stakes using either garden twine or narrow strips of cloth.

☐ **Lawns**—If your grass is dry, do not mow until you have watered or until it rains. Mowing a dry lawn will further stress the turf and expose it to the drying effects of the wind and sun. Clippings fertilize your turf and should be left in place. Mowing more frequently and allowing the clippings to remain will provide extra protection to root systems and less need for supplemental fertilizer.

☐ **Water**—Plants setting berries, such as hollies and pyracanthas, benefit greatly from extra water during late summer dry spells. Azaleas and camellias are also setting their flowerbuds for next year's blooms at this time and will perform much better if not stressed by excessive dryness.

Roses—For a show of fall flowers, prune and fertilize everblooming roses now. Remove dead stems and shorten healthy canes by about one-third. Feed with a rose fertilizer, and mulch to conserve moisture. Water well once each week if it doesn't rain.

PLANT

☐ **Annuals**—Spruce up your flowerbeds with fresh plantings of marigolds, lantana, narrow-leaf zinnias, impatiens, coleus, pentas, and salvias, available now in large sizes at garden centers.

☐ **Fall crocus**—Colchicums or fall crocus are also available at garden centers. Plant now, and you will be rewarded with a multitude of beautiful fall blooms for years.

☐ **Iris and daylilies**—Now is a good time to divide these spring-blooming perennials. Not only will this help existing plants, but it will also provide you with a multitude of new plantings. Dig clumps that have become crowded and have not been blooming as fully as in past years. Divide tubers and roots; trim dead portions. Use younger, vigorous sections for replanting. Amend soil in new beds

with composted pine bark and sphagnum peat moss to a depth of 8 to 10 inches. Group plants for impact.

☐ **Transplants**—Now is the time to set out zinnias, celosias, marigolds, sunflowers, gomphrena, and cosmos for great garden color this fall. Replanting these warm-weather annuals will provide color until it is time to put out cool-weather annuals, such as pansies and ornamental kale.

◄ **Vegetables**—It's time to plant fall vegetables in the Upper South. Set out transplants of broccoli, cauliflower, and collards. Sow seeds of beets, lettuce, English peas, spinach, turnips, and mustard. In the Coastal South, now is the time to set out tomatoes, pepper, eggplants, cucumbers, and summer squash. Seeds of cucumbers, squash, and snap beans sprout quickly if sown directly into the garden.

FERTILIZE

☐ **Azaleas and camellias**—Mulch to conserve moisture as azaleas and camellias are now beginning to set flowerbuds for next spring. Continue to apply an acid-type fertilizer for azaleas and camellias according to the label directions. If leaves are yellow, it means that iron deficiency is present. Apply chelated or granular iron to the soil.

☐ **Basil**—Fertilize basil with a liquid fertilizer, such as 20-20-20, to keep plants productive into fall. Trim off seedheads so plants can use their energy on foliage.

☐ **Impatiens**—These popular and versatile annuals tend to get leggy by late summer, so trim them back to half their height now. Then feed them with a general-purpose, water-soluble fertilizer, such as 20-20-20. They'll quickly start to leaf out and get bushier and covered with vibrant blooms.

Wildflowers—In the Upper, Middle, and Lower South, plant bluebonnets and other wildflower seeds for spring color. Cultivate soil surface to a depth of 1 to 2 inches, scatter seeds evenly, and firm soil. In addition to bluebonnets, other good choices include coreopsis, Indian paintbrush (*Castilleja indivisa*), gaillardia, and Drummond phlox.

Divide—Now is a good time to divide daylilies, amaryllis, and crinums in the Coastal South. Use a garden fork to lift a clump from the ground. Then cut the clump into sections, making sure each has both foliage and roots. Replant divisions, and water often until they become established.

CONTROL

☐ **Chinch bugs**—These tiny pests cause yellow and brown patches of dying grass, particularly in St. Augustine lawns. Hot, dry weather worsens the problem. You can test for chinch bugs by pressing a can with both ends cut out into an affected spot, and then filling the can with water. If present, the ⅙-inch-long black bugs with white wings will float to the top. To control these bugs, keep lawns well watered during dry spells. Apply a granular lawn insecticide according to label directions.

☐ **Hornworms**—Keep an eye out for these large, green caterpillars that have white stripes on the side. They feed voraciously on tomatoes, peppers, eggplants, and pentas. If you find just a few, simply pick them off and dispose of them. For large infestations, spray plants with *Bacillus thuringiensis kurstaki* (DiPel, Thuricide) according to the label directions.

TIP OF THE MONTH

For years, squirrels decimated my outdoor potted plants. So I tried applying a few tablespoons of blood meal to the surface of the soil in the pots. The pots have been undisturbed ever since.

JUSTIN J. BUCKLEY
FAIRFAX, VIRGINIA

coneflowers
summer survivors

These goof-proof flowers come in all sizes and stand up to the heat.

About the time summer gets really hot, coneflowers *(Rudbeckia* sp.) come into their own—laughing at the sun with radiant flowers and reckless abandon. They're commonly called black-eyed Susans, a name that speaks of the cone's color and applies to only a few selections. Others proudly wear brown eyes, and some even don green ones. Invite one into your border, and you'll probably want others to come along.

EASY CARE

Coneflowers require little attention, making them a great choice for color in the mid- to late-summer garden. Regardless of the selection you choose, the care is simple and the same. Basically, these stalwart plants require two things. First, they need adequate sunlight. Four hours of direct sunshine is the minimum needed for good flower production. They sturdily stand up to all-day sun but become lanky and weak in the shade. Their second absolute is well-drained soil. Coneflowers enjoy a well-watered location, provided the soil does not get soggy. They are also fiercely drought tolerant. When foliage wilts from lack of rain, a thorough soaking perks them up and gets them through another rainless week.

Coneflowers have varying appetites, depending on the type. Fertilize repeat-blooming selections, such as 'Indian Summer' *(R. hirta),* throughout the summer to maintain flower production. The selections that bloom once, such as 'Goldsturm,' require feeding only if the lush green leaves appear pale. A granular timed-release fertilizer works well on all coneflowers with a supplemental liquid, such as 20-20-20, applied if needed. ▶

BY ELLEN RILEY / PHOTOGRAPHY RALPH ANDERSON

WHAT'S IN A NAME

Many of us have nicknames—a more easygoing or familiar moniker than our formal given name. The same is true in the world of flowers. To some of us, a coneflower is a yellow *Rudbeckia*. To others, a coneflower is the hot pink number that is an *Echinacea*. To others, coneflowers are all of the above. You can never go wrong learning a plant's botanical name.

When coneflowers are flourishing in your garden, gather a bunch to bring their bright rays of sunshine indoors.

BLACK EYES

The most widely known selection, 'Goldsturm' *(R. fulgida),* may be the true black-eyed Susan. Perfect for the middle of a border, this 2-foot-tall perennial remains stocky and upright without support. Medium-size flowers sport thin golden-colored petals in a single crown surrounding a jet-black cone. This vigorous selection requires division every few years during winter dormancy.

Another choice is the more voluptuous cousin: *R. hirta*. A popular selection called 'Indian Summer' produces large blossoms with thick yellow-orange petals. This black-eyed Susan is short-lived, generally coming back for only a few years. It blooms from seed the first year, and it will self-sow if flowers are left on the plant at the end of the growing season. This selection may require stakes to support the 3-foot stems and heavy heads. Remove spent blooms to encourage fresh buds to form.

BROWN EYES

At first glance, *R. triloba* seems to be throwing a wild party where all the guests have small brown eyes and dance on top of tiny petals. There are masses of them, bouncing on multibranched stems, covering gangly plants. This plant could be accused of being weedy, but the sheer number of flowers redeems it. It may grow up to 4 feet tall, requiring a stake to keep it upright. Brown-eyed Susans are also short-lived, but they rampantly reseed when comfortable. Allow the last blooms of the season to remain on the plant; then cut them back when the seeds have fallen into the garden.

GREEN EYES

A cool color and green eyes make 'Herbstsonne' *(R. nitida)* a quieter member of this flashy family. Tall and willowy, it bears flowers on multi-branched stems and blooms later than other selections. This reliable perennial requires a sturdy support to hold its 5- to 6-foot height and brings an airy, striking display to a late-summer border. The mannerly 'Herbstsonne' does not spread or reseed aggressively, but returns reliably year after year.

CLOSED EYES

Every family has at least one prissy, frilly member. This clan is no exception. 'Goldquelle' is a fully double selection, coming from the *R. laciniata* side of the tribe. The cone is concealed by layers of bright yellow petals, forming a flouncy flower atop a fairly sturdy stem. Even though it grows only 2½ to 3 feet tall, it will benefit from support to help hold petal-heavy branches.

Enjoy just one or all of these selections in your garden. A bonus is their willingness to last as a cut flower. A vase bursting with Susans—black-, brown-, or green-eyed—is a pure celebration of summer. ◇

Edging Turf

Rein in creeping grass and straighten up bed lines with these few simple steps.

Warm-season grasses, such as Bermuda, centipede, buffalo grass, St. Augustine, and Zoysia, have a pesky tendency to spread. During the growing season, these turfs send out runners that try to expand their boundaries by creeping into flowerbeds and natural areas. One of the best ways to keep them in their place is to cut a deep trench edge using a square point shovel.

English gardeners have long used deep trench edging to shape their lawns. It gives turf a refined or manicured look and also makes it difficult for grasses to spread into flowerbeds or shrub borders.

The tools needed to shape your lawn are a supple garden hose, a file, and a square point shovel. Use the garden hose to lay out bed lines; this will help you establish the look you want. The hose can also act as a guide, keeping you in line as you edge with your shovel. Try to eliminate sharp angles or curves. Make smooth, wide, sweeping curves that will allow you to easily maneuver your lawnmower.

Check to make sure your shovel has a sharp blade. A shovel's edge becomes blunt with regular use. Use a steel file to sharpen a dull blade. A sharp edge allows the shovel to make clean cuts and slice through any small roots. Try to dig down 4 to 6 inches deep; then lift and remove excess grass and soil. Removed plugs of grass that still have roots may be planted in bare or thin turf areas.

When finished edging with the shovel, clean out the trench with your hands, removing any rocks, roots, or grass clippings. Dress up the clean edge with fresh mulch, such as pine straw or shredded bark. This simple chore gives your grass definition and helps you reclaim your turf's boundaries. It may take a little work but will make your lawn look great. *Charlie Thigpen*

PHOTOGRAPHS: VAN CHAPLIN

Using a square point shovel, you can shape your turf and give it a clean, crisp edge. Dig down 4 to 6 inches with the shovel; then lift to remove turf and soil.

Remove any grass clippings, roots, or loose soil by hand.

Sharpening the shovel blade with a file makes it easier to cut thick turf.

Beneath the canopy of Laura's beloved trees, textured plantings of green and white enclose a private world of serenity.

BEFORE

Made in the Shade

*This Baton Rouge psychologist finds her
own healing space in the garden.*

You enter this white-and-green garden by stepping under a moonflower vine twined around an arch. That door is the passageway between scalding sun and soothing shade, between the nerve-rasping intensity of daily life and the quiet of inner peace. This garden is a sanctuary. And—like the best sanctuaries—it contains just as much laughter as it does tranquility.

Much of Laura L'Herisson's pleasure in her garden stems from the fact she overcame so many challenges in the process. First, she'd never gardened before. Her home in Baton Rouge,

where she lives with husband Bob Mooberry, is the first one she's ever owned. "I've gone to school half my life, and I lived in apartments while working on my degrees. I've kept major houseplants," she says cheerfully, "initially because I couldn't afford furniture. But I never had a piece of land to play with before."

Having grown up in rural Louisiana surrounded by pastures, Laura always wanted a house with plenty of elbowroom between her and any neighbors. "At least a lake," she laughs, "maybe even a mountain!" Because that was not an option, she decided to create the refuge that she craved.

It wasn't easy. Her suburban backyard had no garden at all when she and Bob moved in, only grass and a few trees. There was also a major drainage problem that called for attention. One friend suggested that she plant things that would grow in mud, because it was in such abundance. "We did the first quarter of the yard with wild brown irises found in a ditch in Port Allen and some blue ones found in a ditch in La Place. That was really the start of the garden."

Laura knew she needed more help, so she asked landscape architect Neil Odenwald to consult. "When Neil first saw my yard, it was just a puny little bed of irises and a bunch of elephant's ears," says Laura. "He asked me what I wanted to accomplish, and I told him, 'A total sense of privacy.' I took the lot plan and blew it up on the copier, and Neil started sketching the first of several beds." The pale gravel paths that surround and define the beds were Neil's idea. They're wide enough to let Laura work comfortably and use the wheelbarrow, and they enhance the silvery cool feeling of her shade-loving variegated plants.

Neil also suggested setting aside a budget for tree replacement. "Trees are very important to me. They offer the shade, silence, and healing seclusion that I value so much. I realized they had to be a large part of my garden," explains Laura. "Neil helped me understand that at certain points they'd need to be harvested and renewed."

The worst disaster for her garden, however, was something for which no preparation could have helped. "We'd lived here about three years when several of the large trees just outside the fence surrounding my yard were cut and removed. I went into shock because my sense of enclosure was totally destroyed." Fortunately, the local energy company was willing to replace some of the trees. Four years later, the new plantings are settling in well, and Laura's garden is once again in a world of its own.

A painted sun, inspired by a quilt pattern, adds a touch of gold light behind a shade-loving ginger.

Though she's now a much more knowledgeable gardener, Laura has never lost her joy in expanding the contents of that private world. "I still find myself buying plants for neat foliage, and then somehow I have to find a home for them in the beds." Does she ever worry about experimenting? "A lot of what I do is because I don't know better," Laura admits cheerfully. "But you can't be afraid of things in the garden." *Liz Druitt*

LAURA'S PLANT LIST

- dogwood
- river birch
- oakleaf hydrangea
- dwarf sasanqua camellia
- baby's breath spiraea
- white butterfly ginger *(Hedychium pradhanii)*
- chartreuse angel's trumpet
- windmill palm
- white begonias, impatiens, and pentas
- white variegated liriope
- hostas and ferns

Container Tapestry

Tie your arrangements together with common threads of color, texture, and scale.

What may appear to be a happy accident of intermingled shades and hues is, more often than not, a carefully designed work of art. With a little planning and preparation, a fabulous container blanketed with colorful flowers and bold textures is easy to do.

Every container needs a focal point, and many times it is the tallest element. This arrangement, designed by Russell Gandy of Planters Nursery in Atlanta, presents a massing of 'Victoria Blue' salvia that creates a point of interest. Its mature 24-inch height is the correct scale for the wide, shallow pot. Several plants are grouped together to draw the eye to that point.

The next tier fills the middle. Pink- and rose-colored pentas play together to give the arrangement plenty of flowers and bulk. When you plan a container, choose two colors, and work with assorted shades in those families. This prevents color chaos. In this case, the two pinks complement each other and keep the collection visually interesting, but not busy.

Russell mingles 'Blue Bells' browallia with the pink pentas to carry the thread of blue from the top tier down into the body of the arrangement. This technique weaves the dominant, cool shade throughout the collection, creating color continuity and pulling the grouping together.

The final layer, around the bottom, softens the pot's edge and gently eases color downward. Here, Russell adds a pink ivy geranium to cascade and carry the color with it. A 'Blackie' sweet potato vine picks up the blues and adds a large, broad leaf to the mix. It makes a terrific addition to all the frilly flowers above and around it. Green-and-white variegated ivy also tumbles over the side, giving the arrangement fullness and allowing just enough of the container to peek through.

Apply the same design principles for a shady container. Colorful caladium leaves work well as the tall focal point and come in a variety of summery hues. Use the leaf color as a guide for the middle tier, choosing appropriate shades of impatiens or begonias to fill in this level. Ivy fares well in shade, and a variegated selection will add sparkling foliage to cascade over the pot's edge.

When planning a container of your own, choose two colors, and work with their variations. Use one color as a focal point throughout. Let color and texture tumble down the side, and you've got a beautiful, carefully woven tapestry with an easygoing appearance. *Ellen Riley*

PHOTOGRAPH: VAN CHAPLIN

This container is a wonderful weaving of color and texture. Although casual in appearance, it is a carefully planned arrangement using some basic principles.

BLOOMING GOOD

Take good care of your container, and it will bloom nonstop throughout the summer.

- Water a full-sun container every day and a shady one about twice a week. Saturate the soil until water runs from the bottom of the pot.
- Remove old blooms weekly.
- Feed every 7 to 10 days with a blossom-boosting fertilizer. Moisten soil with clear water before feeding.

If you have an underground irrigation system, be responsible: Make sure it runs at the proper times and check regularly for any leaks.

Water Wisely

Raindrops fall from above and splash to earth. Plants take in the moisture and thrive. If only gardening were really this simple. We can't always rely on Mother Nature, though, to produce rain when we need it. And when we do need to water, we should do it efficiently, so that this precious resource isn't wasted.

Long, hot summers with little rain can bring on water restrictions as supplies dwindle. To make the most of your watering, follow these tips.

■ If you have an underground irrigation system, don't turn your back on it. Check it frequently to make sure all the spray heads are operating properly and spraying in the right direction. Have it serviced at least once a year by a professional irrigation contractor. As plants grow and block spray patterns, you will need to update your system. Always make sure water is hitting only planted areas. If areas in your yard stay damp, reduce the amount of time these locations are being watered.

■ Water plants in the early morning to avoid any evaporation. Never water in the middle of the day. Plants watered late in the evening will stay wet for long periods and will be more susceptible to disease and fungus.

■ Water plants less often, but water deeply. Thorough soakings allow plants to grow deep roots, making them more drought tolerant.

■ Use soaker hoses and drip irrigation so the water stays on the ground. These efficient systems produce little runoff and evaporation.

■ Mulch shrubs, flowers, and trees. Organic mulch, such as shredded bark or pine straw, layered about 3 to 4 inches thick, will help to hold in moisture, while keeping water-robbing weeds out.

■ Select plants for your garden that require little irrigation, such as ivies, ornamental grasses, nandina, and crepe myrtle. Many of our native plants also tend to be drought tolerant. For color beds, select flowering plants such as lantana, narrow-leaf zinnias, coneflowers, and daylilies. ◇

PHOTOGRAPHS: JEAN ALLSOPP

Buggin' Out

*Leftover odds and ends from home-improvement projects
can find new bite in your backyard.*

ABOVE: *Bugs fly from a pot of Confederate jasmine.*
INSET: *Copper pipe and a tee joint make the body
and head of this dragonfly; painted finials serve as
large round eyes. The wings are salvaged copper;
grounding wire forms the legs and antennae.*

I have insects in my yard, house, and creeping around the deck. Some are big and some small; they come in all colors, shapes, and sizes. They hatched in my basement, the perfect breeding ground for such metallic monsters.

But I'm not worried. I made these bugs from scraps leftover from weekend projects. Long nails, bolts, and copper pipes form the bodies; aluminum flashing and bronze screen make the wings. Wire holds them together and also creates lifelike legs and antennae. My bugs have a whimsical look, thanks to their colorful eyes made from beads. The eyes give each one a different personality.

If you don't have a basement full of junk or scraps, buy materials from a local hardware store. Baling wire is great for the legs. It's cheap and sold in bulk rolls but rusts quickly if it gets wet. Aluminum or galvanized wire won't rust, so you have a choice, rusty or nonrusty wire. Thin-gauge wire works well for making slender, whiplike antennae. It's helpful to have various gauges of wire on hand to fashion different appendages.

Aluminum or metal flashing, usually sold in rolls, is great material for the wings. You can also use bronze-colored screen for this. Large nails and copper pipe are good for making the long bodies of linear-shaped bugs. Small dragonflies can be constructed from square concrete nails; make large ones with copper pipe or 10- or 12-inch nails.

Common household tools are all that's needed to assemble these bugs. Tin snips cut easily through the metal or aluminum flashing, but you should wear leather gloves to protect your hands from the sharp edges. A small pair of pliers with cutters are needed to clip and twist the wire. Use a hammer and nail to punch holes in the flashing. Special paint that will adhere to metal is all it takes to make the bugs colorful. Lightly rough up the flashing with sandpaper or steel wool so the paint will stick to its smooth surface.

These metal wonders can add a little surprise or a fun element to your home, deck, or garden. Just don't let the exterminator see them. *Charlie Thigpen*

ABOVE: *Metal flashing and bright paint colors jazz up these bugs.*

LEFT: *Use a hammer and a nail to punch holes in the flashing. Then thread wire through the holes and attach to nails, bolts, or copper pipe.*

A word of caution: Although they look neat, these bugs can have sharp edges, so they don't make good play toys for small children. ◇

Turf *Love*

Say hello to fanatical folks for whom the grass can never be green enough.

Male turf love is rampant. Walk down your street, and you'll likely encounter a weed-free warrior who edges his lawn with a ruby laser and regards thatch as a serious character flaw. But you may be surprised to learn how often this genetic disorder seduces other family members into codependent relationships. Here are a few of their shocking stories.

It's a typical day in Greenville, South Carolina. Andy and Carolyn Anderson are down on their knees. Why? Because a loathsome weed has dared to invade Andy's nearly perfect 'Emerald' Zoysia lawn. While Andy uses needle-nose pliers to hold the offender upright, Carolyn obligingly paints its leaves with a cotton swab dipped in Roundup.

Andy's lawn doesn't just *look* like a putting green—it really is one. His John Deere greens mower cuts as low as ³⁄₁₆ inch, so Carolyn, an avid golfer, can practice putting. Of course, she's not permitted to dig a hole for the cup. How protective of his grass is Andy? A few years ago, he suffered a heart attack at home. As paramedics wheeled him toward a waiting ambulance, they foolishly eschewed the front walk and crossed his sacred lawn. "They put ugly ruts in my freshly mown grass," Andy recalls indignantly. "I gave 'em hell."

Turf love reveals itself in a variety of aberrant practices. Warren Jones of Augusta, Georgia, tests for mole crickets in his immaculate 'Meyer' Zoysia

BY STEVE BENDER
PHOTOGRAPHY
JEAN ALLSOPP, VAN CHAPLIN

David and Dana Brandon direct daughters Christy, Nicole, and Jenni on a search-and-destroy mission against insurgent weeds.

> I told him the only way I could get him to pay attention to me was to wear something from Victoria's Secret and strap myself to the John Deere.
>
> *Diana Bosse*

ABOVE, RIGHT: *Warren Jones tests for bugs by sudsing his lawn. This brightens the blades while it softens hands.* RIGHT AND INSET: *Even a single weed won't do for Andy Anderson. He uses pliers to hold the weed, while his wife, Carolyn, paints it with Roundup.*

lawn by pouring liquid detergent on a small section at a time. The suds irritate the insects and force them to surface. Kathy Meuret of Riverside, Ohio, boasts that her husband, Terry, employs two kinds of suds. "He washes the lawn—yes, *wash* as in *clean*—with ammonia and liquid soap," she says. "And he feeds the lawn with stale beer—not just any cheap beer, but the good stuff." Clearly, Terry needs immediate help.

Terry isn't alone. David and Dana Brandon of Palm Harbor, Florida, regularly send daughters Christy, Nicole, and Jenni on weed-seeking missions. If any are spotted, David encircles them with orange spray paint and applies herbicide, creating rounded dead zones. "It looks just like aliens landed," notes Dana. According to Liz McGuffey of Durham, North Carolina, her former neighbor, Edgar Toms, "combs every blade of grass." Greg Haworth of Oklahoma City uses a shop vacuum to suck up thatch that floats over from his neighbor's yard after a heavy rain. In Galloway, New Jersey, *Southern Living* subscriber Frank Rudisill truly has a lawn to dye for. When watering restrictions result in brown spots, he sprays them with green dye.

In the convoluted mind of a lawn fanatic, ordinary actions become heinous offenses. Ann Haworth once said to husband Greg how wonderful it would be to win the yard-of-the-month award. Greg's response: "The sign would leave holes in the yard, and we just can't have that." At Kathy Meuret's home, "driving on, parking on, and walking on the grass after a heavy rain are capital crimes. And God help you if you even think about lawn ornaments. You violate the Law of the Lawn, and you will face Judge Terry and his Superior Turf Tribunal."

Not that lawn rangers don't goof up themselves. In Brentwood, Tennessee, Joe Buffler used a new chemical to kill the Bermuda grass invading his fescue. The fescue died; the Bermuda did fine. In St. Augustine, Florida, Curt Zimmerman fertilized his grass with Milorganite, a product made from treated sewage sludge. The odor, recalls his wife, Cindy, "made the neighbors think we had an outhouse built on our property."

Such mishaps can result in a siege mentality, turning turf love into turf war. Glenn and Mary Clements built a home in Purvis, Mississippi. "We picked the right builder, the right colors, the right fabrics. We made but one fatal mistake," says Mary. "We did not pour cement over the entire yard. Instead, we planted grass."

Lawn care may stress out Glenn and Mary, but it actually relieves stress for Joe Buffler. This CPA blows off steam by cutting the lawn every chance he gets. Rumor has it that during tax time, he mows the grass every 45 seconds.

Wives are the most frequent victims of turf love. Many feel a little green monster has supplanted them in their husbands' hearts. "I know David takes great pride in his family and job," says Lynn

Greg Haworth of Oklahoma City uses a shop vacuum to suck up unsightly thatch that floats over from his neighbor's yard after a heavy rain.

Wistar of Reisterstown, Maryland, "but I'd hate to ask if his lawn comes first—I might not like the answer!" Diana Bosse of Loveland, Ohio, says this of her husband, Steve: "I tease him about the time he spends in the yard. In our early years of marriage, I told him the only way I could get him to pay any attention to me was to wear something from Victoria's Secret and strap myself to the John Deere."

Despite its heartbreaks, stresses, disasters, and strains, the quest for the perfect lawn has rewards too. "I'll never forget," remembers Andy Anderson, "the time three little boys came by our yard. One knelt down, took his hand, and rubbed the grass. Then he looked at his little buddies and said, "See, I *told* you it was real!" ◇

Having grown up cutting acres of grass, Joe Buffler was ecstatic to finally have his own lawn. But when the water bill exceeded the mortgage, his wife, Kathryn, cut him off.

*When you admire roads graced
with flowers instead of clutter,
thank Lady Bird Johnson and
those she inspires.*

LADY BIRD'S

See the beautiful blooms along our nation's interstates? They are there largely because of former First Lady and native Texan Lady Bird Johnson. She is the inspiration that led to the planting of flowers along America's highways.

"No one had ever understood the concept of highway beautification until she brought it to the forefront when she was First Lady," says John Thomas, president of Wildseed Farms in Fredericksburg, Texas. John grows large quantities of flower seeds used by many state highway transportation departments in their roadside seeding programs.

Nash Castro was with the National Park Service in Washington, D.C., when Mrs. Johnson was First Lady. He was heavily involved with her beautification efforts in the Capital and later became founding president of the National Wildflower Research Center (as it was known before it was named for Lady Bird) in Austin. "Lady Bird left on the nation an imprint of beauty that will live long after all of us," Nash says. "It's quite comforting to know what she did continues to be a part of our culture."

Mrs. Johnson, 88, lives in Austin and spends weekends at the LBJ Ranch in Stonewall, Texas. The family ranch, now a national park, lies west of Austin and the Lady Bird Johnson Wildflower Center, which she established in 1982 along with fellow flower

LEFT: *An ocean of many-colored cosmos attracts the eyes and arms of a flower-lover visiting Wildseed Farms in Fredericksburg, Texas.* RIGHT: *North Carolina shows evidence of a popular flower seeding program.*

LEGACY

BY MARK G. STITH / PHOTOGRAPHY ALLEN ROKACH

PHOTOGRAPH COURTESY OF THE NORTH CAROLINA DIVISION OF TOURISM, FILM, AND SPORTS DEVELOPMENT

devotee and actress Helen Hayes. Although her age has slowed her somewhat, Mrs. Johnson still enjoys going out to the countryside and admiring wildflowers. In fact, it's been a lifelong passion dating back to her childhood.

"I grew up in the country—rather alone—and one of my favorite pastimes was to walk in the woods, exploring, particularly in the springtime, searching for the first wild violets and starry white blossoms of dogwood…," she writes in the foreword to her book, *Wildflowers Across America* (Abbeville Press), coauthored with Carlton Lees. She also recalls touring the Texas Hill Country to see bluebonnets and Indian paintbrush while attending the University of Texas.

Lady Bird carried that love of nature and flowers to Washington, D.C., while husband Lyndon Baines Johnson served as Congressman, Senator, Vice President, and President. She was the driving force behind beautification efforts in the Capital, working with Secretary of the Interior Stewart Udall, Nash Castro, Laurance and Mary Rockefeller, and many others. She urged her husband to introduce legislation that led to the passage of the Highway Beautification Act of 1965.

"Oh, that was referred to as Lady Bird's Bill," recalls Liz Carpenter, former press secretary to Mrs. Johnson and longtime friend. "She was the one who really was behind that. She was so dismayed by the way that junkyards, billboards, and other unsightly places along highways made our country look. When she became First Lady, she was really able to march this issue up on stage."

Although the bill was aimed primarily at reducing roadside signage, the message of beautification was clearly being promoted and encouraged. Lady Bird also invited the participation of governors' wives, bringing them to the Capital and taking them on bus tours of the city. She encouraged them to promote such efforts in their own states.

"I've heard her say that roads are the things we have that connect us town to town," says Dr. Robert Breunig, executive director of the Lady Bird Johnson Wildflower Center. "She feels that people want to have an immediate sense of place, and the view people have from roads is how they get that feeling. What better way to do that than by letting them see the natural beauty of the country and the native plants that make a place unique?"

She promoted that sentiment in Texas in an interesting way. Robert adds, "The Texas Department of Transportation has been planting wildflowers and native plants since the 1920s, and she really wanted to spur that. So for years, she gave a $1,000 prize—and it was her own money—to the person in the highway

LEFT, BELOW, AND RIGHT: *Flaming sweeps of poppies, daisies, and other flowers beautify the interstates of North Carolina.*

> My special cause, the one that alerts my interest
> and quickens the pace of my life, is to preserve
> the wildflowers and native plants that define
> the regions of our land….
>
> *Lady Bird Johnson*

department who did the best job." The Texas Highway Beautification Awards, as they were known, were given by her for 20 years, beginning in 1969.

Herbert Neimann, assistant landscape director with the Texas Department of Transportation, recalls going out with Lady Bird to look at wildflowers several years ago. "She called me at home the Sunday before Easter," he recalls. "It must have been back in 1977 or 1978. She said that she wanted me to go looking at wildflowers with her and some people on Easter Sunday afternoon.

"I met her at the airport in Austin, and we flew down to Washington County. Then we got in a car, and away we all went. She took me because I knew where the wildflowers would be. There was a photographer along with us, and she took pictures of Lady Bird in the wildflowers. Lady Bird brought several changes of clothes, and we'd stop along the way at a business, and she'd introduce herself, then ask if she could change her clothes so they could take a picture. It was something I'll always remember," Herbert says with a laugh. "She was so interested in getting people involved in beautification."

Lady Bird's campaigning spurred concerted efforts within states to improve highways. For example, Texas sows 30,000 to 60,000 pounds of flower seeds (most of them bluebonnets) along highways every year. Each Southern state has some type of flower seeding program. North Carolina has a large-scale effort, according to Michele Harrington, coordinator of the wildflower seeding program for the North Carolina Department of Transportation.

"The public response has been wonderful," says Michele. "People just love it. Last year was the fifteenth year we've been seeding roadsides. First Lady Dotty Martin [wife of Gov. James G. Martin] really encouraged the program, and we've had tremendous support from the Garden Clubs of North Carolina, who give out awards to employees in the [highway] department who do the best job with their area." The state has also been involved in growing native bur marigold in enough quantities to produce seeds for roadside plantings.

Maryland, too, boasts an active flower seeding program. "We give out wildflower seed packets when available at our state welcome centers," says Joan Hurd, supervisor of the I-70 East Welcome Center in Myersville, not far from Camp David, the famous Presidential retreat. "We also have a Highway Wildflower Guide that shows what's blooming and when."

One of the best stories about Lady Bird is related by Denise Delaney, director of horticulture for the Lady Bird Johnson Wildflower Center. "She was doing an interview years ago out at the LBJ Ranch with Dick Ellis, a local television reporter," Denise recalls. "He asked her why she chose beautification as an emphasis when she was First Lady. She just got this look on her face and opened up her arms, and said 'Joy!'"

Thank you for spreading the joy, Lady Bird.

Lady Bird doesn't want to be remembered only as the First Lady who beautified highways, but as someone who contributed significantly toward the environment as a whole and the appreciation of native plants. For more information contact or visit the Lady Bird Johnson Wildflower Center, 4801 La Crosse Avenue, Austin, TX 78739; (512) 292-4200 or www.wildflower.org. Callaway Gardens in Pine Mountain, Georgia, recently dedicated The Lady Bird Johnson Wildflower Trail in conjunction with the Wildflower Center, thus becoming an affiliate of the Center. For more information call Callaway Gardens at 1-800-225-5292, or visit www.callawaygardens.com. ◇

Limestone rock, ornamental grasses, and succulents (See pages 172–173.)

September

Checklist
for
September

EDITOR'S NOTEBOOK

When is being pretty, tough, and easy to grow not enough? When it comes to the chinaberry tree *(Melia azedarach)*. It grows fast (to 45 feet), gives good shade, tolerates drought, and thrives in terrible soil. It features handsome, glossy leaves; fragrant, lilac-colored flowers in spring; and showy yellow fruit in fall. It was even immortalized by the Doobie Brothers in the song "China Grove." So what's the problem? Well, for one thing, it suckers and forms thickets. And the ripened berries can be kind of disgusting when they squish between your toes. Birds eat the berries and disperse lots of seeds, but sometimes the berries ferment first, resulting in wasted warblers losing control and smashing into billboards, tractor trailers, Drew Carey, and other large objects. In an ironic twist, the hard seeds have often been used to make rosary beads—probably for saying last rites over robins that nosedived into Drew.   *Steve Bender*

☐ **Garden planning**—Take a moment to write down your horticultural successes and failures over the past summer. These notes will come in handy next year when planning your garden.

☐ **Houseplants**—If you gave your plants a summer vacation outside, in a few weeks it will be time to bring them back indoors. Cut back on watering, and allow the containers to dry out a bit. Examine carefully for hitchhikers (lizards, bugs, etc.), and then move the plants inside. Terra-cotta pots may need to be cleaned with a solution of 2 tablespoons bleach to 1 gallon of water. Keep solution away from the plant, as the bleach will damage the leaves.

☐ **Maintenance**—Now is the time to pinch back annuals and fall-blooming perennials, such as marigolds, cosmos, zinnias, and salvias, to extend their flowering time. Also pinch back blooms of basil and coleus so that plants can direct their energy to produce foliage. ▶

☐ **Seeds**—Dry the flower heads of zinnias, cosmos, and tithonias (Mexican sunflowers), and store the seeds in a cool, dry place. Sow these seeds in late next spring for your cutting garden.

☐ **Water**—As temperatures begin to cool, plants need less water. Adjust your watering schedule for lawns, borders, and containers. Pay close attention to containers, in particular, as they tend to become waterlogged.

☐ **Bulbs**—In the Coastal South, separate Easter lilies, amaryllis, and iris. Caladium leaves will start to fade this month. They can be left in the ground, or if you want to move them, dig bulbs, and place in a dry, shady location to dry out and store until next year. Plant paperwhites at this time.

☐ **Fall planting**—Begin planting trees and shrubs this month. Planting in autumn allows them time to grow roots and transition into the garden.

☐ **Fall vegetables**—In the Middle and Lower South, it is time to set out transplants or sow seeds of mustard, collards, spinach, lettuce, turnips, and radishes. Apply about a pound of Scotts Vegetable Food or a similar product per every 100 square feet of your garden prior to planting. Water daily until plants are rooted. Then reduce watering to every three to four days.

☐ **Herbs**—This is the best time to plant herbs in the Coastal and Tropical South. Sage, sweet marjoram, thyme, lavender, rosemary, and sweet fennel can be planted now. Nasturtiums bloom beautifully, and the flowers enhance the flavor of salads.

Bulbs—In addition to hyacinths, plant unusual spring bulbs, such as leucojum, ranunculus, anemones, oxalis, and ipheion. Buy now, and store in a cool, dark place in paper bags for four to six weeks before planting.

☐ **Ornamental grasses**—Miscanthus, pennisetum, inland sea oats, muhlenbergia, stipa, and Japanese blood grasses are spectacular in a winter garden. Use them in drifts or masses of three or more, and combine them with perennials and roses. These grasses also help provide cold-weather protection for more tender plants.

☐ **Spring perennials**—In the Middle and Lower South, set out spring-flowering perennials, such as 'Texas Gold' columbine, yarrow, ox-eye daisies, purple coneflower, Louisiana and prairie phlox, and Louisiana and bearded iris now, so that they will have enough time to become established before next spring. Prepare the soil well before planting by mixing in 3 to 5 inches of organic material, such as sphagnum peat moss, along with 4 to 5 pounds of cottonseed or alfalfa meal.

Chrysanthemums—Garden mums of all shapes, sizes, and colors are available at your local garden center now. Use them inside for interior arrangements, outside in containers, or to add definition to a fall border.

PRUNE

☐ **Crepe myrtles**—Continue removing spent flowers from crepe myrtles to encourage one more crop of blooms before frost. Save major pruning jobs for December and January when trees are dormant.

☐ **Roses**—Prep your roses for spring bloom. After your last frost date, prune to remove all dead wood and crossing branches. Shorten remaining growth by about a third. Make cuts at an angle about ¼ inch above an outward-growing bud.

FERTILIZE

☐ **Chrysanthemums**—Fertilize mums with Scotts Blossom Booster or a similar formulation every two weeks until the buds show color. Pinch or clip fading flowers to encourage additional blooms.

☐ **Lawn**—Early in the month in the Tropical South, apply a complete fertilizer, such as a 16-4-8, to dry turf, and water in. Continue to check your lawn for pests this month.

☐ **Trees**—Add fertilizer to trees this month or next in the Coastal and Tropical South. Use a general fertilizer, such as 12-4-8. It is not necessary to remove mulch first. Root prune any trees you plan on moving in the cooler months. Dig a shallow trench around the dripline, and backfill it. This will encourage the roots to grow in toward the trunk.

CONTROL

☐ **Insects**—This can be one of the worst months for pests in subtropical gardens. Watch for mealybugs, mites, aphids, whiteflies, and scale on hibiscus, croteon, citrus, avocado, mango, and other tropical plants. Spray a horticultural oil in late afternoon, making sure to thoroughly coat the stems and both sides of leaves.

☐ **Weeds**—Continue to pull weeds from your garden. Eliminating them now, before the seeds spread, will reduce work next spring.

September notes:

TIP OF THE MONTH

Collards are the number one vegetable in our part of the state. But the worms like them better than we do. You can spray every day, and they still eat. An old farmer once told me that sifting flour onto the leaves would take care of the worms. I didn't have enough flour, so I tried sprinkling baby powder. Guess what? No worms!

JEAN B. PRIDGEN
ROCKY MOUNT, NORTH CAROLINA

no-fail fall color

GARDENING
PLANTS AND DESIGN

Plant flowers now, and fill in next spring for colorful blooms through fall.

Autumn is a season of brilliance, but usually it is in the clarity of the blue sky and the vivid hues of the treetops. In this garden, however, the flower border plays host to a dynamic display that starts small in spring with drifts of bulbs and grows ever taller, fuller, and more robust until annuals and perennials proudly stand shoulder to shoulder in a season when many gardens are simply tired. They spill their color onto the path and present fresh flowers at eye level.

Flowers and foliage of strong, saturated reds, purples, and bronzes mingle with other hues to make a sweep of color that easily endures the strong Southern sun. This garden was planted in the fall and spring, allowing time for plants to fill out and add height to the border. Although this is a large, mature garden, you can enjoy a smaller version by selecting some of the combinations shown here. For a plan to help you plant, see page 166.

COLOR SELECTION
"The colors in this garden were dictated by the light," says garden designer Mary Zahl of Birmingham. "We tried pale pink in the first planting, and it was horrible. The reds, purples, the black-eyed Susan yellow, and the burgundy foliage look great because these deeper, stronger colors absorb the light."

Color choices are personal, just as when choosing your clothing. But the clothes you wear can be influenced by your hair, skin, and even your destination. Naturally, a garden's colors have different influences and results.

"People think they like certain colors, usually the colors they wear," says Mary. "You may think you hate orange, but it may look great in a border. Just because you are a person who doesn't like strong colors doesn't mean that they may not be the best ones to use in your garden."

BY LINDA C. ASKEY
PHOTOGRAPHY VAN CHAPLIN

LEFT: *'Lady in Red' salvia, chartreuse 'Margarita' sweet potato, and white narrow-leaf zinnia*
BELOW: *The flower spikes of the red-leaved coleus echo the form of the spikes on the forsythia sage.*

PROPER PRUNING

Salvias play a major role in this planting, and essential to their success is pruning. Left on its own, fall-flowering forsythia sage may reach 8 feet in height. By cutting back the plant by half in mid-summer, Mary keeps it 4 to 5 feet tall with numerous spikes of flowers. Other plants in the border are also managed this way, including Mexican bush sage *(Salvia leucantha)* and Tatarian aster *(Aster tataricus)*. Salvias in the border that do not require pruning are 'Lady in Red,' 'Indigo Spires,' and pineapple sage *(S. elegans)*.

SUPPORTS FOR GROWTH

Another technique for a full fall bloom is to support these tall-growing plants so they stand upright. Plastic-coated metal grids are placed over the young plants in late spring and early summer. Rather than trying to stake plants after it is too late and risk breaking stems, Mary supports them as they grow. These grids are available at many garden centers and through mail-order companies. Plants that benefit from this care include the salvias, garden phlox, pink boltonia *(Boltonia asteroides* 'Pink Beauty'), switch grass *(Panicum virgatum* 'Heavy Metal'), and yellow shining coneflower *(Rudbeckia nitida* 'Herbstsonne').

TRICKS OF THE TRADE

At 120 feet long, this border is relatively narrow—only 4 feet. Mary compensates by taking space from behind the fence. 'Callaway' crabapple trees with their bounty of red fruit echo the colors of the border and give the illusion of depth.

Gardens with a long season of bloom have foliage from perennials that have already finished flowering—daylilies, iris, and such. However, Mary sees the leaves as assets. They are full, green, and offer vertical form and interest. There are also plants grown strictly for their ornamental foliage—grasses, sweet potatoes, Caribbean copper plant *(Euphorbia cotinifolia),* and coleus.

The stone walk that separates the border from the lawn becomes less of a path as the garden spills onto it. Still, it is probably best to step back and view the border from the lawn. It's almost more than you can absorb at a single glance.

With the help of Mary's tips and favorite plant combinations, you can savor a lush fall border in your garden too. ◇

TO GET THIS LOOK

1. Tatarian aster
2. pineapple sage
3. 'Lady in Red' salvia
4. *Salvia leucantha*
5. 'Indigo Spires' salvia
6. 'Margarita' sweet potato vine
7. forsythia sage
8. narrow-leaf zinnia
9. coleus

This Arbor Has It Covered

What's the primary purpose of an arbor? To provide shade? To act as support for clinging vines? To frame a view? Well, if you're the owner of this handsome arbor on Maryland's Eastern Shore, yours does all three.

A collaboration between landscape designer Jan Kirsh of Bozman, Maryland, and architect Lauren Dianich of Atelier 11 in Easton, the arbor stands beside the pool house, straddling a walk. "The arbor marks a transition between the main house and pool house and frames the entry to the pool area from the garden," Lauren notes.

Although striking and nicely detailed, the structure is fairly simple in design. Built of painted cedar, it consists of 4 x 4 posts supporting 2 x 6 cross beams and 1 x 1 rafters. The posts rest on brick piers. Copper caps atop the posts prevent rainwater from entering the wood, while adding a stylish touch.

An arbor without vines is like a police officer without doughnuts—something doesn't seem right. For this arbor, Jan chose gold flame honeysuckle *(Lonicera heckrottii)*, which combines blue-green leaves with flowers that are coral pink outside and yellow inside.

This attractive painted arbor frames a picturesque view of the garden beyond, while adding interest to the adjacent pool house.

TAKE THAT, SUCKER!

Jan likes using gold flame honeysuckle, but aphids frequently plague it. To control these sucking pests, she applies Ortho RosePride Systemic Rose & Flower Care every six weeks throughout the growing season. The systemic insecticide kills the aphids, while the 8-12-4 fertilizer promotes healthy growth.

ABOVE: *All the wood used to build the structure is cedar.*
LEFT: *Copper wire strung between two bronze eye straps helps the vine to climb up the arbor.*

Although lacking a scent, the blossoms appear from spring until frost.

Jan also devised a clever way to train the vine up the posts to the beams and rafters. Near the tops and bottoms of selected posts, she attached bronze nautical fittings, called eye straps. (Eyebolts may be substituted. Just make sure they're brass, so they don't rust.) She then ran lengths of copper wire taut between the straps and twined the vines around the wire, as well as around the posts. As a result, the honeysuckle ascends easily, looking as though it had done all the work itself.

This arbor demonstrates the importance of good design and placement. Thanks to Lauren's and Jan's creativity, it covers all the bases. *Steve Bender*

ABOVE: *Each container is stamped.* FAR LEFT: *Fall flowers complement terra-cotta.* LEFT: *Great-grandmother Grace helps young Eli get a feel for shaping the damp clay.*

From Terra Firma To Terra-Cotta

Earth is the garden's essential element. Flowers, fruit, and vegetables are its obvious rewards. But with a dose of TLC and a measured amount of skill, the soil can offer more. A clay pot, too, begins with a handful of dirt that, in the skilled hands of a master potter, grows into a fine garden vessel.

The Hewell family has been turning and burning terra-cotta for nearly 100 years in Gillsville, Georgia. They started out making churns, jars, and jugs. With electricity and refrigeration, their wares became obsolete. To continue practicing the trade, they turned to crafting garden pots in the late 1940s.

GROWING A POT

According to Chester, the fifth generation of Hewell potters, creating a container on a pottery wheel is like planting a seed. "A seed starts growing from the inside out, and a pot's the same. You start with a ball of clay and work from the inside, pushing it out to form the walls." And just as the seedling grows stronger as it matures, the walls of the container thicken and strengthen as the pot attains its full height.

"Plants need oxygen to grow," says Chester. "Pottery is very porous and breathes also." This "breathing" helps plants flourish. A clay container absorbs water, allowing the soil within to maintain a fine balance of air and moisture.

TERRA-COTTA TIPS

Clay pots last for years when treated properly. Winter is their enemy, with water and freezing temperatures a damaging combination. "To keep a clay pot outside during the winter, raise it up off the ground a little bit, so water drains out and away from it," Chester says.

"In the bottom of the pot, put some broken pottery or charcoal pieces," he recommends. A layer of pine bark nuggets or even a few pinecones in the bottom of a large pot also will keep moisture draining freely.

POTTING INTO FALL

Terra-cotta's warm umber shades present a perfect envelope for jewel-toned chrysanthemums, croton, and ornamental grasses. Place a few pieces of broken clay over the pot's drainage hole, and fill it with potting soil. Purchase large, full plants, and snuggle them tightly together.

Begin with the tallest element, most likely an ornamental grass. Step down to the chrysanthemums and croton, and then add some ivy to trail over the side. Use the croton's colors to determine your mums' shades. *Ellen Riley*

(*For sources turn to pages 234—235.*)

LADY PALM
At a Glance

Height: slowly reaches to 10 feet
Light: dappled shade to full shade
Soil: well-drained potting soil
Water: keep evenly moist; tolerates some neglect or overwatering
Feed: monthly with liquid fertilizer during growing season
Temperature: bring indoors if below 45 degrees

One Bountiful Lady

Dividing a mature lady palm into several plants is simple to do and saves your dollars for other garden projects.

Graceful fans of dark green fronds arch from an airy center in soft decorator-perfect curves. They stay that way, too; lady palm, the original "Miss Manners" of house-plants, rarely outgrows its designated space.

Unfortunately, the slow growth of lady palm *(Rhapis excelsa)* means there are never enough available to fill the demand. The result is a high price tag—a good-size 3-gallon plant can cost more than $100.

One sensible solution to lady palm sticker shock is buying root-bound specimens that are sending up new plants from the bottoms of their pots. Lady palms are very easy to divide, so by selecting a fat one, you'll have several of these pretty plants without blowing your budget. You also can divide your own well-established lady palms, instead of spending more money.

THE GREAT DIVIDE

To reduce the time the plants' roots are exposed, prepare your supplies before you begin.

Step 1: Slice away the pot with sharp pruning shears, or split it carefully with the edge of the shovel. (Don't just rip the root ball out of the old pot if it's tight—you don't want to lose any valuable baby lady palms by breaking them off with no roots.)

Step 2: Cut through the tough, fibrous root ball with a shovel or shears, dividing the clump of lady palms into two or more plants,

as you choose, ready for repotting. Make sure to include some roots when you separate the little palms suckering at the sides of the main plant.

Step 3: Repot the new divisions, including the little guys, in pots just big enough to hold their roots. Remember, they like to be a little root bound, so don't give them too much space. Fill in firmly around the plants with potting soil, and water thoroughly, several times, until the new soil is well moistened all the way through. You'll want to water daily for the first week or two, adding a little root stimulator to the water (per label instructions) during this time. Then just keep the soil evenly moist, apply a liquid fertilizer bimonthly, and occasionally wipe dust off the foliage.

Lady palms ask for so little, but contribute so much to a setting. They are never inappropriate, so it's not hard at all to find places for your new plants. They prefer low levels of light, so you can add some as an elegant touch under the caves of the patio, or let one spread its handsome fronds in that dark corner behind your reading chair. Just drop their plain pots into decorative outer containers, hiding the inner pot with a top dressing of potting soil, mulch, or Spanish moss. It is impossible to regret having more lady palms, because their beauty is equaled only by their good behavior.   *Liz Druitt*

Bring In the Basil

HARVEST HINT

Basil blackens wherever the leaves are bruised, so handle it carefully to preserve the bright green color. When stripping leaves from stems in the kitchen, wear gloves, or your green thumb will turn black too. Remove stains with lemon juice.

Basil loves the South as much as the South loves this aromatic herb. Although much of the garden can suffer at this point in the season, sweet basil is still determined to bloom. Unfortunately for the gardener, its blooms are not exactly showy, and the plant stops growing those delicious leaves when it flowers and sets seed. Pruning shears are the answer.

The flowers begin as conical clusters atop each stem, quickly lengthening into 8- to 10-inch stalks. You can nip them off at the base, but they quickly would be replaced by more stalks from the side branches. You'll get more leaves by cutting the plant back by about a third, and you can use the flavorful foliage in the kitchen to season many recipes.

To aid in nature's production, water every two weeks with a liquid fertilizer, such as 20-20-20. This will give plants a jump start on new growth, especially in hot weather. You also could use a timed-release granular fertilizer broadcast over the surface of the soil.

Continue to snip a stalk now and then to chop and sprinkle atop sliced tomatoes, but cut the entire plant again in a few weeks to remove new flowers. You'll come to enjoy these harvest days—your kitchen will smell great, and dinner will taste delicious. ◇

ABOVE, LEFT: *When basil starts going to seed, do more than pinch off the bloom. Cut it back by a third, and preserve the foliage to make pesto.*

Don't Mulch Too Much

So much fuss has been made about the benefits of mulch that it's not surprising that some people overdo it. They think if a little around trees and shrubs is good, a lot will be even better. Without checking first to see whether the previous mulch has decomposed, they automatically add a fresh layer each year. Over time, this accumulated mulch can injure or kill the very plants it was put there to help.

How can you tell if your tree or shrub suffers from overmulching? Signs include abnormally small leaves, chlorotic (yellow or blanched) foliage, dieback of branches, dying grass outside the mulch around the plant, and basal cankers on the trunk where it touches the mulch.

■ Don't apply fresh wood mulch over mulch that's already there. Allow the existing layer to decompose first. Apply a maximum of 2 inches at a time.

■ Don't pile up mulch against the trunks of trees and shrubs. This can cause cankers on spruce species and encourage borers on hardwoods.

■ Don't worry about overmulching with pine straw. This material rots quickly and seldom builds up to damaging levels. However, don't apply more than 2 to 3 inches at a time.

Apply fresh pine bark mulch only after the old layer has decomposed. Don't pile it up against the trunk.

PHOTOGRAPHS: VAN CHAPLIN

Buy It Now, Plant It Now

Fall is a great time to plant and the perfect opportunity to take advantage of some unique sales.

Early sun slants through green-clad branches at Hilltop Arboretum. Normally, at this hour, the beautiful autumn light falls only on the serenity of trees, birds, and meadows. This morning, however, the arboretum in Baton Rouge looks like a stirred-up ants' nest and sounds like a party in progress. The famous Hilltop Plantfest! is about to welcome gardeners for the 20th year in a row.

Excited volunteers are helping vendors and arboretum staff, while staking out choice specimens to buy for themselves. The flats and rows of plants are grouped by garden habitat, making it easier for shoppers to match their own growing conditions. The electric feeling in the air reaches a peak as the event opens and customers head for the perennials tent, the hummingbird section, bog plants or even Xeriscape specimens, ornamental grasses, and the fascinating

TOP: *Loaded carts are the norm at the Hilltop Arboretum's autumn plant sale.* ABOVE: *Gardeners share enthusiasm as they discover interesting plants.*

Connoisseurs' Corner, where rare and unusual plants are stashed for the true horticultural addicts. This is the largest plant sale of its kind in the Southeast, and, as such, it puts the spotlight squarely on the value of fall planting for warm-climate gardeners.

"We in the South need to plant in the fall," explains Hilltop's director, Marion Drummond. "The cool weather and rains give the plants such a good head start for next year's blooms. That's why we hold Plantfest! now and why so many other arboretums and botanical gardens hold large fall plant sales."

After answering questions from eager shoppers pulling wagonloads of ginger, hawthorn, viburnum, and salvia, Marion adds that in addition to providing regionally adapted plants at an optimal time for planting, events such as Hilltop Plantfest! help to spread gardening knowledge. "Volunteers take what they learn here back to their own communities and pass it on," she says.

The result? Better Southern gardens and more Southern gardeners eagerly anticipating autumn's arrival.

Liz Druitt

From Shade to Sun

Austin gardener Nancy Webber made the most of an unexpected opportunity when a tree fell and let the sun shine in.

BEFORE

ABOVE: *A heavy storm brought down Nancy's majestic post oak.*
TOP: *Limestone rock, ornamental grasses, and succulents form the backbone of Nancy Webber's ruggedly beautiful front garden.*

It was a dark and stormy night in Austin back in the winter of 1991. High winds and soil-loosening rains combined to bring down the grand old post oak that had sheltered the Webbers' entire front yard. "When that tree fell, I cried," garden designer Nancy Webber remembers. "It was after midnight, and our gas lines were all uprooted and broken. Emergency repair trucks were everywhere, with their lights flashing. I was out with an umbrella, crying over the tree."

But nothing lasts forever, at least not in gardening. By the time the tree finally was cleared away, Nancy was ready to take advantage of the enormous change in growing conditions in her front yard.

Her first priority was to fix the hole left by the root ball of the fallen tree. "We filled it with dirt from the backyard," recalls Nancy, "and I planted agaves, which are still thriving there, 10 years later. I love the textures of succulent and spiny plants. I can't explain it—I just do. They're so structural, give tons of impact just sitting there, and all you have to do is keep the weeds out of them."

The agaves were just the starting point for developing a garden completely different from the shady lawn it replaced. Nancy began selecting plants of all kinds that offered great color and interest, without any water other than rainfall, and arranging them with the help of her professional eye. Ornamental grasses, salvia, and some of Nancy's favorite single (five-petaled) roses are accented by cactus with broad, wavy pads and narrow-leaved yucca.

Carefully placed limestone rocks add definition to different planting areas. The effect, which Nancy claims was not entirely deliberate, is kaleidoscopic. As you walk or drive past the front of her garden, the dramatic plants rapidly shift into new, exciting combinations of color and texture.

"I didn't draw any formal plan," she says,

RIGHT: *Spineless prickly pear, agave, and Caribbean copper plant offer their riches to the eyes of passersby.*
BELOW: *Agarita, autumn sage, purple fountain grass, candlestick tree, and 'Blue Ice' Arizona cypress build layers of striking beauty.*

NANCY'S FAVORITE EASY-CARE PLANTS

Agave: Nancy highly recommends *Agave parryi* or *A. neomexicana*. Both are handsome, moderate-size specimens suitable for gardens or containers, and both of these agaves usually will take cold to at least the mid-twenties, often down to zero.

Purple fountain grass: "Ornamental grasses are so easy," Nancy says. She suggests purple fountain grass (*Pennisetum setaceum* 'Rubrum') as an excellent one to try. It's a quick-growing annual for the Upper, Middle, or Lower South.

Caribbean copper plant: Also sold as red spurge (*Euphorbia cotinifolia* 'Atropurpurea'), this vivid shrub is becoming increasingly popular at garden centers. "It's just the right size to use as an accent plant," says Nancy, "and it isn't fussy about anything but good drainage. It quickly reaches 5 or 6 feet from a 1-gallon container." It acts as an annual for all but the Tropical South.

Candlestick tree: Already a Southern garden favorite, candlestick tree (*Cassia alata*) combines minimal care with dramatic good looks. "You just have to remember it's going to get 10 feet tall, and put it at the back," Nancy advises. It's an annual in all but the Tropical South.

'Blue Ice' Arizona cypress: Native to the Western United States, Arizona cypress (*Cupressus arizonica* 'Blue Ice') is one of the most colorful conifers for the South. "It needs good drainage but not a lot of water," Nancy notes. "This blue cone-shaped evergreen is a wonderful background tree. It's reliable, and it makes plants around it stand out." Works best in the Middle, Lower, and Coastal South.

"because I had to keep adjusting everything over time, gradually expanding the beds from the street toward the house. I've just kept making more beds as I found plants I really wanted to try. I'll never be finished."

Nancy focuses on experimenting with plants that not only offer visual interest, but also are genuinely drought tolerant. "We often travel during the hottest part of summer," she explains, "and I never water a lot, even when I'm home. So, with the new full-sun conditions, everything I plant has to like it pretty dry."

Does Nancy expect to see more changes in her garden in the future? "Hopefully not as catastrophic as losing that tree," she says, "but I have learned to love change. I'm always moving things around, pulling some plants out, putting others in. That's what I like to do.

"In fact," she muses, "now I couldn't bear to live with a landscape that never changed, whether it was just grass or flower-ing plants that bloom on and on. I don't expect everyone to experiment as much as I do, but I've learned from my clients that change in the landscape can be a real pleasure for everyone." Nancy pauses and then smiles. "They all get so excited when some new thing happens in their gardens."

Liz Druitt

Chinese pistache graces a lawn with color (See page 182.)

October

Checklist for October

EDITOR'S NOTEBOOK

Although I personally grow roses because I love to spray, fertilize, agonize, pray, and then spray some more, most people grow them for the flowers. But did you ever think of planting roses for their spectacular autumn fruits? Admit it—when you glanced at the photo above, you thought you were looking at cherries, cranberries, or grape tomatoes. Instead, you're gazing at the scarlet fruits (or "hips") of the rugosa rose (*Rosa rugosa*). Native to Japan and China, this tough rose is incredibly easy to grow and tolerates wind, poor soil, and drought. Fragrant flowers appear from spring to fall, followed by the fruits. Birds love them and so do very, very, very hungry people. Rugosa rose may not be as common as other roses, but you shouldn't have that much trouble finding it. Just visit your local garden or home center. If you can't find it among the roses, look in the produce section. *Steve Bender*

TIPS

☐ **Cannas and dahlias**—In the Upper and Middle South, lift and divide tubers now. Cut stalks to about 1 inch above the tuber, shake off any loose soil, and let the clump dry. Store in a cool, dry place that does not freeze. In the Lower and Coastal South, tubers don't need to be lifted. Just mulch well to overwinter.

☐ **Gourds and miniature pumpkins**—As the rinds harden and leaves wither, cut each fruit with at least an inch of stem attached, and allow to continue curing in a dry, shady area. After several weeks, carefully wipe off the surfaces with a damp cloth, and apply paste wax or lacquer if a higher sheen is desired. Ornamental gourds can be kept and enjoyed for many years.

☐ **Mulch**—Supplies are plentiful now for creating an organic mulch of pine needles or ground leaves. While keeping soil moist and weeds down, mulch slowly decomposes to improve the soil and nourish plants.

☐ **Perennials**—Now is a good time to divide perennials that have declined from overcrowding or ones you wish to have more of in your garden. Lift and divide clumps of daylilies, iris, coneflowers, hostas, daisies, and ferns. Add a bit of organic matter, such as compost, to the soil, reset divided plants at the same soil level, and water well. If you find you have too many divisions to replant, pass along a few to friends, as they will make treasured gifts.

Fall greens—It's not too late to sow seeds of mustard, collards, turnips, and lettuce for a fall garden. In the Upper and Middle South you may want to use transplants of lettuce for best results.

☐ **Save seeds**—Many favorite vegetable and flower seeds can be saved from year to year, which is a way to preserve our gardening heritage. Southern heirloom flowers for saving include zinnias, bachelor's buttons, larkspur, celosias, sweet peas, and sunflowers. Among the easily saved vegetables are okra, green and shell beans, Southern peas, Indian corn, and heirloom tomatoes. Let seeds dry thoroughly before storing in paper envelopes, making sure to write on the outside the plant's name and the date collected. Store them in the lower part of your refrigerator to extend seed life. The percentage of seeds that will germinate decreases after the first year, but many types may be kept for several years.

☐ **Seasonal plants**—Make sure your outdoor lighting doesn't shine on Christmas cactus, kalanchoe, or poinsettia from about 6 p.m. to 8 a.m. Continue to keep them away from night light till late November or early December. This will encourage the plants to set flowerbuds.

PLANT

☐ **Color beds**—Remove spent summer annuals, prepare the soil, and plant cool-weather annuals, such as violas, pansies, snapdragons, red mustard, and ornamental cabbage and kale. Add a balanced slow-release fertilizer and organic matter, such as composted pine bark; then till the bed before planting.

☐ **Poppies**—Sow seeds now for flowers next spring. Select a sunny location, and scatter seeds on a prepared garden bed; then gently rake and water. To ensure even coverage, mix seeds with builder's sand before sowing to make it easier to see where seeds are cast.

☐ **Trees and shrubs**—Remember that fall is the ideal time to plant trees and shrubs. The cool days allow roots to grow and help condition the plants for the following season. Select a mature size tree that will fit well into your landscape. Dig a hole wider but at the same depth as the tree's root ball, fill in around the root ball with soil, and water thoroughly. If necessary, stake the tree to keep it from tilting or falling over. Plan to remove the stakes in about six months. Keep the soil moist around the roots until the tree is firmly rooted.

☐ **Turf**—Overseed warm-season grasses, such as centipede or Bermuda, with annual ryegrass for a green lawn during the upcoming winter months. Be sure to spread evenly (5 pounds per 100 square feet) and keep moist until germination. Mow regularly.

☐ **Vegetables**—In the Lower and Coastal South, plant seeds of mustard, turnips, radishes, mesclun, and lettuce now. These garden vegetables produce quickly and can be sown in succession throughout the winter months. Children especially enjoy having a garden experience with radishes because they have large seeds, sprout quickly, and mature in just a few weeks. Mesclun, a mix of strongly flavored European lettuces and wild greens, can now be purchased in a variety of flavors that range from mild to hot and spicy.

Plant—Scatter poppy, larkspur, and cornflower seeds over a prepared bed that has been tilled at least 6 to 8 inches deep; then lightly rake, and water. Select a sunny location, and be sure to thin the seedlings so that plants are spaced 4 to 6 inches apart. Larkspur and cornflowers provide masses of blue and purple flowers, which contrast well with the red, pink, and salmon shades of the poppies.

FERTILIZE

☐ **Roses**—Roses will benefit from a feeding now to promote high-quality fall blooms. You can use 1 cup of 12-4-8 or similar formula per bush.

☐ **Soil**—Add organic matter, such as sphagnum peat moss or compost, to your garden before fall planting. If you have a new yard or have noticed an area where no plant seems to do well, get a soil test. Then, if necessary, you should adjust the pH based on the results. For more information about soil testing, contact your local Extension office.

CONTROL

☐ **Lawn**—If annual bluegrass and other cool-weather weeds commonly appear in your lawn, apply a pre-emergence herbicide this month. Check to make sure the treatment matches the type of grass you have. If you didn't fertilize cool-season grass last month, do so early this month. Keep an eye on the need to water, as the cooler temperatures can be deceiving.

☐ **Mildew**—As night temperatures decrease, powdery mildew may become a problem on grapes, roses, crepe myrtles, mangoes, and other susceptible plants. Prevent it with a fungicide, such as Funginex for ornamentals and wettable sulfur for fruits and vegetables.

October notes:

TIP OF THE MONTH

I make a drawing of all of my flowerbeds and mark on the drawings where I've planted bulbs. That way, I know exactly where the bulbs are whenever I turn over the soil.

CLAIRE NEWBURG
BENTON, ARKANSAS

Plant a vegetable garden now for a fresh, tasty harvest this season and into winter, and then enjoy lovely blooms in spring.

homegrown garden
of greens

A vegetable garden doesn't have to be a large affair. This one is only 12 x 24 feet, but yielded plenty of produce throughout the fall and winter. Plus, the striking foliage of various colors, sizes, and textures covered the ground like a quilt. Then, in the spring, when the warming temperatures made the unharvested broccoli, greens, cabbage, and kale bolt into bloom, it gave the plot the look of a well-tended flower garden. Here's how we did it.

Because a hungry rabbit discovered our summer garden and sampled some of the produce, we added a small fence before setting out the fall vegetables. The fencing is anchored with four corner posts, which are twice as tall as the fence. We topped the posts with wooden finials to help define the boundaries. The wood frame adds bulk to the thin wire and makes it sturdy.

We made a gated arbor to serve as a welcoming entrance to our vegetable patch. Adapting salvaged shutters, we installed double doors that swung wide enough to allow a wheelbarrow or large tiller into the garden. Then, old windows were added to create a pitched roof as the arbor's finishing touch.

LEFT: *Planting a fall vegetable garden can be productive, delicious, and attractive.* TOP, RIGHT: *In spring many of the plants bolted. The kale and greens produced delicate, sweetly scented yellow blooms.* ABOVE: *This small arbor, made from salvaged shutters and windowpanes, creates a gateway into the garden.* BOTTOM, RIGHT: *Plants of various colors were placed together for interest and contrast.*

BY CHARLIE THIGPEN / PHOTOGRAPHY VAN CHAPLIN

Next, we spread two bales of sphagnum peat moss on top of the ground and tilled them into the soil. If you start a fall garden early enough, you can direct-sow many cool-weather vegetables, such as carrots, greens, lettuce, radishes, spinach, sugar snap peas, and turnips. Our vegetable garden was filled with transplants, some from cell packs and some from 4-inch pots, that were purchased from a local nursery. We outlined the walking path with flat-leaved and curly-leaved parsley and then spaced out Southern giant curled and 'Giant Red' mustard greens, 'Red Bor' kale, 'Bright Lights' Swiss chard, broccoli, lettuce, and cabbage. Plants with dark-colored foliage were placed next to light-colored ones for contrast, and plants with different leaf sizes, textures, and shapes were mixed together to create eye-catching combinations.

Once everything was planted in the ground, we covered the garden with a layer of finely shredded pine bark mulch. That helped to insulate the ground on cold days and prevented any weed seeds that blew in from taking hold and germinating. This also kept the vegetables and greens much cleaner because soil didn't splash on the plants during heavy downpours.

ABOVE: *'Bright Lights' Swiss chard is edible and ornamental. Its stalks produce a rainbow of vibrant colors.* LEFT: *Lettuce transplants are available at many garden centers in the fall, along with lots of other vegetables.*

We fed the garden with a water-soluble liquid fertilizer, such as 20-20-20, every couple of weeks to make sure that the plants rooted in and stayed healthy. With the warm, early-fall days, the vegetables grew rapidly, and we were picking lettuce and greens within just a few weeks. The other vegetables soon followed. For plants to continue producing, they should be harvested every couple of days, and we did so happily. The collards and kale became sweet and flavorful as temperatures cooled, before they were nipped by frost.

We harvested many of the other vegetables well into the winter. By using a floating row cover blanket, we helped the plants survive temperatures that dipped into the teens. The thin, gauzelike fabric can be draped over plants for extended periods to protect cool-weather crops. A lesson: If you decide to try a row cover, you must be sure to secure it firmly to the ground. If a cold front brings high winds, the cover can lift off, exposing tender plants to the elements.

Cabbage was the only vegetable that didn't produce for us; it bolted before it could head up. In the late winter and early spring, too, many of the cool-weather plants became bitter, tough, and unfit to eat. Still, as they flowered, they made the garden look showy. Their large, colorful foliage, mixed with small yellow blooms, made a beautiful springtime ending to this tasty fall garden. ◇

Fall's Finest Flowers

Gardens that look fabulous in spring can still be lovely come autumn, when they get their second wind. Just ask Nancy Porter. In spring, her garden is a glory of roses, peonies, foxgloves, and iris. Her fall garden, though, is equally spectacular.

Each autumn, New England asters and pink mums fill Nancy's yard in Roland, Arkansas. The pink-and-blue combination provides a striking contrast with the yellow-and-red foliage on the trees surrounding her home. This memorable scene doesn't appear by chance. The plants have multiplied over the years, their roots tiptoeing across the soil to form well-established clumps.

As the cooler winds of autumn begin to blow, this garden shows how stunning fall can be.

About a decade ago, a friend gave Nancy a small piece of the New England aster. That little plant flourished, and she was soon dividing and setting it in other locations. While the asters are rather inconspicuous most of the year, the 2½- to 3-foot-tall plants come into their own around mid-September. Their delicate blue petals encircle small yellow centers. Although the centers soon fade to brown, the petals retain color for almost an entire month, blooming so profusely they resemble billowy clouds.

Like many gardeners, Nancy believes that you can't have a true fall garden unless you have mums. Still, she didn't want the clipped basketball-shaped plants found at most nurseries. She felt they were too rigid. So eight years ago, she planted a Korean hybrid mum named 'Ryan's Pink' *(Chrysanthemum* x *morifolium)*. When the plant gets full sun and a good thinning every few years, it produces thousands of fall blooms that look more like blushing pink daisies.

Leggy plants, they tend to sprawl when in bloom, and their 18- to 24-inch stems have a hard time holding up the bulky flower heads. But Nancy doesn't mind; she likes their loose form, which best fits her garden. (For something smaller, look for 'Hillside Sheffield' and 'Apricot Single,' two Korean hybrids about 12 inches tall.)

While asters and mums anchor the display, Nancy fills in with a variety of plants. She likes Mexican bush sage *(Salvia leucantha)*,

TOP: *A combination of light pink mums and blue asters stars in the colorful show in Nancy Porter's fall garden.* ABOVE: *The purple-and-white blooms of Mexican bush sage contrast beautifully with the red spikes of celosia, an annual you can count on to reseed.*

which has velvety purple-and-white blooms and grayish green foliage. Forming a large, rounded mound, it reaches 3 to 4 feet tall. In the Upper and Middle South, it's grown as an annual, and Nancy dries the blooms, which retain their color.

The garden also features 'Autumn Joy' sedum. Its fall blooms start out dark pink and then turn bronzy red. The numerous florets and thick, rubbery leaves make the plant stand out even when not in bloom. This isn't the most stunning plant, but it may be the most dependable. About the only thing that can kill it is too much water or shade.

Finally, 'Plumosa' celosia grows throughout the garden. Planted several years ago, this plant keeps on reseeding, coming up here and there, and Nancy just lets it go. The spiked red flowers provide a pop of color, and the showy leaves look like they've been painted red along the edges.

Now that summer's heat has burned out, it's time to return to the garden. Nancy's yard is living—and lovely—proof of how beautiful autumn flowers can be. *Charlie Thigpen*

Discover Chinese Pistache

This no-fuss tree gets little acclaim right now. We'd like to help change that.

Tired of messy, slow-growing, pest-ridden trees that are about as thrilling to experience as Des Moines after dark? Take my advice. Go out for a little Chinese this weekend—Chinese pistache, that is.

Growing 30 to 40 feet tall with an oval to rounded shape, Chinese pistache *(Pistacia chinensis)* is quite simply one of the garden's prettiest and most trouble-free trees. Acid soil? It likes it. Alkaline soil? Likes that too. Monsoon rain? No problem. Withering drought? No big deal. Bugs and diseases? Just forget about 'em.

CHINESE PISTACHE
At a Glance

Light: full sun
Soil: well drained, any pH
Height: 30 to 40 feet
Growth rate: moderate (2 feet a year)
Pests: none serious
Range: Upper, Middle, Lower, and Coastal South
Comments: drought tolerant, good fall color

PHOTOGRAPHS: VAN CHAPLIN

ABOVE: *Chinese pistache forms a rounded, medium-size tree 30 to 40 feet tall. If you remove some of the lower limbs, grass will grow up to the trunk.*
LEFT: *Fall color is spectacular, ranging from brilliant red to bright yellow.*

And fall color? Well, it's just to die for. Depending on the tree and how much sun it receives, its lacy, dark green leaves turn brilliant yellow, orange, or scarlet in the fall. In fact, it's among the most dependable trees for fall color in the Lower and Coastal South, and it does equally well in the Southeast and Southwest.

Landscape architect Rodney Fulcher, of Gardens of the Southwest in Abilene, Texas, raves about four Chinese pistaches growing at his office. Started from 5-gallon pots planted about 20 years ago, they now stand nearly 40 feet tall and shade a courtyard.

"Except for the first year, we've never watered them," he says. "We've also never sprayed them for insects or disease." He recommends using Chinese pistache to shade the house, driveway, or patio. It also makes a nice lawn tree. If you remove its lower limbs up to about head height, you can grow grass beneath it all the way up to the trunk.

Though most people wouldn't know a Chinese pistache (pronounced pis-TASH) from a Chinese lantern, Rodney believes it will step into the spotlight. "It's one of the trees of the future," he states. "I've never heard anyone say anything bad about it."   *Steve Bender*

(For sources turn to pages 234–235.)

PHOTOGRAPHS: SYLVIA MARTIN

Halloween Cutie: Bat-Faced Cuphea

Deliver us from ghoulies and ghosties, yes, but not from this fascinating shrub.

This plant is ordinary, really, as long as you're standing back. Bat-faced cuphea is just another showy little bush of sizzling red flowers. It's easy to grow and in constant bloom from late spring into fall. Sure, it looks snappy lining a pathway and makes a great accent plant for containers or next to garden gates and benches. Hummingbirds and butterflies both like it, which is good. But it's hard to see what the fuss is about, until, for whatever reason, you get down with the plant, face to face—and discover that it *has* one.

Other members of this popular family, such as the familiar Mexican heather *(Cuphea hyssopifolia)* or the cigar plant *(C. ignea),* have normal flowers. They attract their pollinators and please the gardener's eye without getting quite so creative about it. *C. llavea,* on the other hand, has all the easy-care

aspects of its close kinfolk, with an unusual added attraction for anyone who takes the time to study it. As with so much of Mother Nature's delicate handiwork, the devil—or in this case, the bat face—is in the details.

Lean down close to the flowers, and you can suddenly see the bats. They swoop toward you, red petal ears alert for sonic waves, white stamen tongues thrust fiercely from their tiny purple faces. They're spooky, they're everywhere, and they're perfect for Halloween. So if you want to thrill and chill your gardening friends, forget about pumpkins. Pumpkins have their place, but they don't last—and they don't attract hummingbirds. Point out the extraordinary attributes of bat-faced cuphea, and everyone will want this captivating Halloween cutie that can carry the whole blooming season. *Liz Druitt*

BAT-FACED CUPHEA
At a Glance

Bloom season: late spring to fall
Range: Lower, Coastal, and Tropical South in the ground; Upper and Middle South grown as annuals or in containers (tender perennial)
Soil: any well drained
Water: generous during worst heat of summer, drought tolerant once established
Fertilizer: minimal
Sun: full sun to partial shade
Comments: Pinch back leggy plants for bushier growth.

AUTUMN'S
OUTDOOR ROOM

*Pumpkin topiaries and a warm outdoor fireplace welcome the season
to the Randleman family's side yard.*

The emerald green, warm-season lawn is turning tawny brown as it prepares to go dormant for the winter. Nippy afternoon breeves send multicolored leaves trickling down to the ground, signaling the change of the seasons. It's a great time of year to enjoy the smell of hickory or oak burning, and to feel the warmth of a fire in a garden room embellished with autumn treasures.

All Duane and Lynn Randleman have to do is open French doors on the side of their house to enter a comfortable, enchanting outdoor room. Together with a contractor, they transformed their side yard into a special place

with a level area for their children to play and also a cozy spot for entertaining guests. The result? Their garden literally flows from the kitchen as an extension of the house, and it's used often by the little ones and the adults.

The stacked bluestone walls create boundaries outlining the turf. Behind them, colorful annuals and perennials spill out of large raised beds. The height of the beds eliminates the need to bend over, making them easier to work. Through the seasons, the look of the garden changes. This time of year, large, buttery mums beside the fireplace add a splash of yellow that complements the orange pumpkins and fall foliage.

BY CHARLIE THIGPEN / PHOTOGRAPHY JEAN ALLSOPP / STYLING ALYCE HEAD

Different-size pumpkins randomly lean and nestle along the wall and lawn for a Halloween treat. 'Nellie R. Stevens' hollies form a dark green impenetrable hedge on one side of the garden, while a feathery row of light green Leyland cypress creates privacy on the other. These living evergreen walls provide a dramatic and practical wrapping for the garden.

Atop the entrance columns stand two pumpkin topiaries, reminiscent of festive finials. The white pumpkins sandwiched between orange ones offer contrast for a striking display. A piece of metal rebar secured in a concrete-filled pot

helps position and stabilize the stacked gourds. Bittersweet weaves around the arrangement, its berries glowing like a string of Christmas lights. Burgundy-colored sourwood leaves spread out from under the pumpkins to cover the concrete base. (For instructions, see box at right.)

A decorative wreath draws attention to the outdoor fireplace, located in a corner of the room. The wreath's circular form was fashioned from a few muscadine vines wired together. Five small pumpkins were evenly spaced and bound to the wreath with wire. Bittersweet and autumn-hued leaves

HOW TO BUILD A PUMPKIN TOPIARY

Supplies needed: bag of concrete, terra-cotta pot, small block of wood, metal rebar (See the top photo).

1. Drill a pilot hole in the block of wood a little smaller than the diameter of the rebar. (A small piece of 4 x 4 works great.)

2. Using a hammer, tap a 2½-foot-long piece of rebar into the block of wood until secure.

3. Set the wood into a bowl-shaped terra-cotta container, covering the drain. The rebar and the wood should be centered in the bowl.

4. Pour dry cement around the wooden block 3 to 4 inches deep for a heavy base (See the center photo).

5. Fill the bowl with water, and let the concrete set for 24 hours.

6. Select three pumpkins. Drill small holes in the bottoms and tops of the first two pumpkins, and slide them onto the rebar (See the bottom photo). Drill a small hole only in the bottom of the third pumpkin to cap the arrangement.

7. Use pinecones as spacers if your rebar is taller than your pumpkins.

8. Leaves make a nice cover for the concrete base. Bittersweet or similarly colored branches wrapped around the arrangement add a decorative touch.

tucked around the vines add bulk to the arrangement. The fireplace rising from the neatly stacked walls serves as a natural gathering place when the temperature drops. A gas starter makes fire building quick and easy, and one of the family's favorite activities is roasting marshmallows over the flames while sipping warm mugs of hot chocolate. Just for fun, the Randlemans have even invited some of their neighbors over to cook hot dogs.

The side yard was never meant to be cluttered with furniture. The walls, capped with large, flat stones, were built at a comfortable height for sitting, and the capstones have tumbled edges so there are no sharp points. Outdoor speakers pipe music into the garden, and low-voltage lighting produces a soft glow, allowing visitors to maneuver around the garden at night.

Many homeowners work hard on their front and back yards, never giving their side yard a second thought. Not the Randlemans—they took a little-used area in their garden and made it a gathering place. In truth, they added a large room onto their house—one that has only the sun, clouds, moon, and stars for a ceiling. ◇

Tulips blooming in a container
(See pages 192–194.)

November

Checklist
for
November

EDITOR'S NOTEBOOK

Virginia creeper *(Parthenocissus quinquefolia)* is one of my favorite native vines. It grows well about anywhere—sun or shade, city or country, good soil or bad. It climbs fast, to the top of whatever it's growing on, but doesn't strangle trees like wisteria will or smother them like kudzu. It latches onto almost any surface, including wood, brick, stone, and concrete. In the fall, it's spectacular, as the leaves change from green to crimson. Unfortunately, many people confuse Virginia creeper with another highly ornamental native—poison ivy. If you're not sure, there's an easy way to distinguish the two. Each leaf of Virginia creeper has five leaflets; leaves of poison ivy have three. Still undecided? Here's a foolproof test. Rub the foliage from one of them all over your body. If you wake up the next morning in intensive care, congratulations—you've positively identified poison ivy.

Steve Bender

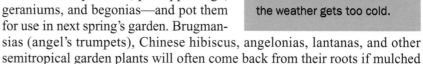

TIPS

☐ **Foliage plants**—Move houseplants inside now in the Coastal and Tropical South. Place them in an area with bright light to avoid shock, and turn them regularly to encourage even growth. Water soil when dry.

☐ **Leaves**—After a rain, piles of leaves can become wet blankets and suffocate your lawn. Rake regularly, and use fallen leaves now for a natural mulch around your trees and shrubs. Or add them to your compost pile for use in the garden later.

☐ **Mulch**—Add pine straw, pine bark, or hardwood mulch around tender plants to help protect from the cold weather. Make sure mulch is not deeper than 2 inches.

☐ **Preparation**—Get your garden ready for winter. Take cuttings or divisions of tender favorites—such as coleus, ornamental sweet potatoes, pineapple sage, geraniums, and begonias—and pot them for use in next spring's garden. Brugmansias (angel's trumpets), Chinese hibiscus, angelonias, lantanas, and other semitropical garden plants will often come back from their roots if mulched now in the Lower South.

☐ **Seedlings**—Larkspur, poppy, and cornflower seedlings need to be thinned so that each plant has 4 to 6 inches of space to grow and bloom. The extra plants may be placed elsewhere in the garden, but water them well for the first few weeks. Mesclun, lettuce, mustard, and other greens should also be thinned now. Use the extra plants as additions to salads.

Winter color—Pansies (above), violas, and snapdragons, available now in garden centers, will help you welcome winter with bright, warm colors for the cool months ahead. Find a sunny, well-drained location, and set out transplants now so they can become established before the weather gets too cold.

PLANT

☐ **Bulbs**—Plant spring-flowering bulbs, such as daffodils, hyacinths, snowdrops, and crocus, now. Make sure to choose a sunny location, and remember that areas under deciduous trees will be sunny in the winter. Add bonemeal or bulb booster to your soil as recommended on the label. Tip: For a natural look, take handfuls of bulbs, and let them gently drop on the ground to create a random pattern of spring blooms. Plant the bulbs where they fall.

☐ **Herbs and vegetables**—In the Middle and Lower South, onions, parsley, cilantro, arugula, cabbage, French sorrel, and chard may be set out now in ornamental borders as well as in the vegetable garden. Their colors and textures make them useful as decorative elements, especially when they are massed between flowering displays. Parsley is great in a cool-weather border.

◄**Narcissus**—Many forms of daffodils—such as Campernelles, jonquils, and most of the smaller flowering types—are well adapted to the South. These hardy, fragrant perennials can create memorable scenes in late winter and early spring as broad drifts of color in open areas and under deciduous trees. They are even compatible with turf if their foliage is allowed to mature and begin dying down naturally before lawn-mowing season begins.

☐ **Paperwhites**—To force these bulbs to bloom inside, start in mid-November for fragrant blossoms throughout the holiday season. It takes about two to three weeks from planting to flowering. Paperwhite kits can make great holiday gifts for your children's teachers.

☐ **Peonies**—Now is the time to plant peonies in the Upper, Middle, and Lower South. Select a sunny location with fertile, well drained soil. Choose a permanent spot because peonies prefer to be undisturbed for many years. Time-tested selections include 'Festiva Maxima' (white) and 'Sarah Bernhardt' (pink).

☐ **Roses**—Add these to your garden this month in a sunny, well-drained area. Dig a hole deep enough for the root ball and slightly wider. Water the root ball and hole, and backfill with sphagnum peat moss or other organic matter. Then add 3 inches of mulch, and water again. Good floribunda choices include 'El Capitan,' 'Fashion,' and 'Allgold.' Hybrid tea selections such as 'Tropicana' or 'Lady Elgin' are also nice additions to the garden.

☐ **Strawberries**—Set out early in the month to allow plants time to establish roots before the weather cools. It is important to plant at the proper depth. Set in the ground so that the crown is even with the surrounding soil level. If planted too deep, they'll rot. If planted too shallow, they'll dry out.

☐ **Trees and shrubs**—Now is the ideal time to plant trees and shrubs in the South. The cool months ahead allow plants to establish root systems before next year's growing season. Select one that will be the right height for the location at maturity. Dig a hole wider than the root ball but the same depth. Backfill with good soil, water well, and stake, if needed. Water daily the first month; then check, and water when dry.

PRUNE

☐ **Spring-flowering shrubs**—It is too late to prune shrubs that flower in the spring, such as azaleas, spiraeas, quince, and forsythias. They have already set their flowerbuds, and pruning now would remove next year's blooms.

☐ **Trees**—Now is a good time to prune deciduous trees. Remove crossing branches, and thin out the tree so light can reach the center when leaves reappear. There should only be one main trunk (leader), so eliminate or reduce any potential competitors. Be sure to water when soil is dry. Rake and add leaves to compost pile. ▶

CONTROL

☐ **Pests**—Check buds and the undersides of leaves and stems on fall annuals for mites, aphids, and caterpillars. Control mites and aphids with a soap and water solution or horticultural oil spray. Most caterpillars can be picked off.

TIP OF THE MONTH

My amaryllis bulbs failed to bloom outdoors for several years. I figured that unusually mild winters might be responsible. So I dug up the bulbs in the fall, placed them in the refrigerator for about six weeks, and then replanted them. It worked. They bloomed the next spring.

JANICE C. MOFFITT
HILTON HEAD ISLAND,
SOUTH CAROLINA

tulips

TRIED AND TRUE

Now's the time to plant our choices for surefire success next spring.

Teardrop-shaped tulip bulbs, sleeping and devoid of roots, pushed down into the dormant winter soil will rise to produce one of spring's most coveted flowers. Their satin-soft petals come in almost every color imaginable. Unlike the daffodil, found nearly everywhere, tulips have a certain air about them. They look a bit aristocratic standing straight with their heads held high.

As the sun warms the soil, roots grow from the base of each awakening bulb. Soft green foliage with pointed tips breaks through the earth first. Then tightly pressed buds appear, looking like small eggs balanced on delicate, pencil-thin stems. As the stems stretch, the blooms grow bigger and fatter each day. These stunning, long-stemmed, chalice-shaped flowers can usually last up to a month. Even as the blooms decline in the warming sun, they bow out gracefully. Gradually the petals flare back and peel away, drifting lightly to the ground. The fallen petals topping the garden floor resemble colorful confetti and signal the end of the tulip's metamorphosis.

The tulips I'm referring to aren't the small species selections or the fancy or multiple petal ones. They're the large-cupped selections, the ones that have a simple yet classic appearance. Each year we plant thousands of bulbs in the fall and winter. We test them to see how they grow and look in our gardens. Over the years we've noticed that a few tulips—such as 'Apricot Beauty,' 'Ivory Floradale,' 'Golden Oxford,' 'Mrs John T. Scheepers,' and 'Pink Impression'—consistently perform well. We've gathered our favorites for you in a box on page 194.

We treat these bulbs as annuals and pull them up once they've finished blooming. The large-flowering tulips don't perennialize well in the South because of warm temperatures. But their presence in the garden is unmatched, so they're worth the effort.

Tulips can be purchased from mail-order catalogs or from your local garden center. The bulbs usually begin arriving at stores around October, and they are often sold in bulk in plastic mesh bags. Most bulbs are covered or partially covered

BY CHARLIE THIGPEN / PHOTOGRAPHY VAN CHAPLIN

FAR LEFT: *The silky flowers of 'Ivory Floradale' start out cream-colored and bleach to a bright white.*

BELOW: *'Pink Impression' has large, long-lasting blooms atop sturdy stems, making it one of the most popular tulips.*

with brown paper-thin sheaths. Carefully inspect bulbs before purchasing them. They should be fat and fleshy like an onion and free of mold.

Bulbs should be refrigerated until time to plant. (Never put them in the freezer.) In the Lower and Coastal South, chill bulbs for eight weeks before setting them out in early January. Don't refrigerate bulbs in sealed plastic bags. Instead, store them in a paper bag in the vegetable bin, away from any fruit. Ripening fruit can release ethylene and cause bulbs to bloom prematurely. In the Upper and Middle South, the best time to plant tulips is around Thanksgiving. They prefer a sunny or slightly shaded, well-drained site. They can stand alone or be mixed with annuals such as pansies. For the greatest impact, plant large blocks of the same selection together.

Tulip bulbs should be planted pointy end up. In the Upper South, place bulbs 8 to 10 inches deep, and they may bloom for several years, even though the flower size will decline each spring. Because they don't perennialize in the Middle, Lower, and Coastal South, you can bury them only 3 to 4 inches deep. Add a bulb fertilizer to the soil to give them a jump start. You can till it into the ground before planting or just sprinkle a little in each hole. Special tools are made for bulb planting, but we prefer to use a small handheld mattock. If you have only a few bulbs to plant, a small garden trowel will

TESTED TULIPS

- orange—'Daydream,' 'Juan,' 'Princess Irene'
- pink—'Pink Impression'
- salmon—'Apricot Beauty'
- red—'Dynamite,' 'Come-back,' 'Kingsblood'
- white—'Ivory Floradale,' 'Maureen'
- yellow—'Golden Oxford,' 'Mrs John T. Scheepers'

LEFT: *Look for bulbs that are fat and fleshy (top). Avoid ones that are moldy or dried (bottom).* BELOW, LEFT: *Plant tulips with pansies for a nice spring show. A small handheld mattock is useful when planting bulbs.*

work fine.

One of the easiest and most effective ways to use tulips is in a planter or container alone or mixed with annuals. It doesn't take many bulbs to make a big show. Planters positioned around your entryway, patio, or deck will elevate the flowers, making them more prominent.

Tulips also look right at home in a flower border—but because of their height, be sure to plant them toward the center of the border. Use annuals, such as pansies, alyssum, or English daisies in the foreground; place iris, foxgloves, or ornamental grasses as a tall backdrop.

No matter how you decide to use tulips, always plant a few extras for cutting. Their strong stems and flowers hold up well when cut. Many are fragrant, so bringing them inside allows you the opportunity to breathe in their sweet scent.

Believe it or not, fall is the time to start thinking about your spring garden. Buy a few sleepy tulip bulbs now, and you'll be glad you did when they rise and burst into bloom, filling your yard with their distinctive bell-shaped beauty.

(For sources turn to pages 234–235.)

ABOVE, LEFT: *Tulips are attractive flower arrangements, so plant extras for cutting. White tulips, blue phlox, and some greenery make a stunning combination.* ABOVE, CENTER: *'Golden Oxford' has lemony yellow petals and looks great in a container mixed with white pansies.* ABOVE, RIGHT: *'Apricot Beauty' has salmon blooms and a sweet fragrance.*

PHOTOGRAPHS: VAN CHAPLIN

Good Soil Is Job #1

Whether you're a seasoned gardener or just a beginner, one simple truth remains—the better your soil, the better your garden.

It's true. Good soil absolutely means lusher growth, less fertilizing, fewer pests, and stronger plants.

My neighbor Chris McDaniel found this out when he decided to redo the foundation planting in front of his house. His kindly builder had stripped away every ounce of original topsoil, and then generously applied a compacted layer of red clay subsoil over the entire yard. Plastic plants might have done okay in that stuff, but I think it's safe to say the living ones wouldn't be living for long.

Chris wanted to yank out all the old, scraggly plants and start over that summer. I convinced him to wait until fall. It is an ideal time for planting in most of the South, because while plants stop growing up top, down below they're still working on roots. By the time next spring rolls around, they have a head start on trees and shrubs planted in spring.

When starting out with awful soil, you have three options—dig out and replace the original soil (which can be both time-consuming and expensive); build raised beds filled with new soil atop the original soil; or improve the original soil. Chris and I chose the last option.

Chris's front beds extend out about 20 feet on either side of the steps. Our first order of business was bringing in a pickup truck filled with good topsoil and spreading half on each side of the steps. One tip for beginners—know the source of the topsoil and/or inspect it before you order it. You want good, clean, loose, dark earth—not clay, rocks, branches, and trash. Never substitute uncomposted cow or horse manure, unless you want seedlings of everything the animal ate coming up in your yard.

Topsoil isn't enough by itself. It usually lacks the organic matter that most plants crave. So Chris added sphagnum peat moss—about 1 (4-cubic-foot) bale for every 30 square feet of bed. Composted manure is an acceptable alternative. Some folks substitute pine bark, but I don't like using it up against the house. Wood attracts termites, and I'd just as soon they schedule their picnic at somebody else's place.

After using a hard rake to spread the peat moss, Chris added the final ingredient—sand. He spread 3 to 4 (40-pound) bags on each side of the steps. Though sand is inert, it loosens soil and aids aeration and drainage, as does or-

TOP, LEFT: *Fall is a great time for planting, but you need to prepare the soil.* TOP, CENTER: *High-quality topsoil is loose, crumbly, and brown. It shouldn't contain trash, clay, rocks, or limbs.* TOP, RIGHT: *Sphagnum peat moss is a good source of organic matter, which loosens heavy soil and enriches it.* ABOVE: *Tilling in sand improves aeration and drainage, making it easier for roots to grow.*

ganic matter. And when dealing with clay soil, good aeration and drainage are just what the gardener ordered.

Now it was time to mix together the topsoil, peat moss, and sand. Chris rented a heavy-duty power tiller for the job. These machines can be a handful to control, but Chris is a big, very macho guy. (Just ask him.) However, smaller tillers, weighing as little as 25 pounds, are readily available and more easily operated.

Blessed with practically perfect soil, Chris was now ready to plant trees and shrubs—and not a single one was plastic.
Steve Bender

Color
THANKSGIVING
WITH
Mums

*Try these simple arrange-
ments for a fresh look for
the holidays.*

BY ELLEN RILEY
PHOTOGRAPHY
RALPH ANDERSON

Chrysanthemums are fall's flowers, bringing the season into your home with inexhaustible blooms. Easily dismissed as rigid and out-of-date, they are, in fact, the best cut-flower bargain around. Mums offer shades that equal the flaming foliage of maples and oaks or mirror the colors of an autumn sunset. Enjoy them, and use them liberally.

ABOVE: *A warm welcome awaits with this tapestry of flowers on the front door.* LEFT: *A partitioned box provides an easy way to display some of the harvest's prettiest players.*

RIGHT: *These tiny 'Kermit' mum spheres round out Thanksgiving decorations.*
FAR RIGHT: *Long and overflowing, this centerpiece is an inviting part of each guest's place setting.*
BELOW: *Lady apples and pomegranates intermingle with large mums and bright, frilly kale.*

While chrysanthemums are perfectly suited to easy arrangements reflecting Thanksgiving's bountiful hospitality, some of their other endearing qualities are ready availability and economical price. Purchase plentiful bouquets while you're grocery shopping—you'll get an abundance of flowers for a very small investment. Or visit your local flower shop for more novel selections.

GREETINGS

A wreath on the door packed with brilliant blooms greets guests with a spirited welcome. 'Viking,' a brown-eyed daisy type, is placed in rows around the wreath as if it were a ribbon wound around the form. In between, similarly shaded mums fill in, with each flower touching the next.

Try this colorful flower ring in other ways, perhaps as a focal point on the mantel along with branches of fall foliage. Or place it in a large, shallow saucer as a centerpiece. Fill the middle with small pumpkins, gourds, and squash, or add a cluster of pillar candles in deep shades of burgundy, rust, and gold.

A HARVEST TABLE SETTING

Capture the spirit of your Thanksgiving dinner with an overflowing centerpiece. Our arrangement is contained in an old-fashioned chicken feeder filled with florist foam. You might

WHO'S WHO AMONG MUMS

There are several different flower styles to choose from. Here are the names that go with the blooms.

Cushion mums: This type of bloom has no visible disk. It is purely petals, tightly packed from the center to the edges.

Button mums: A smaller version of the cushion mum, this usually grows no larger than the size of a quarter.

Daisy mums: This style blossom has a round, central disk with petals surrounding it. Almost always yellow, newer hybrids may have a different "eye" color, such as 'Viking,' with a brown center.

Football mums: This is the big boy we all remember from high school football games. About the size of a softball, the blooms are held high on thick, sturdy stems.

also use a weathered wooden toolbox, or simply place blocks of the foam in saucers lengthwise down the table.

Again, it's easy to purchase your materials while grocery shopping. Choose large pompon football mums and a bunch or two with smaller blooms in complementary tones.

From the produce section, bring home heads of colorful kale and selections of persimmons, pomegranates, lady apples, and artichokes. To make arranging simple and avoid a structured look, purchase odd numbers of these items.

Beginning with the kale, secure leaves in the florist foam down the length of the container, alternating sides.

Fill in between with the large chrysanthemums, and attach the fruit and vegetables with wooden florist picks or skewers. Cluster the smaller flowers, filling in any gaps.

Trickle a few blossoms and other elements onto the table surrounding the centerpiece. Monitor the florist foam, keeping it moist to preserve the flowers' freshness.

ROUNDING IT OUT

Smaller arrangements also have a place in this holiday's decor. Give chrysanthemums a fresh look in an unexpected way. Brilliant green, button-type 'Kermit' mum spheres mimic osage oranges and add an autumnal accent to a window ledge. Placed on a narrow breadboard with candles and red daisy mums, they create a feel of easy elegance. This easy-to-make arrangement also works well on a mantel or long table.

Fill an old sectioned wooden box with kumquats, cranberries, flowers, pears, and candles in complementary colors. This versatile arrangement could either serve as a centerpiece on a small dining table, or it can be placed on a sideboard or tea caddy in order to complement other arrangements.

Chrysanthemums are the quintessential fall flower. Use them to add easy, fabulous color to your Thanksgiving celebration. See page 200 for hands-on instructions for making the wreath and spheres.

Choose green button-type 'Kermit' mums for an unusual display.

Easy Does It Thanksgiving

Fast and simple, try these decorations for big impact at your holiday table.

The Thanksgiving arrangements featured on pages 196–199 are all quick and easy. Here, we provide instructions for the spheres and wreath. Our projects use many flowers, but the beauty of mums is their low price.

SPHERES

Florist foam balls are available in an assortment of sizes. We used 2-inch spheres for our project. When surrounded with flowers, the balls appear almost twice that size.

Soak the forms in a mixture of water and flower food diluted according to label directions. Cut flower stems short—about an inch under the bloom head. Push the stems into the form, with flowers touching or slightly overlapping. Add flowers until the sphere is completely covered.

THE WREATH

Begin with a foam wreath form, and soak it thoroughly in water. As with the spheres, add a small pack of flower food to the water.

Wrap a piece of florist tape in one area around the wreath several times to reinforce the form, and then fasten a piece of wire over it to make a hanger. Position the wire loop at the form's plastic back for easy hanging.

As before, cut each flower underneath the bloom head, leaving a stem about 1 inch long. Push the stems into the florist foam so that the blossoms hug the surface of the foam. Fill the form completely, grouping together similar colors.

In our wreath, we repeated the brown-eyed 'Viking' mum around the form to establish a color pattern. Then we filled in around them with flowers in complementary shades.

NICE TO KNOW

Florist foam spheres and wreath forms come in a number of sizes. When deciding how large a wreath should be, consider weight. Once the foam is moist and filled with flowers, the arrangement will become heavier. For your first go at this, think small. Once you are familiar with the weightiness of the matter, you can try other sizes.

The arrangements will last about a week or longer if the florist foam is kept moist, so water them every two days. A simple method is to place them in the kitchen sink and spray gently to moisten the foam. Allow to drain completely.

Ellen Riley

SUPPLIES

Many grocery stores have complete floral departments. This is a good source for basic flower supplies. Crafts stores also stock a reasonable assortment of equipment, or consult your local florist for the items mentioned here.

A good mail-order source for supplies is Dorothy Biddle Service. To request a catalog, contact them at 348 Greeley Lake Road, Greeley, PA 18425, (570) 226-3239 or by E-mail at retail@dorothybiddle.com.

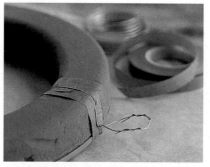

ABOVE, LEFT: *Wrap florist tape around the form to prevent the hanging wire from slicing through it.* **ABOVE, RIGHT:** *Pack flowers tightly for a full display.*

ABOVE: *'Midnight' is a great choice for a space away from direct light. Dropping no leaves, it will remain bushy and full.*
LEFT: *The stature of 'Too Little' makes it a perfect plant for a prominent place, such as this table.*

TROUBLESHOOTING

Your ficus will tell you if it is unhappy. Here are the clues.

■ **Yellow leaves dropping:** A change in light or location will cause leaf drop. Give it time, and it will adjust. If you have not moved the plant recently, it is asking for more water. The more light the plant receives, the more water it requires.

■ **Green leaves dropping:** Too much water, so back off a little. Be sure the roots are not sitting in water.

A New Face for Ficus

Nothing stays the same. There's always something new coming along, whether it's a fashion trend, a fresh taste in food, or a stylish car. The plant world is no different, with growers hard at work hybridizing old favorites into novel selections to keep gardeners interested.

A great example of this effort is the common ficus tree *(Ficus benjamina)*. The next time you go shopping for houseplants, look for two new introductions that will remind you of this familiar tree, but with a twist.

The first time you see 'Too Little,' you'll think, "I know it's a ficus, but it's so small." This dwarf tree matures to a height of only 14 inches, with a head about 10 inches across. 'Too Little' produces masses of tiny, shiny green leaves with slightly curled edges. It is a true ficus tree in miniature, and like the big one, needs very bright light and water before the soil becomes dry.

Display 'Too Little' in a shallow glazed container to evoke the image of bonsai. This diminutive selection gives the appearance of an aged tree, without all the training and fuss of the Oriental art form. Underplant the tree with prostrate foliage plants, such as nerve plant or creeping fig; or leave the shallow surface roots exposed for a true bonsai look.

'Midnight' ficus is another new kid on the block. This selection can be easily recognized by its thick, glossy, almost black leaves. New growth is brilliant green, and the contrast between the two is stunning. 'Midnight' grows thick, bushy, and upright, and it may ultimately reach a height of 8 feet. Be sure to keep its mature size in mind when looking for a spot to put your plant.

This selection's most unique attribute isn't its foliage, but its willingness to withstand lower light. Most ficus trees need direct sun or very bright light, but 'Midnight' adjusts to less light without shedding a leaf. When grown in a darker place, it also requires less water than its bright-light-seeking cousins.

Like all other ficus, feed these new selections with a well-balanced, liquid fertilizer, such as 20-20-20. During fall and winter, once a month is sufficient. Spring and summer are more active growth times, so feed every other week.
Ellen Riley

Regal Rex Begonias

Leaves pretty enough to be a royal robe make this easy-to-grow houseplant one to own.

Within the hierarchy of the begonia family, *Begonia rex* has been crowned king of the clan. Splendid colors, grand texture, and lavishly patterned foliage set the rexes apart from other houseplants. Shades ranging from silver and soft pink to dark purple and magenta with splashes of bright green show off as brilliantly as crown jewels.

Plant size and shape vary greatly; some selections may produce leaves the size of a lady's hand, while others are no larger than a silver dollar. All rex begonias are rhizomatous, meaning their thick stems creep laterally across the soil, producing leaf buds upward and roots downward. A type often associated with rex begonias is the iron

cross—with each lime green leaf emblazoned with a distinct, dark mark. This plant, *B. masoniana,* is also rhizomatous, allowing it into family gatherings with the rexes.

EASY CARE

Rex begonias are not picky once you understand their basic needs. During short winter days, plants require the bright light of a northern window or a little early-morning eastern sun. In summer, light needs diminish.

Being a bit discriminating, a rex begonia craves its comfort; good quality, well-drained potting soil is of utmost importance. This plant likes moist, but not soggy, soil. When it stays too wet, stems turn mushy and leaves drop.

Water thoroughly about once a week or before soil becomes dry, and never allow the plant to sit in a saucer of water.

Rex begonias enjoy high humidity, especially during winter months with drying indoor heat. If misting is your thing, this is an opportunity to indulge a houseplant. Leaves may be sprayed daily and will flourish with this attention. Crispy, dried-out leaf edges are the sign of low humidity.

Feed your begonia monthly during the winter and every other week throughout the rest of the year. An all-purpose liquid fertilizer such as 20-20-20 is a good choice.

Rex begonias are relatively slow growers, usually producing six or

LEFT: *Bright light on a windowsill is a perfect setting for this iron cross begonia (left) and its companion rex begonias.* RIGHT: *Different colors and patterns combine beautifully in this old painted box.* BOTTOM, RIGHT: *The colorful leaves pair well with blooming houseplants, such as this kalanchoe. Keep plants in their individual pots so you can water them easily in the sink and ensure proper drainage.*

seven new leaves a year. Occasionally small flowers occur during summer months. Keep plants actively producing new foliage by removing flowers while they are in bud stage.

SHOW THEM OFF

This plant makes a striking display, whether used as a solitary specimen standing alone in a decorative pot or holding court with other begonias and blooming houseplants. Assemble the plants in pretty color combinations, varying leaf size and shape as well as shades.

In collective arrangements, always keep these plants in separate containers. Remove them from the decorative pot to water and groom, and allow them to drain well before placing them back in the larger vessel.

With the holidays rapidly approaching, we look toward rich color and texture for decorative touches. This easy-to-grow houseplant brings an instant spot of aristocratic elegance to any indoor landscape.

Ellen Riley

(For sources turn to pages 234–235.)

REX BEGONIAS
At a Glance

Light: bright, indirect light, such as a northern window
Water: moist, but not soggy
Feed: in winter, once a month; twice monthly the rest of the year, with all-purpose liquid fertilizer, such as 20-20-20
Comments: enjoys high humidity; mist daily if in dry heat during winter months

Pyracantha branch adds winter color (See pages 212–213.)

December

Checklist
for
December

EDITOR'S NOTEBOOK

You might buy a tree just for its beautiful flowers or leaves, but I bet you've never bought one for its bark. Up until now, we should say. Meet the coral bark Japanese maple *(Acer palmatum* 'Sangokaku'). Athough the leaves of this small tree turn a nice yellow in fall, the plant is really at its best in winter, when leaves drop to reveal spectacular, glowing red bark. In spring 2001, we included several of these trees in our display at the Southeastern Flower Show in Atlanta to introduce our new *Southern Living* Plant Collection from Monrovia. People took one look at the maples and went berserk. Little old ladies were practically hefting them up on their shoulders to spirit them away. To find a nursery near you that carries coral bark Japanese maple and the rest of our collection from Monrovia, call 1-888-752-6848. And if you see a little old lady carrying a maple on her head, be nice, and lend her a hand.

Steve Bender

□ **Cold protection**—Identify plants in your yard that will be susceptible to cold damage. In the Lower and Coastal South, banana bougainvillea, avocado, hibiscus, and poinsettia all need protection. Collect boxes, sheets, newspapers, or burlap, and store in a handy location to place over those plants. Uncover plants as soon as temperatures rise. Add mulch to beds, especially around tender plants. Mulch can raise the temperature a couple of degrees during cold weather. If a freeze is expected in your area, make sure your plants have been watered well. Group plants together on a patio or porch, or move them to a protected location.

□ **Containers**—In the Upper and Middle South, empty clay pots and turn them upside down to prevent them from freezing and cracking. If possible, stack them in a basement or garage.

□ **Cyclamen and poinsettia care**—Both cyclamen and poinsettias like bright, indirect light. Keep out of drafts near windows and away from heater vents. Water plants carefully, and provide them adequate drainage. They should not sit in saucers of water. Clip flowers as they fade. ▶

□ **Garden tools**—Clean, sharpen, repair, and oil your tools before putting them up for the year. Also, have your lawnmower serviced before storing.

Christmas tree care—It is important to keep your tree well watered so it will not dry out and begin shedding needles. Before placing the tree in the stand, make a fresh cut in the trunk about 1 inch above the existing cut. The new cut will allow the tree to absorb water more easily. You may be surprised at how much water the tree will need. Water well and often. Remember that a dry tree is a fire hazard.

□ **Greenery**—Cuttings of magnolia, pine, holly, and boxwood last longer as holiday decorations if you soak the stems in a bucket of water overnight before using them.

□ **Herbs**—Dill, cilantro, parsley, borage, and lovage are ready for harvest this month in the Coastal and Tropical South. When the morning dew has dried completely, trim desired amount to dry or use fresh. Avoid damaged or diseased leaves. Store fresh herbs in the refrigerator and dried ones in airtight containers.

□ **Mulch**—If you have not already mulched them, trees, shrubs, and perennials will benefit from 2 to 3 inches of organic material, such as pine straw, shredded leaves, or shredded bark. This will help prevent cold damage, keep in moisture, and protect roots through winter.

□ **Rosemary**—Middle and Upper South gardeners should be careful not to bring a potted rosemary plant indoors before it receives a light frost. Once indoors, keep it in a cool, well-lit room.

☐ **Bedding plants**—In the Coastal and Tropical South, add a few uncommon bedding plants—such as 'Sunburst' gazanias, Vintage Series stock, or 'Wonderland' Iceland poppies—to your winter garden.

◀ **Bulbs**—Pre-refrigerated tulips and hyacinths are ready to plant during December and early January in the Lower and Coastal South. Choose a sunny site where the soil has been amended by incorporating 3 to 5 inches of organic material—such as sphagnum peat moss, composted pine bark, or compost—into porous, well-drained soil. Incorporate around 3 to 5 pounds of cottonseed, alfalfa meal, or bulb booster fertilizer into 100 square feet of bed area. For continuous spring blooms, set bulbs amid masses of pansies, violas, sweet alyssum, or dianthus.

☐ **Camellias**—In the Middle, Lower, and Coastal South, now is a good time to select and plant camellias for your garden. Plants are blooming, and you can choose the flower colors you prefer. 'Yuletide' camellia *(Camellia sasanqua* 'Yuletide') is an especially nice gift for your gardening friends, as it will bloom during the holidays for years to come and remind them of your generosity.

☐ **Living Christmas trees**—Make sure live trees are right for your climate after the holiday. Leyland cypress, Norfolk Island pine, deodar cedar, or red cedar work well in the Lower, Coastal, and Tropical South. Leave the tree in its original container for display. Water only when dry. It can stay indoors for up to two weeks before being moved outside.

☐ **Winter greens**—In the Lower and Coastal South, you can still sow seeds of radishes, turnips, and mustard for a late-winter or early-spring harvest.

◀ **Fruit trees**—Apple trees can be pruned this month. Be sure to take out branches that are growing inward so that light can reach the middle of the tree. Also, citrus is ready for harvesting now, even if it is still slightly green. Give it a taste test if in doubt. Pick as soon as the fruit has ripened. This will prevent spoilage, which can attract unwanted critters.

☐ **Holly**—Harvest boughs this month making sure to use good pruning practices—they're great to use for seasonal decorating. The natural form of the holly plant should still be obvious after pruning. Many native and Oriental hollies are well adapted to Southern gardens. Low-growing forms (2 to 4 feet) include dwarf yaupon and dwarf Chinese varieties. Intermediate-size hollies include 'Dwarf Burford,' needlepoint, and yaupon selections such as 'Pride of Houston.' Large-growing hollies are ideal for evergreen hedges and specimens. 'Nellie R. Stevens,' 'Greenleaf,' 'Savannah,' standard Burford, and 'William Fleming' weeping yaupon can become small trees after a few years.

December notes:

᳕

TIP OF THE MONTH

I planted nandina bushes in my yard expecting to use the red berries in Christmas arrangements, but the birds seemed to think the berries were just for them. So last year, I hung jingle bells on the stems near the berries. Now the birds go elsewhere for food, and I have beautiful berries.

ELLEN DEMOTT
RINGGOLD, VIRGINIA

Create grand style in no time at all
with this evergreen Southern classic.

Magnolia
Decks the Halls

Magnolia is the quintessential Southern Christmas greenery, with its lustrous leaves coloring our homes in elegant style. Full-figured branches are easy to arrange down the length of a table, on a mantel, or in a wreath. Use them liberally to create generous, great-looking holiday decorations.

TABLE MATTERS

Dinner guests warrant special treatment any time, but during the holidays we want our table decor to really shine. With minimal fuss, using magnolia is an uncomplicated and elegant way to set a spectacular surrounding for your festive meal. Cut branch tips 4 or 5 inches long; arrange them down the table length as you would a fabric runner. Place the tight leaf clusters with their prettiest sides facing diners, hiding the woody stems under glossy foliage. Add polished ruby-colored apples for depth and burnished gold ribbons to glimmer in candlelight. For fun, we used a solid shade of gold and a second patterned gold ribbon, weaving them among the foliage and onto the table. Wired edges help ribbon stay where you place it.

Candles are a must for any celebration. Votives in clear containers tucked here and there along the magnolia runner's perimeter illuminate the setting. Elevate other candles using festive glassware. Place the votives in martini glasses or other wide goblets, and hold them in place with stemless nandina or holly berries. Nudge these taller candles into the centerpiece, allowing them to spread their flickering warmth over the table.

COME INSIDE

The mantel can be a decorating challenge, but you want a look of gracious abundance. Magnolia comes to the rescue with an effortless solution. Cut branches of varying lengths, ranging from 5 to 10 inches long. First, place the longest stems down the mantel's length. Then fill in gaps with the shorter ones, allowing some foliage to rest over the front edge.

Add candles in an odd-numbered cluster as the center of attention, or fill the ledge's length with pillars. Stagger heights, removing

ABOVE: *Guests will feel merry and bright when greeted with this beautiful tablescape. Made from only a few ingredients, the look is festive and luxurious.*
LEFT: *Brightly polished apples, candlelight, and glistening ribbon contribute colorful pizzazz to the magnolia runner.*

BY ELLEN RILEY
PHOTOGRAPHY
JEAN ALLSOPP

any leaves that may come in contact with a burning wick. Tuck various red berries among the magnolia leaves for added color and texture. Nandina clusters hold their own, size wise, among the large, glossy foliage. Bunch smaller holly sprigs together for greater impact.

The final touch is simple; weave shimmering ribbon, in gold or another holiday color, into the arrangement for a bit of glitzy sparkle.

FESTIVE FOLIAGE

Magnolia's fabulous and versatile foliage makes an elegant backdrop for other holiday elements. This Southern favorite is also easy to work with. Follow these 4 quick steps to create the decoration pictured to the right.

STEP 1: *Fill the mantel with freshly cut magnolia branches, that range in size from 5 to 10 inches in length.*
STEP 2: *Add candles to the mix, using odd numbers and varying heights.*
STEP 3: *Tuck clusters of nandina, holly, or other berries among the magnolia.*
STEP 4: *Finally, add a metallic ribbon to weave it all together.*

WELL-CONDITIONED FOLIAGE

If magnolia is abundant, you may choose to refresh your arrangements during the holiday season. Out of water, the thick leaves remain fresh and supple for about five days; then they begin to dry and curl. Placed in a water reservoir, they last significantly longer. Here are a few secrets.

■ Take a bucket of warm water into the garden along with very sharp pruners. Make the cut at a sharp angle, and place foliage immediately into the container.
■ Once indoors, recut the woody stems, and soak them overnight in fresh water.
■ When practical for the arrangement's style, put stems in a vase or moist florist foam for longevity.

WHO'S WHO

If your landscape does not include a magnolia tree, consider planting one or several, if you have space. There are numerous *Magnolia grandiflora* selections, each with its own decorating virtues. Small-leaved selections are beautiful in wreaths and table arrangements. Larger-leaved selections are perfect for filling a fireplace or crafting a grand garland. Here are a few suggestions with Christmas decorations in mind.
'Little Gem': A slow-growing, small magnolia with tight clusters of deep green leaves. Foliage is small, with the leaf undersides a rich velvety-brown. This tree adapts well to containers.
'Bracken's Brown Beauty': Larger than 'Little Gem,' with leaves about 5 inches long. The foliage, with fuzzy brown undersides, is considered one of the small-leaved selections.
'Majestic Beauty': A large-leaved selection with a densely branching form. A luxurious tree providing plentiful decorating material.

LEFT: *Simply rake fallen debris into a shallow row, and push your lawnmower over the material several times to chop it into fine pieces.* ABOVE: *Spread the chopped leaves and pine needles over the surface of your planting beds. It makes excellent, attractive mulch that stays firmly in place. As it decomposes, it enriches the soil.*

Get Your Mulch for Free

TIME TO LIME?

Not all leaves acidify the soil, but oak leaves and pine needles certainly do. This is fine for acid-loving plants, such as azalea, rhododendron, camellia, gardenia, blueberry, and dogwood. However, many vegetables and flowers prefer soil that's only slightly acid or neutral (pH 6.5 to 7.0). Adding lime is an easy way to counteract acidity. Now is a good time to do it.

A simple soil test kit available at garden and home centers can tell you the soil's approximate pH. For a precise recommendation of exactly how much (if any) lime to add to your soil, you'll need to get a soil test kit from your local cooperative Extension service.

It's lucky Moses and the Israelites didn't own houses in the suburbs. Why? Because when manna fell from heaven, they'd probably take a cue from their neighbors and rake it to the curb.

To a gardener, December's fallen leaves and pine needles are just like manna. Each leaf and needle contains a larder of organic matter—absolutely the best material for loosening clay or improving the water- and nutrient-holding capacity of sand. Organic matter feeds legions of plants, earthworms, and micro-organisms. Yet what do most of us do with this treasure? Rake it to the street for the city to take away.

Not me. Maybe it's because I think that landfills are for unrecyclables, such as rusted washing machines or albums by Air Supply. Or maybe it's because I'm cheap and can't stand the thought of buying sphagnum peat moss and ground bark when all this free organic matter is falling down around me.

In any case, I don't rake leaves into the street. Instead, I rake them into long, shallow rows about 6 inches deep. Then I set my lawnmower on its highest setting and run over the pile, making enough passes to completely chop it up.

I like to use a mulching mower, because it's designed to chop leaves into little pieces, but you can use a regular bagging mower—just take off the bag. The first time you run over the leaves, you'll invariably miss some. So rake them all into a pile again, and run over them once more. You'll be amazed at how small that big pile of leaves becomes.

Carefully gather that finely shredded material—it's garden gold. Take it to your flowerbed, shrub border, or vegetable garden, and spread a 2-inch-thick layer over the soil surface and around any existing plants. The shredded leaves make excellent, attractive mulch—they stay in place and don't wash or blow away. Even more important, as the leaves slowly decompose, they add vital organic matter to the soil, improving its ability to support abundant life. Do this every fall, and before long, you'll have the richest soil on the block. And you won't have paid a dime.

Steve Bender

Winter Berry Buffet

Birds and berries both add colorful warmth to a winter garden.

They are not bound by fences or tied, as we are, to the ground. Birds are free and wild. They can also be cold and hungry, especially during long, dark days. By winter, when the cornucopia of autumn seeds is a distant memory, wild birds are deeply grateful to any gardener who planted shrubs with long-lasting, edible berries. They show that gratitude with a colorful, vocal presence—bright bursts of feathered activity accented by running commentary on the ownership of every tiny fruit.

In addition to getting birds to grace your winter garden, you get the pleasure of showy berries when you plant the right shrubs. It's a win-win situation. Many of the standard ornamental shrubs familiar to all Southerners are well-suited to the task.

BY LIZ DRUITT / PHOTOGRAPHY VAN CHAPLIN, SYLVIA MARTIN

pyracantha

yaupon

possumhaw

yellow-berried yaupon

can be either pruned as shrubs or limbed up as small trees. And because they are native, there's almost always another one within pollinating range to help your female holly bushes load up with succulent berries. Birds that forage on holly berries include robins, blue jays, cedar waxwings, Eastern bluebirds, mockingbirds, red-bellied woodpeckers, brown thrashers, rufous-sided towhees, and hermit thrushes, so you'll have plenty of activity to watch as they wrangle and mingle in your yaupons and possumhaws.

If you haven't quite filled your garden with the various hollies, you might find room for a cherry laurel as well. This evergreen shrub or small tree can be an elegant specimen in full sun or blend well into a shady understory planting. This plant's black, shiny fruits attract mockingbirds, robins, cedar waxwings, and Eastern bluebirds, and they also offer a contrast to the reds, yellows, and oranges of the hollies.

Another favorite is pyracantha, or firethorn. It thrives in full sunlight and has a huge feathered following, which includes the species already listed. The orange or red berries that flame in the winter landscape will also warm the little bellies of hungry cardinals, purple finches, and the amazing pileated woodpeckers. It's worth almost any amount of effort to attract these big, angular birds that look like a cross between feathered dinosaurs and Joan Crawford in shoulder pads. Fortunately, too, pyracantha is easy to grow.

Even nandina, though not every bird's first choice, will be nibbled on by mockingbirds, cedar waxwings, and robins. And, if their berries weren't all stripped by hungry beaks in the late fall, you can look for winter action in your ligustrums, privets, cotoneasters, and Chinese photinia, as well as in the native wax myrtles and red cedars.

Just make sure that you include something that will help keep feathers and soul together for the winter birds. They may have the freedom of the air, but only you can offer them the freedom of your garden.

Hollies are the first choice for long-lasting bird forage. As a group, these shrubs provide great cover and nesting sites, as well as edible berries. Because the berries ripen at different rates, even on one bush, they provide food for at least a couple of months.

Burford hollies have the advantage of being self-fertile, producing crops of berries without a separate pollinator. Native hollies (including such favorites as winterberry, possumhaw, yaupon, dahoon holly, and American holly) are equally pretty and perhaps even more versatile in landscapes. Many of them

teach an old wreath new tricks

It may look hard, but all you have to do is stack wreaths of fruit and greenery for a welcoming holiday look.

The most fabulous decorations for your home can begin very simply—with wreaths made from an assortment of fruit and cuttings of evergreen foliage. Combined to create an elegant topiary atop a garden urn, they resemble luxuriant plants encircled with glistening fruit. Give a coordinating, natural look to your home's front door with a similar wreath. If you have double front doors, you can even divide the wreath in half, and place one piece on each door. Follow our step-by-step instructions to make these beautiful front-door accents that herald this season of festivities.

BY JULIA HAMILTON / PHOTOGRAPHY JEAN ALLSOPP
STYLING MARY LEIGH FITTS

Tailor our designs to suit the style and the spirit of your home, and then enjoy your most beautiful season of holiday decorating ever.

TIERED TOPIARIES

Topiaries the size of those we assembled (about 5 feet tall, including the urn) each require six wire or straw wreath forms for greenery and four straw forms for the fruit. You'll need a good quantity of apples, lemons, and oranges and a lot of boxwood, fir, and/or other kinds of fresh foliage.

First, plan your topiary, taking into account the size of the urn or container that will form the base. The bottom wreath should be a few inches larger in diameter than the opening of your container; the other wreaths will look gradually smaller due to the size of the fruit.

Greenery for these topiaries was wired to wreath forms that range in diameter from about 18 inches at the bottom to about 8 inches at the top. If a variety of sizes is unavailable, you can easily add extra greenery to a small wreath form to make it appear larger. Large red apples were attached to a 16-inch straw wreath form. Oranges, lemons, and small green apples were attached to 12-inch wreath forms.

Cut the greenery from your yard, or buy it at a Christmas tree lot. Once you've made the wreaths, simply stack them to form the topiary, starting with the largest rings of foliage and fruit, and then moving to the top, adding wreaths that decrease in size. Stabilize the wreaths with wire, if desired.

step 1

step 2

MATERIALS FOR TOPIARY

straw or wire wreath forms
for greenery

cuttings of greenery
(fir, boxwood, 'Little Gem' magnolia,
and hemlock)

clippers

florist wire and metal florist pins

straw wreath forms for fruit

fresh fruit

slender 12-inch wooden florist stakes
or 6-inch-long wooden florist picks

urn

square piece of wood

STEP 1: Purchase wreaths, or you can choose to make them yourself, using pieces of boxwood, fir, and other evergreens. For small wreaths, cut the greenery into pieces that are about 5 inches long; make them a few inches longer to create larger wreaths. Cluster several strands of greenery together, and bind them with a piece of florist wire. (If you are using a straw wreath form, attach the greenery clusters to the straw with metal

If your house has double doors, try this idea for a wreath that divides in half.

florist pins instead of using florist wire.) When using a wire wreath form, attach the greenery with florist wire. All the greenery clusters should be turned in the same direction. Cover the form thickly, so that each wreath will stand about 4 inches or more high.

Attach a ring of fresh fruit to the outside edge of a straw wreath form. Break slender 12-inch wooden florist stakes in half (or you can use 6-inch-long wooden florist picks). Insert one end into the piece of fruit and the other end into the straw wreath form. Continue attaching fruit until the outside edge of wreath is completely covered.

STEP 2: Place a square of wood over the mouth of the urn. Set the largest wreath of greenery on top of the wood square, and add a wreath of fruit. Continue adding wreaths, alternating greenery and fruit. Finish the topiary by placing two small wreaths of greenery at the top; then add cuttings of magnolia.

MATERIALS FOR WREATH

wreath form cut in half

cuttings of greenery
(magnolia, fir, and boxwood)

red apples

florist stakes or picks

florist wire

DOOR WREATH

If you have one front door, use a wire or straw wreath form in the size you prefer. If your home has double front doors, you'll need a form that will hold its shape when cut in half. (We used a green plastic wreath filled with florist foam and had it cut at a lumberyard.)

Attach fir, magnolia, and boxwood to each half of the wreath (or to an uncut wreath); cover the foam completely. Use florist stakes or picks to attach the desired fruit.

Attach each wreath half to one of double doors, using wire to suspend it from nails. Also, wire the bottom of each piece to the door knob to keep it stationery. (For an uncut wreath, slip wreath hanger over the top of the door, or wire the wreath to a nail or door knocker.)

PHOTOGRAPHS: VAN CHAPLIN

LEFT: *From left to right, golden false cypress, Colorado blue spruce, bird's nest spruce, white pine, and blue rug junipers* BELOW: *Sun exposure gives a gold tinge to the needles of hinoki false cypress* (Chamaecyparis obtusa *'Aurea'*).

Colorful Conifers For Your Winter Garden

When you look out on your winter landscape, are you taking in a pleasing scene that invites you outside, or does it make you want to draw the blinds and wait until March? Perhaps it's time to consider adding a few conifers to your garden.

This time of the year is perfect for analyzing the design of your landscape. If you rely on deciduous trees, shrubs, and perennials, your garden is probably looking a tad bleak right now. Conifers, most of which are evergreen, can change that. A broad group of plants that bear cones and have needle-like leaves, they come in a wide range of sizes, shapes, and textures that can provide year-round interest to any setting. Although they are included in the conifer family, keep in mind that exceptions—such as dawn redwood, bald cypress, and larch—drop their needles in winter.

On a small mountain overlooking downtown Bowling Green, Kentucky, homeowner Jerry Baker has amassed an extensive collection of evergreens on his arboretum-like property. With

If your garden has a case of the blahs, try perking things up with a conifer or two—or three.

the help of landscape architect Mitchell Leichhardt, he has planted numerous conifers. "I love how the foliage colors change with the season," Jerry says. "That's one of the most interesting things about these plants. Some conifers get bright yellow in summer but fade to green in winter, and some are bluish green in summer but turn purple in winter."

Gardeners in the Upper South, like Jerry, are particularly blessed when it comes to growing conifers, such as spruces, firs, arborvitae, and false cypress, which are strong enough to handle any winter temperatures the region has to offer. But even these typically hardy plants appreciate some protection from harsh winds or sudden freezing or thawing. To handle the hot summers found in the Lower and Coastal South, gardeners there are better off planting a juniper, cypress, cedar, cryptomeria, or rugged Japanese black pine.

Virtually all conifers, from the Upper South to the Coastal South, prefer well-drained soil and full sun. If your yard is mostly shady with clay

soil, try some smaller conifers in raised beds or, better still, containers that can be placed in a sunny spot. To prevent needle burn or even dead plants, it's best to avoid chemical fertilizers. A mild organic fertilizer or a top dressing of compost applied in late fall or spring is all that is needed.

Unless you have a large garden like Jerry's or you are ready to become a full-fledged conifer collector, it might be best to limit your palette to just three or four favorite selections. It's like the "too much of a good thing…" speech your mother gave you about ice cream when you were young. Consider yourself forewarned. Many a crazed conifer collector began with the innocent purchase of a few small shrubs.

Glenn R. DiNella

Easy Amaryllis

Create your own splendor in the grass to enhance the glory of this bulb.

TOP: *'Charisma' amaryllis sports festive mottled blooms.* ABOVE: *After amaryllis has begun to send up bloom spikes, sprinkle on a thin layer of wheatgrass seeds.*

Amaryllis are truly one of the simple joys of the holidays. These large bulbs can be easily enticed to bloom inside during the season and beyond. Their blossoms come in an array of forms and colors—singles, doubles, and miniatures in red, white, pink, salmon, and even chartreuse. And just when you think they've completed their performance, another bloom spike shoots up with more buds for a glorious encore. Certainly all that would seem to be enough, but you can make the show even more dramatic. Sow grass seeds in the soil around the base of the bulb to create a natural-looking display and cover the soil.

WHAT YOU WILL NEED

■ **Amaryllis**: Many types are available during the holidays from catalogs, home and garden centers, or by mail-order. You can begin with a simple bulb, or you can buy an already potted one. *Note:* We placed two bulbs in one pot for this project.

■ **Wheatgrass seeds:** Look for these at health food stores, home and garden centers, or by mail-order. *Note:* You can substitute annual ryegrass (which has a slightly finer texture). Annual ryegrass is often used to overseed lawns during the winter. If you have any leftover from overseeding your lawn, you can use just a handful for this project.

■ **Simple clay pot and saucer:** We used an old 7-inch clay pot with a colorful vintage plate as a saucer.

You may have never thought of growing grass inside. Just getting it to grow outside is enough of a challenge for most folks. Still, the truth is, it's easy, easy, easy. Plus, watching things grow will calm you. With the holiday rush pulling us in so many directions, we sometimes forget to slow down, relax, and enjoy the season.

WHAT TO DO

If you have purchased a potted amaryllis bulb, you will have one less step. Generally the larger the bulb, the larger the flower and the more bloom spikes. Our selection, 'Charisma,' had three bloom spikes for each bulb over a six-week period.

Amaryllis likes to be crowded, so buy a pot that is only about $1\frac{1}{2}$ inches larger than the bulb all the way around. Plant the bulb in a well-drained potting mix with some organic matter, such as sphagnum peat moss. The soil level should be about 1 inch below the rim of the container, and at least a third of the bulb should sit above the soil level. Firm the soil mix, water well, and then place your potted amaryllis bulb in a warm and sunny room. You need to keep the soil only slightly moist until the bulb begins to send up its bloom spike. The time it takes your amaryllis to bloom can vary, depending on the conditions of light, temperature, and water. Some selections of this plant grow several feet tall and may need staking.

Once the spike appears and the flowerbuds are swelling, water well and let drain. Then lightly sprinkle a layer of wheatgrass seed, and pat into the soil. Under good conditions, your grass seed will germinate quickly, and you should soon have a lush bed crowned by a glorious amaryllis.

BY GENE B. BUSSELL / PHOTOGRAPHY VAN CHAPLIN

'Charisma' amaryllis, underplanted by a green bed of wheatgrass, will brighten any room during the holidays.

Brookgreen Gardens, Murrells Inlet, South Carolina (See page 226.)

Favorites

A CUT ABOVE

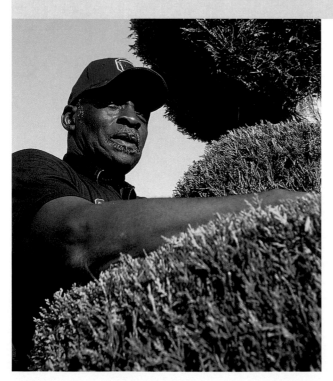

We know you've never met anyone like this artist. In his gifted hands, ordinary plants become extraordinary.

Pearl Fryar is the best thing that ever happened to a juniper. Left to its own devices, this lowly shrub might be doomed to a life of decorating the front of a drive-in bank. But in Pearl's hands, it becomes a Picasso—an abstract expression of the plant's full potential.

If you haven't heard of Pearl Fryar yet, you will. The work of this self-taught master of topiary (the art of pruning trees and shrubs into different forms) has been acclaimed throughout North America and Europe. His topiaries are displayed at the American Visionary Art Museum in Baltimore, the Museum of Fine Arts in Boston, and at Spoleto Festival USA in Charleston. He has appeared on the Discovery Channel,

BY STEVE BENDER / PHOTOGRAPHY ALLEN ROKACH

ABOVE: *Pearl will clip just about any plant that doesn't run, including a pair of live oaks that look like kissing turtles.* LEFT: *He refuses to trim plants to fit preformed wire frames, preferring to dream up his own creations.*

It was an award a younger Pearl Fryar never would have conceived might be his. As a youth, he saw athletics as the only way to escape poverty. "I was going to be the next Roy Campanella," he says ruefully. "If only I'd spent as many hours with my books as I spent behind a plate catching baseballs."

Two women set him on the right track. The first was Mallie Butler Stock. "She was my role model," he says, "the first black lady in my community to go to college. I ended up going to the same college that she did: North Carolina Central in Durham." There, in his first art appreciation class, Pearl discovered Pablo Picasso.

"When I saw the work of Picasso, it changed my life," he reveals. "I saw some of his work before he became famous and saw that he stayed with it to the point where he believed in himself, and then got the attention of the people who could make the difference."

HGTV, and PBS's *The Victory Garden.* And he is in constant demand on the garden lecture circuit.

But Pearl bestows his most precious gift on his community of Bishopville, South Carolina. Holding up his life as an example to at-risk schoolchildren from low-income families, this sharecropper's son inspires them to believe in themselves so they, too, may reach their potentials.

In a funny way, the Pearl Fryar phenomenon owes its existence to the Bishopville Yard-of-the-Month award. Pearl and Metra, his wife of 34 years, had lived in North Carolina, New York, and Georgia but never had a yard. When they moved to Bishopville in 1976, Pearl decided the Yard-of-the-Month was going to be his. There was a problem: At the time, the award was limited to city residents, and Pearl's yard lay outside city limits.

"I needed a reason for the city to make an exception," Pearl recalls. "So I started cutting up plants and got a lot of attention. One thing led to another until I decided, 'I'm going to cut up every plant in my yard—pine trees, oak trees, blue spruce. You name it.'" His strategy worked. The powers-that-be made an exception, and Pearl got his award.

The second woman to influence Pearl was Polly Laffitte, former art curator for the South Carolina State Museum. In 1997, she was looking for self-taught artists to feature at an exhibition, and she visited Pearl. "It blew me away," Polly says of his garden. "He pushed beyond anybody's expectations of what you could do with topiary. What he was doing was sculpture." When she subsequently commissioned him to create topiaries for the museum, Pearl felt affirmed as an artist.

Today, his 3-acre topiary garden showcases hundreds of evergreen and deciduous plants pruned into fanciful forms. He prefers creating abstract shapes, feeling they afford him more creativity. He prunes according to his mind's design, refusing to trim plants to fit frames: "That kind of topiary looks fantastic, but it takes no skill at all."

He is just as good a gardener as he is an artist. In addition to the pruned junipers and yews you'd expect to find in his yard, he trains blue spruce, Norway spruce, Canadian hemlock, and Fraser fir—cool-weather conifers that you'd never imagine would survive in the Lower South. He succeeds by digging a

You can accomplish anything in life if you believe in yourself.

Pearl Fryar

6-inch-deep trench around each tree a few feet out from the trunk, and then mounding pine straw around the base. The trench forces roots to go deeper into the soil. The pine straw aids drainage and aeration and also keeps roots cool and moist.

When he isn't trimming greenery, Pearl spends much of his time reshaping the attitudes of minority children. He lectures at schools and teaches topiary in his garden. His message: "You can accomplish anything in life if you believe in yourself.

"These are kids that feel that society has left them out," he says. "If you want to motivate them, you cannot send them to a doctor or a lawyer. They'll look at him and say, 'Well, you had money.' But I'll walk in and say, 'Look, I grew up on a farm and walked several miles to school. But I taught myself to be an artist, something I could make a living at. So don't let anyone dictate your life.'"

Pearl continues, "My favorite advice is this: 'He or she who does no more than average never rises above the average.' That's like my garden. Most plants I have are the same as you'd find in any garden in Bishopville. The difference is, I believed in my art and went one step further." *(For sources turn to pages 234–235.)*

Beloved Flowers

Rudbeckia 'Summer Sun'

spiderwort

narrow-leaf zinnia

Asking a *Southern Living* garden editor to choose a favorite flower is like taking a kid to a candy store and offering to buy one piece. The inevitable response: "Only one? Can't I pick two? Please?" Although it was hard to narrow it down, some of us have bitten the bullet and chosen a favorite—at least for today.

RUDBECKIA
If you could grab a handful of sunshine and roll it into a flower, a black-eyed Susan *(Rudbeckia* sp.) would surely emerge. I love these flowers for their unflinching color. They are neither soft nor subtle—but neither are Southern summers. These plants withstand hot, dry days without missing a beat, and they bloom with foolish abandon during our most brutal gardening months.

There are numerous selections to choose from, each with a different personality. I like tall, willowy *Rudbeckia* 'Herbstsonne' for height in my border. Its soft yellow flower has a green cone and multiple blooms per stem. The occasionally annual 'Indian Summer' has fat, voluptuous flowers that appear throughout those hot months. And 'Goldsturm' is like an old friend—it lasts through thick and thin.

Add *Rudbeckia* to your garden—and treat yourself to more than one selection. When they bloom, cut a bouquet of black-eyed Susans for your kitchen table. You will be charmed by elegant simplicity, I promise. *Ellen Riley*

NARROW-LEAF ZINNIA
When they say big things come in small packages, they're talking about narrow-leaf zinnia *(Zinnia angustifolia).* I don't like fussy plants, and this low-growing zinnia doesn't fuss. It creates billowy masses of orange, white, or yellow blooms from spring till fall. Over the past five years, I have found this zinnia to be the most dependable flowering annual for sunny locations. It needs very little water, excels in containers, and unlike other zinnias, is not susceptible to powdery mildew. It's also very disease-resistant. How could this plant not be a favorite? *Charlie Thigpen*

SPIDERWORT
With an exotic name like spiderwort *(Tradescantia virginiana),* this plant is intriguing from the start. I first became enamored with the little three-petaled violet-blue beauty when I lived and worked at the Isabelle Bowen Henderson House & Garden in Raleigh. These 2-foot-tall unassuming perennials with bright green straplike leaves still flourished there even after 20-something years. I decided right then that even I could grow spiderworts. Their only requirement is moist soil.

More refined gardeners might consider them invasive, but I've always found them easy to control by digging the bulblets up with a shovel. If you want something more challenging and exotic looking, try one of the white, magenta, red, or pink cultivated varieties sold at nurseries. Like daylilies, the flowers last only a day, but they are replaced the next morning with another cluster. Unlike daylilies, the petals are so small, they simply shrivel, disappear, and don't need deadheading. *Glenn R. DiNella*

Must-See Southern Gardens

But don't take our word for it. Go for a drive and look—you'll like what's out there.

Our Garden staff are not the only ones devoting their lives to the pursuit of gardening for the masses. Whatever you need help with, public gardens are ready to lend a hand. There are hundreds of great ones around the South, but here are the five we consider the cream of the crop.

CHEEKWOOD BOTANICAL GARDEN AND MUSEUM OF ART, NASHVILLE

The public gardens I most enjoy are those with a private beginning. On an intimate scale, Cheekwood blends the older personal grounds of a magnificent home with newer public areas. The original estate gardens have been renovated, giving a glimpse into the style of elegant and beautifully appointed private spaces. Additional gardens have recently been developed to serve as both picturesque destinations and learning resources. Lush flower borders, an herb garden, and a sculpture trail are part of the growing developments on the 55 acres. Old stables have been transformed into an educational facility enjoyed by children and adults. This garden, rich in history, is growing rapidly into the new century. For more information call (615) 356-8000, or visit www.cheekwood.org.   *Ellen Riley*

LADY BIRD JOHNSON WILDFLOWER CENTER, AUSTIN

I like just about every garden I've ever seen, but there are a few that stand out as places I'll revisit every time I get the chance. The Lady Bird Johnson Wildflower Center is one of my all-time favorites. Here the architecture suits the flowers: Buildings of rough native limestone are a perfect backdrop for the Texas Hill Country plantings. The seasonal changes of these native plants—sometimes vivid, sometimes subtle—are far more satisfying to me, somehow, than the "in-your-face" bright but artificial beds that decorate some other public gardens. This garden is a terrific place to get centered again as a Texan, to understand why you live where you live, and to learn how to incorporate a little of that incredible wild Texas beauty into your own living space. For more information call (512) 292-4200, or visit www.wildflower.org.

Liz Druitt

MISSOURI BOTANICAL GARDEN, ST. LOUIS

If I called the Missouri Botanical Garden the finest botanical garden in America, some folks might quibble, but none could really argue. Established in 1859, it ranks at the top in so many categories: the first geodesic dome greenhouse; the country's foremost research program dealing with tropical rain forests; an outstanding collection of garden sculpture, including works by Henry Moore and Carl Milles; community education programs that enlighten more than 100,000 citizens a year; and, of course, 79 acres of glorious gardens that showcase roses, daylilies, wildflowers, bulbs, cacti, tropical plants, and much more. This is a must-stop for anyone visiting the Gateway City. For more information call (314) 577-9400, or visit www.mobot.org.

Steve Bender

BROOKGREEN GARDENS, MURRELLS INLET, SOUTH CAROLINA

The powerful beauty of Brookgreen Gardens is probably best captured by the words of Archer Huntington, who created the gardens from several ad-

ABOVE: *Missouri Botanical Garden geodesic dome, St. Louis*
BELOW, LEFT AND RIGHT: *Lady Bird Johnson Wildflower Center, Austin*

joining Lowcountry rice plantations in 1929. He described the mission of the more than 9,000-acre gardens as a "quiet joining of hands between science and art." His wife, Anna, an accomplished sculptor, laid out a plan in the shape of a massive butterfly and thus set the groundwork for a superbly designed coastal garden. For almost 70 years, visitors have had the pleasure of wandering paths that wind by fountains, through artfully arranged displays of lush plantings, into peaceful courtyards, and past more than 500 sculptures by American artists. Brookgreen boasts the largest collection of outdoor sculpture in the U.S., and every work of art seems to be paired with a planting that was made for it. The Lowcountry Wildlife Trail offers a glimpse into the untamed beauty of the local flora and fauna. Everywhere you turn, there is a new breathtaking view, and the overall effect is simply stunning. For more information call 1-800-849-1931, or visit www.brookgreen.org. *Glenn R. DiNella*

BIRMINGHAM BOTANICAL GARDENS

The Birmingham Botanical Gardens is one of my favorite places because I've been able to enjoy it for so many years. When my grandmother would take me there as a child, we would always end up in the Japanese garden, where I looked for koi swimming in the pond. Now my son, Jacob, runs ahead to see the brightly colored fish. Birmingham also features a rose garden, fern glade, wildflower walk, conservatory, vegetable areas, and many other display gardens. Covering 67 acres, the gardens provide a pleasant green belt for a busy city. They're also special to me because I helped develop the *Southern Living* Garden located on the grounds. I planted many of the original trees, shrubs, and perennials about 20 years ago, and now I get to see them all grown up. To find out more information call (205) 414-3950, or visit www.bbgardens.org. *Charlie Thigpen*

Why We Love Gardening In the South

The Old South used to be all about roots, about who your people were. The New South is a richer, more balanced blend of folks, including many warm and wonderful ones who are Southerners by choice, not by birth. But for gardeners, the South is still—and always will be—about roots.

Because of the relative warmth of our climate, soil never gets deeply affected by frost. Even in winter, a Southern garden is alive. You can stand in the middle of a cold, quiet garden and almost feel the action—all those roots vibrating deep in the unfrozen ground beneath your feet.

There is, in fact, no absolute dormant season for most of us in the Middle and Lower South. You can get by with ignoring your garden, perhaps, during the worst heat of summer and for the whole two weeks of winter. It might ease up enough then, if you're lucky, and you'll be able to catch back up. It's sort of like running for a freight train as it slows for a level crossing. There are pauses as one clutch of plants plays out and another bunch is still in the process of springing up to replace it. But the Southern garden, just like that steaming freight train, never comes to a full stop.

Consequently, neither does the Southern gardener. Sometimes it seems there's just too much to deal with. Mud and floods and fire ants, droughts that crack the cotton-depleted soil, wild temperature swings, and wilder weeds are just a few of our regular gardening companions. It can make you want to fling your trowel into the azaleas and head back into the air conditioning. But in exchange, we are given the most remarkable gift of constancy—constant color, constant growth, constant participation in nature—the constancy of those never-sleeping roots.

A lot of folks say there's no rest for the weary. What I've learned, as a Southern gardener, is that there's really no rest for the blessed. And this certainly is where I want my garden to grow—right here in the South, where I will always, every day, be able to feel the living roots.

Liz Druitt

Editors' Picks

While logging long hours in the garden dreaming up new ideas for *Southern Living,* we have developed penchants for certain helpers that we can't, or simply refuse to, live without. We thought we'd share our favorite garden companions with you.

PAID BACK IN SPADES
Like a faithful old dog, my English garden spade sits outside my back door waiting for me. I use it for everything: edging the beds, planting what I bought at the nursery that day, and burying the "garbage" (a crude term, which I inherited from my father, for kitchen vegetable scraps). We have nothing so romantic at my house as spreading "compost." Perhaps most often, the little spade even cheerfully performs the dirty job of cleaning up after the dogs.
Glenn R. DiNella

GONE TO THE DOGS
When I head out the back door for my garden, I can't get a step outside without Zelda and Jeff, my two dogs, in pursuit. They tag along to check on my progress—successes and failures. They're seasoned animals and gladly hang close. We discuss what needs to be done, and they rarely disagree with me. Sometimes Jeff will pick up a glove or an empty pot (or even a full one on occasion) and run with it to tease and taunt. But they are my constant companions and great gardening buddies.
Ellen Riley

FLIPPING OUT
You can hear me in the yard as I take on many of my gardening chores. The slap, slap is the sound of my flip-flops. My wife used to call me the the barefoot gardener, but over the years my tender feet have encountered too many sweet gum balls, holly leaves, and rosebushes. Some days it's too cold for my flip-flops, and some jobs do require boots. But most days in the yard, you can hear me coming.
Charlie Thigpen

FASTEST PRUNERS AROUND
I don't understand, personally, how anyone could garden without a sharp pair of pruners ready at hand. I know I can't. There are spent flowers to clip off, bits of deadwood to prune away, bushes that need their shapes adjusted a little bit, always something! And I favor my beloved Felco 8s because they are so nicely shaped and so light, yet sturdy. My Felcos, after all, are *always* right there in my now slightly frayed back pocket. When I want to garden, I want to garden *now*. So I just grab my 8s and go.

Happiness: a new pair of Felcos and a nice rosebush to clip.
Liz Druitt

MY FROSTY COMPANION
My favorite thing to take out to the garden, I'm not ashamed to say, is a beer. That's because the only real time I have to be out there is when I'm dog tired from work. But a good beer makes it bearable. With one sip, I can overlook the black spot on my roses. With another sip, the spider mites sucking the life out of the verbena no longer vex me. By the time I finish the bottle, the fact that I am called a "garden guru" yet have the most desolate, dead-looking yard in North-Central Alabama does not wrack me with shame. Now, some of you think that I could achieve the same serenity with a tall glass of iced tea. But, then again, you haven't seen my yard.
Steve Bender

MY TIP BAG
My mother couldn't go out without her purse; she felt like something was missing. That's how it is when I garden with my Tip Bag. Having that bag standing by my side organizes my effort and makes cleanup easy. It's light, easy to carry, and quick to empty into the compost or trash. Best of all, it lasts—certainly longer than I do on a hot day.
Linda C. Askey

Favorite Tips

PHOTOGRAPH: JEAN M. ALLSOPP

PHOTOGRAPHS: VAN CHAPLIN

ABOVE: *Spray plants with horticultural oil or insecticidal soap before taking them indoors to keep any insects from infesting your other houseplants.* FAR LEFT: *Put paths where they naturally fall, and garden around them.* LEFT: *Mulch around existing perennials first; then plant your annuals.*

The garden editors at *Southern Living* are all enthusiastic, hands-on gardeners. Their collective experience is impressive and diverse, based on their individual interests. Here's what they've learned after all these years.

- If you're planting in the ground, make the time to prepare your soil. Just doing this will take care of 90% of the work needed for having a healthy garden.
- One universal tip from our garden editors is to get a soil test so you know what you're dealing with.
- In areas with rocky or poor soils, don't fight Mother Nature. Making raised beds to grow vegetables and flowers is easier than struggling to fix problem soil.
- Look at plants when they are blooming, and buy them when they're not. By the time they're in bloom at the nursery, they are past the perfect planting stage.
- Whether you're planting a cell-pack annual or a potted shrub, be sure to water the plant thoroughly before sticking it in the ground.
- Always check out a nursery's guarantee and return policy before making a major plant purchase. Some will warrant trees and shrubs for a year and replace a dead plant; some will not.
- If you're buying lots of one kind of azalea or crepe myrtle, buy them all in bloom. That way you won't be stuck with 14 red plants and 2 lavender ones.
- If you're using pine straw as mulch, consider shredding it first. The chopped needles are easy to dust off any plants that might have gotten buried.
- The key to watering if you don't have an irrigation system is to get a good-quality, kink-free hose.
- Add organic material as you start a new flowerbed, and replenish seasonally, before each planting.
- Always plant annuals with a timed-release fertilizer.
- Near the end of July, cut back flowering annuals halfway. Feed with a liquid blossom booster, and you'll have fabulous flowers in September and October.
- Wait until fall and winter to move established plants that need relocating.
- If you've just moved to a house with a preexisting garden, watch the garden through a full cycle of seasons. Then you'll know what's really there, like hidden clumps of bulbs or low spots that hold water after rain.
- Spring is great, but learn to love autumn. It's a superb season in the Southern garden, with gorgeous flowers and great weather. It's also the best time to plant perennials, roses, trees, and shrubs.

Finally, our editors offer some unusual gems of advice.

- Ellen Riley: Always stretch a bit before taking on any big gardening task.
- Glenn DiNella: Try planting a tall rosebush next to your birdbath. As the blooms fade and drop into the bowl, it creates a floating potpourri.
- Charlie Thigpen: Use branches and twigs to stake up flowers that have fallen over. The natural shapes work well in the garden, and you can't beat the price.
- Liz Druitt: Build a compost heap. Experienced gardeners always have one and pretend it's to improve the soil. Actually it's a guilt-free place to put the corpses of plants we've inadvertently killed.
- Steve Bender: Design the garden you like, and don't worry about what the neighbors will say. People are going to talk about you anyway. ◇

Getting an edge: *What are some effective ways of edging flowerbeds?*

ALISON PEICK
WAVERLY, TENNESSEE

Brick edging usually works well, because it's a natural material and easy to use in either straight or curving lines. While you can mortar the bricks in place, remember that once the cement dries, you're stuck. So if you're not sure of your final design, simply butt the bricks up against each other, and leave them unmortared. This way, you can easily change the design if you want. Flexible steel edging works well for straight or curving beds, too. Just be sure to anchor it at least an inch or two in the ground, and don't leave it bowed atop the ground, looking like a piece of metal spaghetti. Finally, one of our favorite methods for putting an edge between a flowerbed and lawn is to dig a trench about 8 inches deep and 12 inches wide, then fill the trench with pine straw. For more information about edging options, see page 347 of *The Southern Living Landscape Book.*

Flowering ground covers: *We have a cabin in the woods in Middle Tennessee. The ground is filled with rocks and red clay. What kinds of flowering ground covers can we plant that will thrive in sun or shade?*

SANDY REYNOLDS
GERMANTOWN, TENNESSEE

Poor soil limits your choices, but there are a few ground covers to suggest. For sun, try liriope, creeping phlox (thrift), and carpet bugleweed (ajuga). For shade, try liriope, carpet bugleweed, and common periwinkle *(Vinca minor).*

Non-blooming camellia: *On the north side of my house, I have a camellia growing in a pot on a screened porch. It has never bloomed. Any ideas?*

CONNIE LITTLE
ACKWORTH, GEORGIA

Your camellia may not be getting enough sunlight. Camellias bloom better if they get at least a half-day of sun. And try to be patient. It takes some plants a couple of years to really start blooming well.

Climbing hydrangea: *I've been looking for a climbing vine to grow on a shady masonry wall. Does climbing hydrangea need sun? How about support on which to climb?*

DAWN THOMSON
PISGAN FOREST, NORTH CAROLINA

Climbing hydrangea *(Hydrangea anomala petiolaris)* will grow fine on your wall. It doesn't need a trellis or wires. It climbs by means of aerial roots that grip a surface, much like English ivy climbs. But you may have a problem getting the vine to flower. It needs at least partial sun in order to bloom well.

Bulb bunnies: *As my tulips emerge from the earth in spring, rabbits eat them to the ground. What should I do?*

MARY THOMAS
CAPE MAY, NEW JERSEY

Do you like rabbit stew? Just a thought. If not, you could try placing a temporary chicken wire fence around your tulip bed in spring. The fence needn't be tall—18 to 24 inches should do—because rabbits don't climb. Or plant your tulips in large containers that can be moved out of harm's way.

Blooms for tight spots: *What kinds of perennials can I plant that have bright, showy flowers but stay small for the tight spaces in my garden?*

MICHAEL CLELAND
BAXLEY, GEORGIA

You have numerous plants from which to choose. Those that fit your criteria include the many types of pinks *(Dianthus)*, sedums, creeping phlox (also called thrift), catmint, thyme, coral bells, society garlic, Japanese roof iris, ajuga, liriope, chives, and mazus.

Rose woes: *I have four 7-year-old rosebushes that produce green foliage, but never any flowers. I have fertilized them regularly for two seasons with no luck. I need some help!*

LIZ RUFFING
ROWLETT, TEXAS

The first thing to check is whether your roses are getting enough sun. Most roses prefer full sun. The next

thing to think about is when and how you prune. Hybrid tea roses bloom repeatedly during the growing season, so you can prune them just about anytime. But many climbers and old-fashioned roses bloom just once a year in spring. The best time to prune them is early summer. If you prune them in late summer, fall, or winter, you'll cut off most of the flowerbuds for next year. A third possibility is that the good part of the rose—the top portion above the graft union—has died, and the foliage is coming from the rootstock. An indicator of this is if the foliage has changed color or shape in recent years. If this is the case, you'll have to replace your roses.

The grass is always greener: *What, other than grass, can you plant in the drain field of a septic tank?*

NANCY SIMMONS
JONESBORO, GEORGIA

Erma Brombeck wrote, "The grass is always greener over the septic tank," and she was right. The problem with planting anything else is that it has to have very shallow roots to avoid interfering with the septic systems. You could try a ground cover, such as English ivy, common periwinkle, liriope, or mondo grass. This might also be a good spot for annual bedding plants. Just think, you'd never have to fertilize them again.

Slugfest: *Slugs have eaten just about all of the flowers around my front porch. I've put out slug bait and beer, but I still seem to have a million of them. Any better ideas?*

SHERRYL MYRICK
CUMMING, GEORGIA

Sure—stop wastin' good beer on those slugs. You should waste it on your husband instead. Then try to eliminate hiding places for slugs, such as rocks, bricks, and pieces of wood. Spreading slug bait should help, provided you follow the label directions carefully. Another effective control is called diatomaceous earth, a talc-like powder that causes slugs to dry out and then die. You can find this at many home centers and nurseries.

Killer kudzu: *Every year, my yard becomes overrun with kudzu. It takes us most of the summer to get it under control. How do I get rid of it for good?*

TRACY MATTHEWS
BIRMINGHAM, ALABAMA

The best way to eradicate any plant is to make it the focal point of your garden, thereby assuring its immediate demise. But if you don't want to go that route, try this. Cut off near the ground all vines climbing up trees. Then spray all the vines attached to the ground with Roundup or Brush-B-Gon. Follow label directions carefully. Kudzu is deeply rooted, so you will probably have to spray more than once.

Gooey begonias: *Please tell me what could have eaten my begonias at the base and caused them to fall over as if they were rotted.*

PAT MORRE
WEST COLUMBIA, SOUTH CAROLINA

It sounds like your begonias rotted away due to wet soil and poor drainage. To fix the problem, fix your soil. Amend it with lots of organic matter (peat, compost, bark) and coarse sand. Make the bed slightly higher than the surrounding area, so that excess water runs off, and leave a little space between plants. Jamming them together restricts air circulation, which increases the chances of rot and other diseases.

Dead bushes: *We just landscaped this spring. The azaleas, boxwoods, and wax-leaf ligustrums are dead. We watered them every other day because the temperatures were over 100 degrees. When I dug up the plants, the ground was extremely moist. What do you think is the cause?*

STORMY GILLIAM
COLLEGE STATION, TEXAS

While heat and drought undoubtedly contributed to your plants' demise, another factor may have been the potting soil in the pots. This potting soil is often lighter and of a much different texture than garden soil. Water doesn't like to move between vastly different types of soil, so when you water, the original root ball remains dry, even though the surrounding soil is moist. Eventually, the plant will die of thirst. To prevent this from happening again, be sure to work lots of organic matter into your planting bed this fall. This will improve drainage and also change the texture to be more like potting soil. Be sure to water each plant thoroughly before setting it in the ground. Ease the plant out of the pot, and use a pencil to gently loosen the outer roots and keep them from wrapping around the root ball. Plant your bushes so that the top of the root ball is even with the soil surface, water the bed thoroughly, and then mulch.

Warding off wasps: *What can I do to get the wasps off of the 'Autumn Joy' sedum in my garden? Wasps cover it almost all the time.*

DOLORES MULLINS
MOUNT WASHINGTON, KENTUCKY

Wasps are drawn to the nectar and the pollen in the flowers. They won't pay any attention to you if you just leave them alone. But you can't really keep them away. If you're afraid of wasps, try moving the sedum farther back in the border, so that the insects won't be as close. Or you might want to remove the sedum all together.

Mole control: *How can we get rid of moles who have made our backyard a mess?*

AMY WILDER
CLEMMONS, NORTH CAROLINA

The novel solution we've heard about is placing used kitty litter in the mole tunnels. The moles don't like the smell (can't say we blame them) and go someplace else. Other people recommend rolling up pieces of Juicy Fruit chewing gum and dropping them in the tunnels. Moles eat this and die. Or you could try applying an insecticide such as GrubEx to kill the grubs the moles are hunting. Be sure to follow label directions carefully.

Twice as nice: *Are there any azaleas that bloom twice a year?*

JOANN SHEPHERD
VIRGINIA BEACH, VIRGINIA

Go to your garden or home center and see if they sell the new Encore azaleas. These hybrids bloom in both fall and spring and come in colors of red, pink, orange, and purple. They're fine for growing in the Lower and Coastal South (where you live), but may need winter protection in the Upper and Middle South.

In the shade: *One side of my home is shady, and the soil is constantly moist. Please tell me what kinds of plants could thrive there. Even my fescue has a hard time!*

KAREN GOEBEL
BROKEN ARROW, OKLAHOMA

More plants like sun and well-drained soil than the other way around, but you still have plenty from which to choose. Shrubs and perennials that might work in your situation include summersweet (*Clethra alnifolia*), cardinal flower (*Lobelia cardinalis*), silver variegated Japanese sedge (*Carex morrowii* 'Variegata'), cinnamon fern, lady fern, royal fern, and sensitive fern. And instead of grass, plant a ground cover that tolerates wet feet and shade, such as sweet woodruff (*galium odoratum*).

Aster disaster: *What causes the asters I plant to turn totally brown every summer except for the upper 25% of the stems?*

SARITA NAEGEL
CINCINATI, OHIO

It appears your asters were attacked by powdery mildew, a fungus that causes the leaves to turn brown and shrivel. To prevent its return next year, cut off and destroy all aster leaves and stems after your plants go dormant this fall. Then after they leaf out next spring, spray them according to label directions with either Funginex or Immunox. You may have to spray every few weeks in rainy, humid weather.

February

BARE FACTS FOR PLANTING BARE-ROOT ROSES
Page 32: **Bare-root roses** available from Arena Rose Company; The Roseraie at Bayfields; Edmunds' Roses; Heritage Roses of Tanglewood Farm; Jackson & Perkins; Sam Kedem Nursery; Petaluma Rose Company; Teas Nursery Company, Inc.

STARTING SEEDS
Page 33: **Seed starting kit** available from Park Seed. **Paper Pot Maker** available from Gardener's Supply Company.

March

NATURALIZING DAFFODILS
Pages 58–59: **Daffodil bulbs** available from Brent and Becky's Bulbs, Old House Gardens Heirloom Bulbs, McClure & Zimmerman. (All companies have fall delivery dates for daffodil bulbs.)

April

ATAMASCO LILY
Page 71: **Atamasco lily bulbs** *(Zephyranthes atamasco)* available from Plant Delights Nursery.

QUEEN OF THE ROAD
Page 72: **Queen Anne's lace** *(Daucus carota)* available from Dabney Herbs, Niche Gardens.

UPPING THE STAKES
Page 73: **Ceramic spheres** available from Robin VanValkenburgh.

May

ONE TOUGH, SHOWY ROSE
Page 93: **Chestnut roses** available from Antique Rose Emporium, Chamblee's Rose Nursery.

FIESTA IN LUCINDA'S GARDEN
Pages 96–101: To order *The Herb Garden Cookbook,* contact Lucinda Hutson.

June

SCENTED GERANIUMS
Pages 106–108: **Scented geraniums** available from The Herb of Grace, GardenSmith Greenhouse & Nursery, Papa Geno's Herb Farm & Prairie Perennials.

ICE BLUE SALVIA
Page 109: **Mealy-cup sage** selections available as plants from many retail nurseries, as plants or seeds from Goodwin Creek Gardens.

EASY-CARE LILIES
Page 115: **Lily-of-the-Nile** available in containers at most garden centers. To find a source for 'Midknight® Blue' and the other plants in the *Southern Living* Plant Collection, call Monrovia.

July

FRAGRANT HOSTAS
Pages 126–127: **Hostas** available from Plant Delights Nursery; Goodness Grows; Savory's Gardens, Inc.

September

FROM TERRA FIRMA TO TERRA COTTA
Page 168: Large **Hewell garden pot** available through *Southern Living* At Home. Other styles available from Hewell's Pottery.

October

DISCOVER CHINESE PISTACHE
Page 182: **Chinese pistache** available from Louisiana Nursery, Inc.; Woodlanders, Inc.

November

TULIPS TRIED AND TRUE
Pages 192–194: **Tulips** available from Brent and Becky's Bulbs, Dutch Gardens, McClure & Zimmerman.

REGAL REX BEGONIAS
Pages 202–203: **Rex begonias** available from Logee's Greenhouses, Ltd.; **wooden box, old iron dog, and glass and silver vessels** from Tricia's Treasures.

Southern Living Favorites

A CUT ABOVE
Pages 222–224: Contact Pearl Fryar.

Antique Rose Emporium
9300 Lueckemeyer Road, Brenham,
TX 77833; (800) 441-0002;
www.weAREroses.com

Arena Rose Company
P.O. Box 3096, Paso Robles, CA
93447; (888) 466-7434;
www.arenaroses.com

Brent and Becky's Bulbs
7463 Heath Trail, Gloucester, VA
23061; (877) 661-2852;
www.brentandbeckysbulbs.com;
free catalog

Chamblee's Rose Nursery
10926 U.S. Highway 69 North, Tyler,
TX 75706-8742; (800) 256-7673;
www.chambleeroses.com

Dabney Herbs
P.O. Box 22061, Louisville, KY
40252; (502) 893-5198;
www.dabneyherbs.com

Dutch Gardens
P.O. Box 2037, Lakewood, NJ 08701;
(800) 818-3861;
www.dutchgardens.com

Edmunds' Roses
6235 SW Kahle Road, Wilsonville,
OR 97070; (888) 481-7673;
www.edmundsroses.com

Gardener's Supply Company
128 Intervale Road, Burlington, VT
05401; (800) 955-3370;
www.gardeners.com

GardenSmith Greenhouse & Nursery
231 Hogan's Mill Road, Jefferson, GA
30549; (706) 367-9047;
www.gardensmithonline.com

Goodness Grows
332 Elberton Road (P.O. Box 311),
Lexington, GA 30648;
(706) 743-5055

Goodwin Creek Gardens
P.O. Box 83, Williams, OR 97544;
(800) 846-7359;
www.goodwincreekgardens.com

The Herb of Grace
Located at 1951 Highway 63, Spring
Creek Township, NC; mailing
address: 1951 Highway 63, Hot
Springs, NC 28743; (828) 622-7319;
www.theherbofgrace.com

Heritage Roses of Tanglewood Farm
16831 Mitchell Creek Drive, Fort
Bragg, CA 95437; (707) 964-3748

Hewell's Pottery
6035 Highway 52, Gillsville, GA
30543; (770) 869-3469;
www.hewellspottery.com

Jackson & Perkins
1 Rose Lane, Medford, OR 97501;
(800) 292-4769;
www. jacksonandperkins.com

Logee's Greenhouses, Ltd.
141 North Street, Danielson, CT
06239; (888) 330-8038;
www.logees.com

Louisiana Nursery, Inc.
5853 Highway 182, Opelousas, LA
70570; (337) 948-3696;
www.durionursery.com

Lucinda Hutson
P.O. Box 300607, Austin, TX 78703;
www.onr.com/user/lucinda, or write
via E-mail lucinda@onr.com

McClure & Zimmerman
P.O. Box 368, Friesland, WI 53935;
(800) 883-6998; www.mzbulb.com;
free catalog

Monrovia
(888) 752-6848; www.monrovia.com.

Niche Gardens
1111 Dawson Road, Chapel Hill, NC
27516; (919) 967-0078;
www.nichegardens.com

Old House Gardens Heirloom Bulbs
536 Third Street, Ann Arbor, MI
48103-4957; (734) 995-1486;
www.oldhousegardens.com;
catalog $2

**Papa Geno's Herb Farm &
Prairie Perennials**
Roca, NE; (402) 423-5051;
http://papagenos.com

Park Seed
1 Parkton Avenue, Greenwood, SC
29649; (800) 845-3369;
www.parkseed.com

Pearl Fryar
145 Broad Acres Road, Bishopville,
SC 29010; (803) 484-5581

Petaluma Rose Company
P.O. Box 750953, Petaluma, CA
94975; (877) 738-2586;
www.petrose.com

Plant Delights Nursery
9241 Sauls Road, Raleigh NC 27603;
(919) 772-4794;
www.plantdelights.com; Minimum
order is $25; catalog price is 10
stamps or a box of chocolates

Robin VanValkenburgh
79 Rosecrest Street, Asheville, NC
28804; (828) 253-5456;
www.gardenballs.net

The Roseraie at Bayfields
P.O. Box R, Waldoboro, ME 04572;
(207) 832-6330; www.roseraie.com

Sam Kedem Nursery
12414 191st Street East, Hastings,
MN 55033; (651) 437-7516;
www.kedemroses.com

Savory's Gardens, Inc.
5300 Whiting Avenue, Edina, MN
55439; (952) 941-8755; ships only in
spring and fall; catalog $3

Teas Nursery Company, Inc.
P.O. Box 1603, Bellaire, TX 77402;
(800) 446-7723;
www.teasnursery.com

Tricia's Treasures
1433-5 Montgomery Highway,
Birmingham, AL 35216;
(205) 822-0004

Woodlanders, Inc.
128 Colleton Avenue, Aiken, SC
29801; (803) 648-7522;
www.woodlanders.net

www.southernlivingathome.com

*Unlisted items are one of a kind or un-
available.*

Index

Plant Hardiness Zone Map

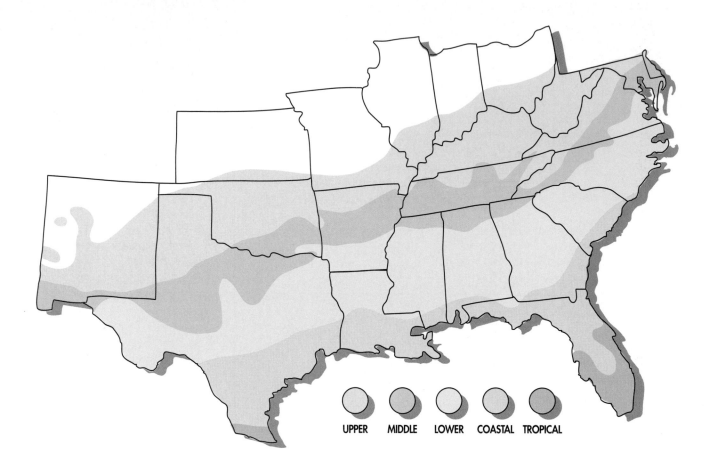

UPPER   MIDDLE   LOWER   COASTAL   TROPICAL

The United States Department of Agriculture has charted low temperatures throughout the country to determine the ranges of average low readings. The map above is based loosely on the USDA Plant Hardiness Zone Map, which was drawn from these findings. It does not take into account heat, soil, or moisture extremes and is intended as a guide, not a guarantee.

The southern regions of the United States that are mentioned in this book refer to the following:

Upper South: -10° to 0°F minimum
Middle South: 0° to 5°F minimum
Lower South: 5° to 15°F minimum
Coastal South: 15° to 25°F minimum
Tropical South: 25° to 40°F minimum